BEOWULF

W.W. NORTON & COMPANY, INC.
also publishes

THE NORTON ANTHOLOGY OF AMERICAN LITERATURE
edited by Nina Baym et al.

THE NORTON ANTHOLOGY OF CONTEMPORARY FICTION
edited by R. V. Cassill

THE NORTON ANTHOLOGY OF ENGLISH LITERATURE
edited by M. H. Abrams et al.

THE NORTON ANTHOLOGY OF LITERATURE BY WOMEN
edited by Sandra M. Gilbert and Susan Gubar

THE NORTON ANTHOLOGY OF MODERN POETRY
edited by Richard Ellmann and Robert O'Clair

THE NORTON ANTHOLOGY OF POETRY
edited by Alexander W. Allison et al.

THE NORTON ANTHOLOGY OF SHORT FICTION
edited by R. V. Cassill

THE NORTON ANTHOLOGY OF WORLD MASTERPIECES
edited by Maynard Mack et al.

THE NORTON FACSIMILE OF
THE FIRST FOLIO OF SHAKESPEARE
prepared by Charlton Hinman

THE NORTON INTRODUCTION TO LITERATURE
edited by Carl E. Bain, Jerome Beaty, and J. Paul Hunter

THE NORTON INTRODUCTION TO THE SHORT NOVEL
edited by Jerome Beaty

THE NORTON READER
edited by Arthur M. Eastman et al.

THE NORTON SAMPLER
edited by Thomas Cooley

BEOWULF

A *New Prose Translation by*

E. TALBOT DONALDSON

YALE UNIVERSITY

W · W · NORTON & COMPANY

New York · London

Library of Congress Catalog Card No. 66–11783

PRINTED IN THE UNITED STATES OF AMERICA

4 5 6 7 8 9 0

ISBN 0-393-09687-4

Contents

Introduction

The Poem

Beowulf, the oldest of the great long poems written in English, was probably composed more than twelve hundred years ago, in the first half of the eighth century. Its author may have been a native of what was then West Mercia, the West Midlands of England today, though the late tenth-century manuscript, which alone preserves the poem, originated in the south in the kingdom of the West Saxons. In 1731, before any modern transcription of the text had been made, the manuscript was seriously damaged in the fire that destroyed the building in London which housed the extraordinary collection of medieval English manuscripts made by Sir Robert Bruce Cotton (1571–1631). As a result of the fire and of subsequent deterioration of the manuscript, a number of lines and words have been lost from the poem, but even if the manuscript had not been damaged, the poem would still have been difficult, because the poetic Old English (or Anglo-Saxon) in which it was written is itself hard, the style is allusive, the ideas often seem remote and strange to modern perceptions, and because the text was inevitably corrupted during the many transcriptions which must have intervened in the two and a half centuries between the poem's composition and the copying of the extant manuscript. Yet despite its difficulty, the sombre grandeur of Beowulf is still capable of stirring the hearts of readers, and because of its excellence as well as its antiquity, the poem merits the high position that it is generally assigned in the study of English poetry.

While the poem itself is English in language and origin, it deals not with native Englishmen, but with their Germanic forebears, especially with two south Scandinavian tribes, the Danes and the Geats, who lived on the Danish island of Zealand and in southern Sweden, respectively. Thus, the historical period it concerns—insofar as it may be said to refer to history at all—is some two centuries before the poem was written; that is, it concerns a time following the initial invasion of England by Germanic tribes in 449, but before the Anglo-Saxon migration was completed, and perhaps before the arrival of the ancestors of the audience to whom the poem was sung: this audience may have considered itself to be of the same Geatish stock as the hero, Beowulf. The one datable fact of history mentioned in the poem is a raid on the Franks made by Hygelac, the king of the Geats at the time Beowulf was a young man, and this raid occurred in the year 520. Yet despite their antiquity, the poet's materials must have been very much alive to his audience, for the elliptical way in which he alludes to events not directly concerned with his plot demands of the listener a wide knowledge of traditional Germanic history. This knowledge was probably kept alive by other heroic poetry, of which little has been preserved in English, though much must once have existed. As it stands, *Beowulf* is not only unique as an example of the Old English epic, but is also the greatest of the surviving epics composed by the Germanic peoples.

It is generally agreed that the poet who put the old materials into their present form was a Christian, and that his poem reflects a Christian tradition: the conversion of the Germanic settlers in England had largely been completed during the century preceding the one in which the poet wrote. But there is little general agreement as to how clearly *Beowulf* reflects a Christian tradition or, conversely, the actual nature of the Christian tradition that it is held to reflect. Many specifically Christian references occur, especially to the Old Testament: God is said to be the Creator of all things and His will seems recognized (sporadically if not systematically) as being identical with Fate (*wyrd*); Grendel is described as a descendant of Cain, and the sword that Beowulf finds in Grendel's mother's lair has engraved on it the story of the race of giants and their destruction by flood; the dead await God's judgment, and Hell and the Devil are ready to receive the souls of Grendel and his mother, while believers will find the Father's embrace; Hrothgar's speech of advice to Beowulf (section XXV) seems to reflect patristic doctrine in its emphasis on conscience and the Devil's lying in wait for the unwary. Yet there is no reference to the New Testament—to Christ and His Sacrifice which are the real bases of Christianity in any intelligible sense of the term. Furthermore, readers may well feel that the poem achieves rather little of its emotional power through invocation of Christian values or of values that are consonant with Christian doctrine as we know it. Perhaps the sense of tragic waste which pervades the Finnsburg episode (section XVI) springs from a Christian perception of the insane futility of the primitive Germanic thirst for vengeance; and the facts that Beowulf's chief adversaries are not men but monsters and that before his death he is able to boast that as king of the Geats he did not seek wars with neighboring tribes may reflect a Christian's appreciation for peace among men. But while admitting such values, the poet also invokes many others of a very different order, values that seem to belong to an ancient, pagan, warrior society of the kind described by the Roman historian Tacitus at the end of the first century. It should be noted that even Hrothgar's speech about conscience is directed more toward making Beowulf a good Germanic leader of men than a good Christian. One must, indeed, draw the conclusion from the poem itself that while Christian is a correct term for the religion of the poet and of his audience, it was a Christianity that had not yet by any means succeeded in obliterating an older pagan tradition, which still called forth powerful responses from men's hearts, despite the fact that many aspects of this tradition must be abhorrent to a sophisticated Christian. In this connection it is well to recall that the missionaries from Rome who initiated the conversion of the English proceeded in a conciliatory manner, not so much uprooting paganism in order to plant Christianity as planting Christianity in the faith that it would ultimately choke out the weeds of paganism. And the English clung long to some of their ancient traditions: for instance, the legal principle of the payment of *wergild* (defined below) remained in force until the Norman Conquest, four centuries after the conversion of the English.

In the warrior society whose values the poem constantly invokes, the most important of human relationships was that which existed between the warrior—the thane—and his lord, a relationship based less on subordination of one man's will to another's than on mutual trust and respect. When a warrior vowed loyalty to his lord, he became not so much his servant as his voluntary companion, one who would take pride in defending him and fighting in his wars. In return, the lord was expected to take affectionate care of his thanes and to reward them richly for their valor: a good king, one like Hrothgar or Beowulf, is referred to by such poetic epithets as "protector of warriors" and "dispenser of treasure" or "ring-giver," and the failure of bad kings is ascribed to their ill-temper and avarice, both of which alienate them from their retainers. The material benefit of this arrangement between lord and thane is obvious, yet under a good king the relationship seems to have had a significance more spiritual than material. Thus the treasure that an ideal Germanic king seizes from his enemies and rewards his retainers with is regarded as something more than mere wealth that will serve the well-being of its possessor; rather, it is a kind of visible proof that all parties are realizing themselves to the full in a spiritual sense—that the men of this band are congenially and successfully united with one another. The symbolic importance of treasure is illustrated by the poet's remark that the gift Beowulf gave the Danish coast-guard brought the latter honor among his companions, and even more by the fact that although Beowulf dies while obtaining a great treasure for his people, such objects as are removed from the dragon's hoard are actually buried with him as a fitting sign of his ultimate achievement.

The relationship between kinsmen was also of deep significance to this society and provides another emotional value for Old English heroic poetry. If one of his kinsmen had been slain, a man had the special duty of either killing the slayer or exacting from him the payment of *wergild* ("man-price"): each rank of society was evaluated at a definite price, which had to be paid to the dead man's kinsmen by the killer who wished to avoid their vengeance—even if the killing had been accidental. Again, the money itself had less significance as wealth than as a proof that the kinsmen had done what was right. Relatives who failed either to exact *wergild* or to take vengeance could never be happy, having found no practical way of satisfying their grief for their kinsmen's death. "It is better for a man to avenge his friend than much mourn," Beowulf says to the old Hrothgar, who is bewailing Aeschere's killing by Grendel's mother. And one of the most poignant passages in the poem describes the sorrow of King Hrethel after one of his sons had accidentally killed another: by the code of kinship Hrethel was forbidden to kill or to exact compensation from a kinsman, yet by the same code he was required to do one or the other in order to avenge the dead. Caught in this curious dilemma, Hrethel became so disconsolate that he could no longer face life.

It is evident that the need to take vengeance would create never-ending feuds, which the practice of marrying royal princesses to the kings or princes of hostile tribes did little to mitigate, though the purpose of such marriages was to replace hostility by alliance. Hrothgar wishes to make peace with the Heatho-Bards by marrying his daughter to their king, Ingeld, whose father was killed by the Danes; but as Beowulf predicts, sooner or later the Heatho-Bards' desire for vengeance on the Danes will erupt, and there will be more bloodshed. And the Danish princess Hildeburh, married to Finn of the Jutes, will see her son and her brother both killed while fighting on opposite sides in a battle at her own home, and ultimately will see her husband killed by the Danes in revenge for her brother's death. Beowulf himself is, for a Germanic hero, curiously free of involvement in feuds of this sort, though he does boast that he avenged the death of his king, Heardred, on his slayer Onela. Yet the potentiality—or inevitability—of sudden attack, sudden change, swift death is omnipresent in *Beowulf*: men seem to be caught in a vast web of reprisals and counterreprisals from which there is little hope of escape. This is the aspect of the poem which is apt to make the most powerful impression on the reader—its strong sense of doom.

Beowulf himself is chiefly concerned not with tribal feuds but with fatal evil both less and more complex. Grendel and the dragon are threats to the security of the lands they infest just as human enemies would be, but they are not part of the social order and presumably have no one to avenge their deaths (that Grendel's mother appeared as an avenger seems to have been a surprise both to Beowulf and to the Danes). On the other hand, because they are outside the normal order of things, they require of their conqueror something greater than normal warfare requires. In each case, it is the clear duty of the king and his companions to put down the evil. But the Danish Hrothgar is old and his companions unenterprising, and excellent though Hrothgar has been in the kingship, he nevertheless lacks the quality that later impels the old Beowulf to fight the dragon that threatens his people. The poem makes no criticism of Hrothgar for this lack; he merely seems not to be the kind of man—one might almost say he was not fated—to develop his human potential to the fullest extent that Fate would permit: that is Beowulf's role. In undertaking to slay Grendel, and later Grendel's mother, Beowulf is testing his relationship with unknowable destiny. At any time, as he is fully aware, his luck may abandon him and he may be killed, as, indeed, he is in the otherwise successful encounter with the dragon. But whether he lives or dies, he will have done all that any man could do to develop his character heroically. It is this consciousness of testing Fate that probably explains the boasting that modern readers of heroic poetry often find offensive. When he boasts, Beowulf is not only demonstrating that he has chosen the heroic way of life, but is also choosing it, for when he invokes his former courage as pledge of his future courage, his boast becomes a vow; the hero has put himself in a position from which he cannot withdraw.

Courage is the instrument by which the hero realizes himself. "Fate often saves an undoomed man when his courage is good," says Beowulf in his account of his swimming match: that is, if Fate has not entirely doomed a man in advance, courage is the quality that can perhaps influence Fate against its natural tendency to doom him now. It is this complex statement (in which it is hard to read the will of God for Fate) that Beowulf's life explores: he will use his great strength in the most courageous way by going alone, even unarmed, against monsters. Doom, of course, ultimately claims him, but not until he has fulfilled to its limits the pagan ideal of a heroic life. And despite the desire he often shows to Christianize pagan virtues, the Christian poet remains true to the older tradition when, at the end of his poem, he leaves us with the impression that Beowulf's chief reward is pagan immortality: the memory in the minds of later men of a hero's heroic actions. The poem itself is, indeed, a noble expression of that immortality.

The Translation

The chief purpose of this translation is to try to preserve for the reader what the translator takes to be the most striking characteristic of the style of the original: extraordinary richness of rhetorical elaboration alternating with—often combined with— the barest simplicity of statement. The effect of this, impressive though it is, is difficult to analyze; perhaps the principal thing it accomplishes is to keep us constantly aware that while the aspirations of the people concerned are high-heroic, the people themselves are merely people—men with almost all the limitations (Beowulf's great physical strength is an exception) of ordinary mortals. That is, men may rise to the heroism of the rhetorical style, but they are nevertheless always the human beings of the plain style. In order to try to reproduce this effect, it has seemed best to translate as literally as possible, confining oneself to the linguistic and intellectual structure of the original. It is perfectly true that a literal translation such as this is bound to result in a style of modern English prose that was never seen before on land or sea and is not apt to be again—a good example of what Ben Jonson would surely call "no language." But no received English style that I know, modern or archaic, sounds anything like *Beowulf:* there seems to be no accepted alternate to a literal rendering.

For a good many years prose translators of *Beowulf* chose to use a "heroic" style which at least sounded archaic, for it borrowed liberally from Milton, Pope, Shakespeare, and the King James Bible, as well as from later imitators of these. A good many serviceable translations were thus produced, but in general the homogeneousness of their style necessarily proved false to the original by elevating even its simplest statements into highly adorned ones: the hero can perform the commonest actions— like sitting down—only by means of an elaborate periphrasis. More recent translators have eschewed the artificiality of such style and have rendered the poem into what is called "modern colloquial English." This has resulted in bringing out very effectively the starker side of the poem, its understatements and its directness, but has also given the unfortunate impression that the heavily rhetorical side is excrescent and unnecessary: heaped-up epithets are reduced, like fractions to be simplified, to one or two terms, the "whale-road" is resolved into what it surely is, the sea, and "*þaet waes god cyning*" becomes, colloquially but rather donnishly, "He was an excellent king." Decorum expects translators to maintain a consistent point of view through their style, but the *Beowulf* poet (along with most great poets) forges a complex style that simultaneously discloses differing aspects of the same situation; lacking his vision and his language (not to mention his talent), we tend to emphasize one aspect at the expense of the other.

One sentence will illustrate the kind of difficulty the translator of *Beowulf* constantly encounters. It occurs during the hero's fight with Grendel's mother in her under-water hall. The sword Hrunting has failed him; he has grappled with the monster-woman and thrown her to the floor; then he himself stumbles and falls. At this point the poet says, "*Ofsaet þa þone selegyst*": "Then she sat upon the hall-guest." This is a reasonable action, for she is much bigger than he, and is preparing to stab him. Yet if one is using a consistently heroic style, the simple verb "sat"—especially in juxtaposition with the seemingly "epic" epithet "hall-guest"—will simply not do; in order to preserve the translator's and the hero's dignity, Grendel's mother must throw, hurl, fling, or otherwise precipitate herself upon her adversary. If, on the other hand, one is using the colloquial style, then "hall-guest" is an embarrassment, and one is apt to go through the (perfectly correct) semantic process of *hall-guest* = *hall-visitor* or *hall-stranger* = *visitor* or *stranger in the hall* = *intruder*. And "intruder" is in many ways quite satisfactory, but it lacks whatever potential for quick, grim humor the expression "hall-guest" has. Surely something specious has been added if Grendel's mother acts more dramatically than just sitting upon Beowulf, and something good has been lost if he becomes other than a hall-guest.

An honest translator must confess that while he has tried to avoid the defects of his predecessors, he has probably introduced defects of which they were free. My resolute avoidance of such terms as bill, buckler, and byrnie undoubtedly gives the impression that the poet's vocabulary was limited in words for sword, shield, and mail-shirt: actually it was so rich that bill, buckler, and byrnie lend only paltry, stopgap aid, and I have thought it better to make the poet monotonous than quaint. At times I have been guiltily aware that an Old English word might be more exactly translated by a polysyllabic Latinate synonym than by the word's modern English monosyllabic descendant which I have preferred, but one is so often absolutely compelled to use Latinisms that I have tried to avoid them whenever there was the slightest possibility of doing so. With words whose potential translations range from the colorless to the highly colored—such as "man: warrior: hero" —I have generally preferred the more modest of the alternates, though it might be argued that I have thus behaved anti-heroically. I am not sure that my feeling that *thou* and *thee* are inappropriate in a modern translation may not be idiosyncratic, but it has at least enabled me to evade such monstrosities as "thou achievedest." I am sorry we have lost the interjection "lo" from modern English: it is enormously useful, and hard to get around for Old English *hwaet*, though I have got around it when I could. While my translation is not intended to be in purely "natural" English, I have avoided unnatural expressions unless they performed some function in rendering the Old English style.

I cannot boast that I have been able to resolve with entire honesty every dilemma presented by the original. Like most translators, I have put in proper names in some places where the poet used only pronouns, have occasionally changed difficult constructions to easy ones, and have altered word order—and thus the poet's emphasis—in sentences where to preserve the literal would be to obscure the sense. I have also occasionally introduced glosses into the text. For instance, after the Danes and Geats have journeyed from Heorot to Grendel's mere and have found it boiling with blood—and Aeschere's head upon the shore—the poet says, "Again and again the horn sang its urgent war-song. The whole troop sat down." Seen from a realistic point of view, there is nothing surprising about this: the warriors have had a hard trip, and nothing is, for the moment, to be gained by remaining standing. Yet even one who believes that heroic warriors need not always be in furious motion experiences a sense of anticlimax here, and I have wilfully added a gloss: "The whole troop sat down to rest." A problem of a different sort, to be solved only by suppression of sense, occurs in the Danish coast-guard's speech to the arriving Geats. After marveling at their boldness and warlike appearance, he says to them (literally): "Hear my simple thought: haste is best to make known whence your comings are." The thought is, indeed, simple enough, but the expression is highly elaborate, a plain question put in a most formal way that shows at once respect for and defiance of the Geatish warriors. I know of no way to render such shades of meaning in modern English, and my translation makes of the coast-guard a plainer, blunter man than the poet probably conceived. In general I hope, however, that I have not played false too often, and that the reader unfamiliar with Old English may derive from this translation some real sense of the poem's extraordinary qualities.

I should like to thank Miss Mary Carruthers for her great help in checking the translation, correcting errors, and suggesting improvements. To several of my friends who are enormously learned in Old English I am also much indebted for their patient kindness in answering my sometimes naïve questions, but since they did not see the manuscript, I shall not embarrass them by naming them. Two colleagues who did see the manuscript— William Wiatt of Indiana and Albert H. Marckwardt of Princeton —offered most helpful suggestions; I am grateful, both for those that I used and those that I didn't. I tried not to consult other translations during the course of my own work (except in the case of several venerable cruxes), but I was familiar with several of them —especially Clark Hall's—before I began, and I know that they often helped me when I was not aware of their doing so. The translation is based on F. Klaeber's third edition of the poem (1950); in general, the emendations suggested by J. C. Pope, *The Rhythm of Beowulf*, second edition (1966), have been adopted.

E. Talbot Donaldson

BEOWULF

Beowulf

[*Prologue: The Earlier History of the Danes*]

Yes, we have heard of the glory of the Spear-Danes' kings in the old days—how the princes of that people did brave deeds.

Often Scyld Scefing [1] took mead-benches away from enemy bands, from many tribes, terrified their nobles—after the time that he was first found helpless.[2] He lived to find comfort for that, became great under the skies, prospered in honors until every one of those who lived about him, across the whale-road, had to obey him, pay him tribute. That was a good king.

Afterwards a son was born to him, a young boy in his house, whom God sent to comfort the people: He had seen the sore need they had suffered during the long time they lacked a king. Therefore the Lord of Life, the Ruler of Heaven, gave him honor in the world: Beowulf [3] was famous, the glory of the son of Scyld spread widely in the Northlands. In this way a young man ought by his good deeds, by giving splendid gifts while still in his father's house, to make sure that later in life beloved companions will stand by him, that people will serve him when war comes. Through deeds that bring praise, a man shall prosper in every country.

Then at the fated time Scyld the courageous went away into the protection of the Lord. His dear companions carried him down to the sea-currents, just as he himself had bidden them do when, as protector of the Scyldings,[4] he had ruled them with his words —long had the beloved prince governed the land. There in the harbor stood the ring-prowed ship, ice-covered and ready to sail, a prince's vessel. Then they laid down the ruler they had loved, the ring-giver, in the hollow of the ship, the glorious man beside

1. The meaning is probably "son of Sceaf," although Scyld's origins are mysterious.
2. As is made clear shortly below, Scyld arrived in Denmark as a child alone in a ship loaded with treasures.
3. This is not the hero of the poem, who is a Geat, but the grandfather of the Danish King Hrothgar, whose hall the Geat hero is to free from Grendel's attacks.
4. I.e., the Danes ("descendants of Scyld").

the mast. There was brought great store of treasure, wealth from lands far away. I have not heard of a ship more splendidly furnished with war-weapons and battle-dress, swords and mail-shirts. On his breast lay a great many treasures that should voyage with him far out into the sea's possession. They provided him with no lesser gifts, treasure of the people, than those had done who at his beginning first sent him forth on the waves, a child alone. Then also they set a golden standard high over his head, let the water take him, gave him to the sea. Sad was their spirit, mournful their mind. Men cannot truthfully say who received that cargo, neither counsellors in the hall nor warriors under the skies.

(I.) [5] Then in the cities was Beowulf of the Scyldings beloved king of the people, long famous among nations (his father had gone elsewhere, the king from his land), until later great Healfdene was born to him. As long as he lived, old and fierce in battle, he upheld the glorious Scyldings. To him all told were four children born into the world, to the leader of the armies: Heorogar and Hrothgar and the good Halga. I have heard tell that [. . . was On]ela's queen,[6] beloved bed-companion of the Battle-Scylfing.

[*Beowulf and Grendel*]

[THE HALL HEOROT IS ATTACKED BY GRENDEL]

Then Hrothgar was given success in warfare, glory in battle, so that his retainers gladly obeyed him and their company grew into a great band of warriors. It came to his mind that he would command men to construct a hall, a mead-building large[r] than the children of men had ever heard of, and therein he would give to young and old all that God had given him, except for common land and men's bodies.[7] Then I have heard that the work was laid upon many nations, wide through this middle-earth, that they should adorn the folk-hall. In time it came to pass—quickly, as men count it—that it was finished, the largest of hall-dwellings. He gave it the name of Heorot,[8] he who ruled wide with his words. He did not forget his promise: at the feast he gave out rings, treasure. The hall stood tall, high and wide-gabled: it would wait for the fierce flames of vengeful fire; [9]

---

5. The numbering of sections is that of the manuscript, which makes, however, no provision for Section XXX.
6. The text is faulty, so that the name of Healfdene's daughter has been lost; her husband Onela was a Swedish (Scylfing) king.
7. Or "men's lives." Apparently slaves, along with public land, were not in the king's power to give away.
8. I.e., "Hart."
9. The destruction by fire of Heorot occurred at a later time than that of the poem's action, probably during the otherwise unsuccessful attack of the Heatho-Bard Ingeld on his father-in-law Hrothgar, mentioned in the next clause.

the time was not yet at hand for sword-hate between son-in-law and father-in-law to awaken after murderous rage.

Then the fierce spirit [1] painfully endured hardship for a time, he who dwelt in the darkness, for every day he heard loud mirth in the hall; there was the sound of the harp, the clear song of the scop.[2] There he spoke who could relate the beginning of men far back in time, said that the Almighty made earth, a bright field fair in the water that surrounds it, set up in triumph the lights of the sun and the moon to lighten land-dwellers, and adorned the surfaces of the earth with branches and leaves, created also life for each of the kinds that move and breathe.—Thus these warriors lived in joy, blessed, until one began to do evil deeds, a hellish enemy. The grim spirit was called Grendel, known as a rover of the borders, one who held the moors, fen and fastness. Unhappy creature, he lived for a time in the home of the monsters' race, after God had condemned them as kin of Cain. The Eternal Lord avenged the murder in which he slew Abel. Cain had no pleasure in that feud, but He banished him far from mankind, the Ruler, for that misdeed. From him sprang all bad breeds, trolls and elves and monsters—likewise the giants who for a long time strove with God: He paid them their reward for that.

(II.) Then, after night came, Grendel went to survey the tall house—how, after their beer-drinking, the Ring-Danes had disposed themselves in it. Then he found therein a band of nobles asleep after the feast: they felt no sorrow, no misery of men. The creature of evil, grim and fierce, was quickly ready, savage and cruel, and seized from their rest thirty thanes. From there he turned to go back to his home, proud of his plunder, sought his dwelling with that store of slaughter.

Then in the first light of dawning day Grendel's war-strength was revealed to men: then after the feast weeping arose, great cry in the morning. The famous king, hero of old days, sat joyless; the mighty one suffered, felt sorrow for his thanes, when they saw the track of the foe, of the cursed spirit: that hardship was too strong, too loathsome and long-lasting. Nor was there a longer interval, but after one night Grendel again did greater slaughter—and had no remorse for it—vengeful acts and wicked: he was too intent on them. Thereafter it was easy to find the man who sought rest for himself elsewhere, farther away, a bed among the outlying buildings—after it was made clear to him, told by clear proof, the hatred of him who now controlled the hall.[3]

1. I.e., Grendel.
2. The "scop" was the Anglo-Saxon minstrel, who recited poetic stories to the accompaniment of a harp.
3. I.e., Grendel.

Whoever escaped the foe held himself afterwards farther off and more safely. Thus Grendel held sway and fought against right, one against all, until the best of houses stood empty. It was a long time, the length of twelve winters, that the lord of the Scyldings suffered grief, all woes, great sorrows. Therefore, sadly in songs, it became well-known to the children of men that Grendel had fought a long time with Hrothgar, for many half-years maintained mortal spite, feud, and enmity—constant war. He wanted no peace with any of the men of the Danish host, would not withdraw his deadly rancor, or pay compensation: no counselor there had any reason to expect splendid repayment at the hands of the slayer.[4] For the monster was relentless, the dark death-shadow, against warriors old and young, lay in wait and ambushed them. In the perpetual darkness he held to the misty moors: men do not know where hell-demons direct their footsteps.

Thus many crimes the enemy of mankind committed, the terrible walker-alone, cruel injuries one after another. In the dark nights he dwelt in Heorot, the richly adorned hall. He might not approach the throne, [receive] treasure, because of the Lord; He had no love for him.[5]

This was great misery to the lord of the Scyldings, a breaking of spirit. Many a noble sat often in council, sought a plan, what would be best for strong-hearted men to do against the awful attacks. At times they vowed sacrifices at heathen temples, with their words prayed that the soul-slayer [6] would give help for the distress of the people. Such was their custom, the hope of heathens; in their spirits they thought of Hell, they knew not the Ruler, the Judge of Deeds, they recognized not the Lord God, nor indeed did they know how to praise the Protector of Heaven, the glorious King. Woe is him who in terrible trouble must thrust his soul into the fire's embrace, hope for no comfort, not expect change. Well is the man who after his death-day may seek the Lord and find peace in the embrace of the Father.

[THE COMING OF BEOWULF TO HEOROT]

(III.) So in the cares of his times the son of Healfdene constantly brooded, nor might the wise warrior set aside his woe. Too harsh, hateful and long-lasting was the hardship that had come upon the people, distress dire and inexorable, worst of night-horrors.

---

4. According to old Germanic law, a slayer could achieve peace with his victim's kinsmen only by paying them *wergild*, i.e., compensation for the life of the slain man.
5. Behind this obscure passage seems to lie the idea that Grendel, unlike Hrothgar's thanes, could not approach the throne to receive gifts from the king, having been condemned by God as an outlaw.
6. I.e., the Devil. Despite this assertion that the Danes were heathen, their king, Hrothgar, speaks consistently as a Christian.

A thane of Hygelac,[7] a good man among the Geats, heard in his homeland of Grendel's deeds: of mankind he was the strongest of might in the time of this life, noble and great. He bade that a good ship be made ready for him, said he would seek the war-king over the swan's road, the famous prince, since he had need of men. Very little did wise men blame him for that adventure, though he was dear to them; they urged the brave one on, examined the omens. From the folk of the Geats the good man had chosen warriors of the bravest that he could find; one of fifteen he led the way, the warrior sought the wooden ship, the sea-skilled one the land's edge. The time had come: the ship was on the waves, the boat under the cliff. The warriors eagerly climbed on the prow—the sea-currents eddied, sea against sand; men bore bright weapons into the ship's bosom, splendid armor. Men pushed the well-braced ship from shore, warriors on a well-wished voyage. Then over the sea-waves, blown by the wind, the foam-necked boat traveled, most like a bird, until at good time on the second day the curved prow had come to where the seafarers could see land, the sea-cliffs shine, towering hills, great headlands. Then was the sea crossed, the journey at end. Then quickly the men of the Geats climbed upon the shore, moored the wooden ship; mail-shirts rattled, dress for battle. They thanked God that the wave-way had been easy for them.

Then from the wall the Scyldings' guard who should watch over the sea-cliffs saw bright shields borne over the gangway, armor ready for battle; strong desire stirred him in mind to learn what the men were. He went riding on his horse to the shore, thane of Hrothgar, forcefully brandished a great spear in his hands, with formal words questioned them: "What are you, bearers of armor, dressed in mail-coats, who thus have come bringing a tall ship over the sea-road, over the water to this place? Lo, for a long time I have been guard of the coast, held watch by the sea so that no foe with a force of ships might work harm on the Danes' land: never have shield-bearers more openly undertaken to come ashore here; nor did you know for sure of a word of leave from our warriors, consent from my kinsmen. I have never seen a mightier warrior on earth than is one of you, a man in battle-dress. That is no retainer made to seem good by his weapons—unless his appearance belies him, his unequalled form. Now I must learn your lineage before you go any farther from here, spies on the Danes' land. Now you far-dwellers, sea-voyagers, hear what I think: you must straightway say where you have come from."

7. I.e., Beowulf the Geat, whose king was Hygelac.

(IV.) To him replied the leader, the chief of the band un-locked his word-hoard: "We are men of the Geatish nation and Hygelac's hearth-companions. My father was well-known among the tribes, a noble leader named Ecgtheow. He lived many winters before he went on his way, an old man, from men's dwellings. Every wise man wide over the earth readily remembers him. Through friendly heart we have come to seek your lord, the son of Healfdene, protector of the people. Be good to us and tell us what to do: we have a great errand to the famous one, the king of the Danes. And I too do not think that anything ought to be kept secret: you know whether it is so, as we have indeed heard, that among the Scyldings I know not what foe, what dark doer of hateful deeds in the black nights, shows in terrible manner strange malice, injury and slaughter. In openness of heart I may teach Hrothgar remedy for that, how he, wise and good, shall overpower the foe—if change is ever to come to him, relief from evil's distress—and how his surging cares may be made to cool. Or else ever after he will suffer tribulations, con-straint, while the best of houses remains there on its high place."

The guard spoke from where he sat on his horse, brave officer: "A sharp-witted shield-warrior who thinks well must be able to judge each of the two things, words and works. I understand this: that here is a troop friendly to the Scyldings' king. Go forward, bearing weapons and war-gear. I will show you the way; I shall also bid my fellow-thanes honorably to hold your boat against all enemies, your new-tarred ship on the sand, until again over the sea-streams it bears its beloved men to the Geatish shore, the wooden vessel with curved prow. May it be granted by fate that one who behaves so bravely pass whole through the battle-storm."

Then they set off. The boat lay fixed, rested on the rope, the deep-bosomed ship, fast at anchor. Boar-images [8] shone over cheek-guards gold-adorned, gleaming and fire-hardened—the war-minded boar held guard over fierce men. The warriors hastened, marched together until they might see the timbered hall, stately and shining with gold; for earth-dwellers under the skies that was the most famous of buildings in which the mighty one waited—its light gleamed over many lands. The battle-brave guide pointed out to them the shining house of the brave ones so that they might go straight to it. Warrior-like he turned his horse, then spoke words: "It is time for me to go back. The All-Wielding Father in His grace keep you safe in your undertakings. I shall

---

8. Carved images of boars (sometimes represented as clothed like human war-riors) were placed on helmets in the belief that they would protect the wearer in battle.

go back to the sea to keep watch against hostile hosts."

(V.) The road was stone-paved, the path showed the way to the men in ranks. War-corselet shone, hard and hand-wrought, bright iron rings sang on their armor when they first came walking to the hall in their grim gear. Sea-weary they set down their broad shields, marvelously strong protections, against the wall of the building. Then they sat down on the bench—mail-shirts, warrior's clothing, rang out. Spears stood together, sea-men's weapons, ash steel-gray at the top. The armed band was worthy of its weapons.

Then a proud-spirited man [9] asked the warriors there about their lineage: "Where do you bring those gold-covered shields from, gray mail-shirts and visored helmets, this multitude of battle-shafts? I am Hrothgar's herald and officer. I have not seen strangers—so many men—more bold. I think that it is for daring—not for refuge, but for greatness of heart—that you have sought Hrothgar." The man known for his courage replied to him; the proud man of the Geats, hardy under helmet, spoke words in return: "We are Hygelac's table-companions. Beowulf is my name. I will tell my errand to Healfdene's son, the great prince your lord, if, good as he is, he will grant that we might address him." Wulfgar spoke—he was a man of the Wendels, his bold spirit known to many, his valor and wisdom: "I will ask the lord of the Danes about this, the Scyldings' king, the ring-giver, just as you request—will ask the glorious ruler about your voyage, and will quickly make known to you the answer the good man thinks best to give me."

He returned at once to where Hrothgar sat, old and hoary, with his company of earls. The man known for his valor went forward till he stood squarely before the Danes' king: he knew the custom of tried retainers. Wulfgar spoke to his lord and friend: "Here have journeyed men of the Geats, come far over the sea's expanse. The warriors call their chief Beowulf. They ask that they, my prince, might exchange words with you. Do not refuse them your answer, gracious Hrothgar. From their war-gear they seem worthy of earls' esteem. Strong indeed is the chief who has led the warriors here."

(VI.) Hrothgar spoke, protector of the Scyldings: "I knew him when he was a boy. His father was called Ecgtheow: Hrethel of the Geats [1] gave him his only daughter for his home. Now has his hardy offspring come here, sought a fast friend. Then, too, seafarers who took gifts there to please the Geats used to say that he has in his handgrip the strength of thirty men, a man

---

9. Identified below as Wulfgar.
1. Hrethel was the father of Hygelac and Beowulf's grandfather and guardian.

famous in battle. Holy God of His grace has sent him to us West-Danes, as I hope, against the terror of Grendel. I shall offer the good man treasures for his daring. Now make haste, bid them come in together to see my company of kinsmen. In your speech say to them also that they are welcome to the Danish people."

Then Wulfgar went to the hall's door, gave the message from within: "The lord of the East-Danes, my victorious prince, has bidden me say to you that he knows your noble ancestry, and that you brave-hearted men are welcome to him over the sea-swells. Now you may come in your war-dress, under your battle helmets, to see Hrothgar. Let your war-shields, your wooden spears, await here the outcome of the talk."

Then the mighty one rose, many a warrior about him, a company of strong thanes. Some waited there, kept watch over the weapons as the brave one bade them. Together they hastened, as the warrior directed them, under Heorot's roof. The war-leader, hardy under helmet, advanced till he stood on the hearth. Beowulf spoke, his mail-shirt glistened, armor-net woven by the blacksmith's skill: "Hail, Hrothgar! I am kinsman and thane of Hygelac. In my youth I have set about many brave deeds. The affair of Grendel was made known to me on my native soil: sea-travelers say that this hall, best of buildings, stands empty and useless to all warriors after the evening-light becomes hidden beneath the cover of the sky. Therefore my people, the best wise earls, advised me thus, lord Hrothgar, that I should seek you because they know what my strength can accomplish. They themselves looked on when, bloody from my foes, I came from the fight where I had bound five, destroyed a family of giants, and at night in the waves slain water-monsters, suffered great pain, avenged an affliction of the Weather-Geats on those who had asked for trouble—ground enemies to bits. And now alone I shall settle affairs with Grendel, the monster, the demon. Therefore, lord of the Bright-Danes, protector of the Scyldings, I will make a request of you, refuge of warriors, fair friend of nations, that you refuse me not, now that I have come so far, that alone with my company of earls, this band of hardy men, I may cleanse Heorot. I have also heard say that the monster in his recklessness cares not for weapons. Therefore, so that my liege lord Hygelac may be glad of me in his heart, I scorn to bear sword or broad shield, yellow wood, to the battle, but with my grasp I shall grapple with the enemy and fight for life, foe against foe. The one whom death takes can trust the Lord's judgment. I think that if he may accomplish it, unafraid he will feed on the folk of the Geats in the war-hall as he has often done on the flower of men. You will not need to hide my head [2]

2. I.e., "bury my body."

if death takes me, for he will have me blood-smeared; he will bear away my bloody flesh meaning to savor it, he will eat ruthlessly, the walker alone, will stain his retreat in the moor; no longer will you need trouble yourself to take care of my body. If battle takes me, send to Hygelac the best of war-clothes that protects my breast, finest of mail-shirts. It is a legacy of Hrethel, the work of Weland.[3] Fate always goes as it must."

(VII.) Hrothgar spoke, protector of the Scyldings: "For deeds done, my friend Beowulf, and for past favors you have sought us. A fight of your father's brought on the greatest of feuds. With his own hands he became the slayer of Heatholaf among the Wylfings. After that the country of the Weather-Geats might not keep him, for fear of war. From there he sought the folk of the South-Danes, the Honor-Scyldings, over the sea-swell. At that time I was first ruling the Danish people and, still in my youth, held the wide kingdom, hoard-city of heroes. Heorogar had died then, gone from life, my older brother, son of Healfdene—he was better than I. Afterwards I paid blood-money to end the feud; over the sea's back I sent to the Wylfings old treasures; he[4] swore oaths to me.

"It is a sorrow to me in spirit to say to any man what Grendel has brought me with his hatred—humiliation in Heorot, terrible violence. My hall-troop, warrior-band, has shrunk; fate has swept them away into Grendel's horror. (God may easily put an end to the wild ravager's deeds!) Full often over the ale-cups warriors made bold with beer have boasted that they would await with grim swords Grendel's attack in the beer-hall. Then in the morning this mead-hall was a hall shining with blood, when the day lightened, all the bench-floor blood-wet, a gore-hall. I had fewer faithful men, beloved retainers, for death had destroyed them. Now sit down to the feast and unbind your thoughts, your famous victories, as heart inclines."

[THE FEAST AT HEOROT]

Then was a bench cleared in the beer-hall for the men of the Geats all together. Then the stout-hearted ones went to sit down, proud in their might. A thane did his work who bore in his hands an embellished ale-cup, poured the bright drink. At times a scop sang, clear-voiced in Heorot. There was joy of brave men, no little company of Danes and Weather-Geats.

(VIII.) Unferth spoke, son of Ecglaf, who sat at the feet of the king of the ´Scyldings, unbound words of contention—to

3. The blacksmith of the Norse gods.   Wylfings Hrothgar had settled.
4. Ecgtheow, whose feud with the

him was Beowulf's undertaking, the brave seafarer, a great vex-
ation, for he would not allow that any other man of middle-
earth should ever achieve more glory under the heavens than
himself: "Are you that Beowulf who contended with Breca, com-
peted in swimming on the broad sea, where for pride you explored
the water, and for foolish boast ventured your lives in the deep?
Nor might any man, friend nor enemy, keep you from the
perilous venture of swimming in the sea. There you embraced the
sea-streams with your arms, measured the sea-ways, flung forward
your hands, glided over the ocean; the sea boiled with waves,
with winter's swell. Seven nights you toiled in the water's power.
He overcame you at swimming, had more strength. Then in the
morning the sea bore him up among the Heathoraemas; from
there he sought his own home, dear to his people, the land of
the Brondings, the fair stronghold, where he had folk, castle, and
treasures. All his boast against you the son of Beanstan carried
out in deed. Therefore I expect the worse results for you—though
you have prevailed everywhere in battles, in grim war—if you
dare wait near Grendel a night-long space."

Beowulf spoke, the son of Ecgtheow: "Well, my friend Un-
ferth, drunk with beer you have spoken a great many things
about Breca—told about his adventures. I maintain the truth that
I had more strength in the sea, hardship on the waves, than
any other man. Like boys we agreed together and boasted—we
were both in our first youth—that we would risk our lives in the
salt sea, and that we did even so. We had naked swords, strong
in our hands, when we went swimming; we thought to guard
ourselves against whale-fishes. He could not swim at all far from
me in the flood-waves, be quicker in the water, nor would I move
away from him. Thus we were together on the sea for the time
of five nights until the flood drove us apart, the swelling sea,
coldest of weathers, darkening night, and the north wind battle-
grim turned against us: rough were the waves. The anger of the
sea-fishes was roused. Then my body-mail, hard and hand-linked,
gave me help against my foes; the woven war-garment, gold-
adorned, covered my breast. A fierce cruel attacker dragged me
to the bottom, held me grim in his grasp, but it was granted
me to reach the monster with my sword-point, my battle-blade.
The war-stroke destroyed the mighty sea-beast—through my hand.

(IX.) "Thus often loathsome assailants pressed me hard. I
served them with my good sword, as the right was. They had
no joy at all of the feast, the malice-workers, that they should
eat me, sit around a banquet near the sea-bottom. But in the
morning, sword-wounded they lay on the shore, left behind by
the waves, put to sleep by the blade, so that thereafter they

would never hinder the passage of sea-voyagers over the deep water. Light came from the east, bright signal of God, the sea became still so that I might see the headlands, the windy walls of the sea. Fate often saves an undoomed man when his courage is good. In any case it befell me that I slew with my sword nine sea-monsters. I have not heard tell of a harder fight by night under heaven's arch, nor of a man more hard-pressed in the sea-streams. Yet I came out of the enemies' grasp alive, weary of my adventure. Then the sea bore me onto the lands of the Finns, the flood with its current, the surging waters.

"I have not heard say of you any such hard matching of might, such sword-terror. Breca never yet in the games of war— neither he nor you—achieved so bold a deed with bright swords (I do not much boast of it), though you became your brothers' slayer, your close kin; for that you will suffer punishment in hell, even though your wit is keen. I tell you truly, son of Ecglaf, that Grendel, awful monster, would never have performed so many terrible deeds against your chief, humiliation in Heorot, if your spirit, your heart, were so fierce in fight as you claim. But he has noticed that he need not much fear the hostility, not much dread the terrible sword-storm of your people, the Victory-Scyldings. He exacts forced levy, shows mercy to none of the Danish people; but he is glad, kills, carves for feasting, expects no fight from the Spear-Danes. But I shall show him soon now the strength and courage of the Geats, their warfare. Afterwards he will walk who may, glad to the mead, when the morning light of another day, the bright-clothed sun, shines from the south on the children of men."

Then was the giver of treasure in gladness, gray-haired and battle-brave. The lord of the Bright-Danes could count on help. The folk's guardian had heard from Beowulf a fast-resolved thought.

There was laughter of warriors, voices rang pleasant, words were cheerful. Wealhtheow came forth, Hrothgar's queen, mindful of customs, gold-adorned, greeted the men in the hall; and the noble woman offered the cup first to the keeper of the land of the East-Danes, bade him be glad at the beer-drinking, beloved of the people. In joy he partook of feast and hall-cup, king famous for victories. Then the woman of the Helmings went about to each one of the retainers, young and old, offered them the costly cup, until the time came that she brought the mead-bowl to Beowulf, the ring-adorned queen, mature of mind. Sure of speech she greeted the man of the Geats, thanked God that her wish was fulfilled, that she might trust in some man for help against deadly deeds. He took the cup, the warrior fierce in

battle, from Wealhtheow, and then spoke, one ready for fight—
Beowulf spoke, the son of Ecgtheow: "I resolved, when I set out
on the sea, sat down in the sea-boat with my band of men, that
I should altogether fulfill the will of your people or else fall
in slaughter, fast in the foe's grasp. I shall achieve a deed of
manly courage or else have lived to see in this mead-hall my
ending day." These words were well-pleasing to the woman, the
boast of the Geat. Gold-adorned, the noble folk-queen went to
sit by her lord.

Then there were again as at first strong words spoken in the
hall, the people in gladness, the sound of a victorious folk, until,
in a little while, the son of Healfdene wished to seek his evening
rest. He knew of the battle in the high hall that had been plotted
by the monster, plotted from the time that they might see the
light of the sun until the night, growing dark over all things, the
shadowy shapes of darkness, should come gliding, black under
the clouds. The company all arose. Then they saluted each other,
Hrothgar and Beowulf, and Hrothgar wished him good luck,
control of the wine-hall, and spoke these words: "Never before,
since I could raise hand and shield, have I entrusted to any
man the great hall of the Danes, except now to you. Hold now
and guard the best of houses: remember your fame, show your
great courage, keep watch against the fierce foe. You will not
lack what you wish if you survive that deed of valor."

[THE FIGHT WITH GRENDEL]

(X.) Then Hrothgar went out of the hall with his company
of warriors, the protector of the Scyldings. The war-chief would
seek the bed of Wealhtheow the queen. The King of Glory—
as men had learned—had appointed a hall-guard against Gren-
del; he had a special mission to the prince of the Danes: he kept
watch against monsters.

And the man of the Geats had sure trust in his great might,
the favor of the Ruler. Then he took off his shirt of armor, the
helmet from his head, handed his embellished sword, best of
irons, to an attendant, bade him keep guard over his war-gear.
Then the good warrior spoke some boast-words before he
went to his bed, Beowulf of the Geats: "I claim myself no
poorer in war-strength, war works, than Grendel claims himself.
Therefore I will not put him to sleep with a sword, so take
away his life, though surely I might. He knows no good tools
with which he might strike against me, cut my shield in pieces,
though he is strong in fight. But we shall forgo the sword in the

night—if he dare seek war without weapon—and then may wise God, Holy Lord, assign glory on whichever hand seems good to Him."

The battle-brave one laid himself down, the pillow received the earl's head, and about him many a brave seaman lay down to hall-rest. None of them thought that he would ever again seek from there his dear home, people or town where he had been brought up; for they knew that bloody death had carried off far too many men in the wine-hall, folk of the Danes. But the Lord granted to weave for them good fortune in war, for the folk of the Weather-Geats, comfort and help that they should quite overcome their foe through the might of one man, through his sole strength: the truth has been made known that mighty God has always ruled mankind.

There came gliding in the black night the walker in darkness. The warriors slept who should hold the horned house—all but one. It was known to men that when the Ruler did not wish it the hostile creature might not drag them away beneath the shadows. But he, lying awake for the fierce foe, with heart swollen in anger awaited the outcome of the fight.

(XI.) Then from the moor under the mist-hills Grendel came walking, wearing God's anger. The foul ravager thought to catch some one of mankind there in the high hall. Under the clouds he moved until he could see most clearly the wine-hall, treasure-house of men, shining with gold. That was not the first time that he had sought Hrothgar's home. Never before or since in his life-days did he find harder luck, hardier hall-thanes. The creature deprived of joy came walking to the hall. Quickly the door gave way, fastened with fire-forged bands, when he touched it with his hands. Driven by evil desire, swollen with rage, he tore it open, the hall's mouth. After that the foe at once stepped onto the shining floor, advanced angrily. From his eyes came a light not fair, most like a flame. He saw many men in the hall, a band of kinsmen all asleep together, a company of war-men. Then his heart laughed: dreadful monster, he thought that before the day came he would divide the life from the body of every one of them, for there had come to him a hope of full-feasting. It was not his fate that when that night was over he should feast on more of mankind.

The kinsman of Hygelac, mighty man, watched how the evil-doer would make his quick onslaught. Nor did the monster mean to delay it, but, starting his work, he suddenly seized a sleeping man, tore at him ravenously, bit into his bone-locks, drank the blood from his veins, swallowed huge morsels; quickly he had eaten all of the lifeless one, feet and hands. He stepped closer, then felt with his arm for the brave-hearted man on the bed, reached out towards him, the foe with his hand; at once in fierce response Beowulf seized it and sat up, leaning on his own arm. Straightway the fosterer of crimes knew that he had not encountered on middle-earth, anywhere in this world, a harder hand-grip from another man. In mind he became frightened, in his spirit: not for that might he escape the sooner. His heart was eager to get away, he would flee to his hiding-place, seek his rabble of devils. What he met there was not such as he had ever before met in the days of his life. Then the kinsman of Hygelac, the good man, thought of his evening's speech, stood upright and laid firm hold on him: his fingers cracked. The giant was pulling away, the earl stepped forward. The notorious one thought to move farther away, wherever he could, and flee his way from there to his fen-retreat; he knew his fingers' power to be in a hateful grip. That was a painful journey that the loathsome despoiler had made to Heorot. The retainers' hall rang with the noise—terrible drink [5] for all the Danes, the house-dwellers, every brave man, the earls. Both were enraged, fury-filled, the two who meant to control the hall. The building resounded. Then was it much wonder that the wine-hall withstood them joined in fierce fight, that it did not fall to the ground, the fair earth-dwelling; but it was so firmly made fast with iron bands, both inside and outside, joined by skillful smith-craft. There started from the floor—as I have heard say—many a mead-bench, gold-adorned, when the furious ones fought. No wise men of the Scyldings ever before thought that any men in any manner might break it down, splendid with bright horns, have skill to destroy it, unless flame should embrace it, swallow it in fire. Noise rose up, sound strange enough. Horrible fear came upon the North-Danes, upon every one of those who heard the weeping from the wall, God's enemy sing his terrible song, song without triumph—the hell-slave bewail his pain. There held him fast he who of men was strongest of might in the days of this life.

(XII.) Not for anything would the protector of warriors let the murderous guest go off alive: he did not consider his life-days of use to any of the nations. There more than enough of Beowulf's earls drew swords, old heirlooms, wished to protect the life of their dear lord, famous prince, however they might. They did not know when they entered the fight, hardy-spirited warriors, and when they thought to hew him on every side, to seek his soul, that not any of the best of irons on earth, no war-sword, would touch the evil-doer: for with a charm he had made

---

5. The metaphor reflects the idea that the chief purpose of a hall such as in.

victory-weapons useless, every sword-edge. His departure to death from the time of this life was to be wretched; and the alien spirit was to travel far off into the power of fiends. Then he who before had brought trouble of heart to mankind, committed many crimes—he was at war with God—found that his body would do him no good, for the great-hearted kinsman of Hygelac had him by the hand. Each was hateful to the other alive. The awful monster had lived to feel pain in his body, a huge wound in his shoulder was exposed, his sinews sprang apart, his bone-locks broke. Glory in battle was given to Beowulf. Grendel must flee from there, mortally sick, seek his joyless home in the fen-slopes. He knew the more surely that his life's end had come, the full number of his days. For all the Danes was their wish fulfilled after the bloody fight. Thus he who had lately come from far off, wise and stout-hearted, had purged Heorot, saved Hrothgar's house from affliction. He rejoiced in his night's work, a deed to make famous his courage. The man of the Geats had fulfilled his boast to the East-Danes; so too he had remedied all the grief, the malice-caused sorrow that they had endured before, and had had to suffer from harsh necessity, no small distress. That was clearly proved when the battle-brave man set the hand up under the curved roof—the arm and the shoulder: there all together was Grendel's grasp.

[CELEBRATION AT HEOROT]

(XIII.) Then in the morning, as I have heard, there was many a warrior about the gift-hall. Folk-chiefs came from far and near over the wide-stretching ways to look on the wonder, the footprints of the foe. Nor did his going from life seem sad to any of the men who saw the tracks of the one without glory—how, weary-hearted, overcome with injuries, he moved on his way from there to the mere [6] of the water-monsters with life-failing footsteps, death-doomed and in flight. There the water was boiling with blood, the horrid surge of waves swirling, all mixed with hot gore, sword-blood. Doomed to die he had hidden, then, bereft of joys, had laid down his life in his fen-refuge, his heathen soul: there hell took him.

From there old retainers—and many a young man, too—turned back in their glad journey to ride from the mere, high-spirited on horseback, warriors on steeds. There was Beowulf's fame spoken of; many a man said—and not only once—that, south nor north, between the seas, over the wide earth, no other man under the sky's expanse was better of those who bear shields,

6. Lake.

more worthy of ruling. Yet they found no fault with their own dear lord, gracious Hrothgar, for he was a good king. At times battle-famed men let their brown horses gallop, let them race where the paths seemed fair, known for their excellence. At times a thane of the king, a man skilled at telling adventures, songs stored in his memory, who could recall many of the stories of the old days, wrought a new tale in well-joined words; this man undertook with his art to recite in turn Beowulf's exploit, and skillfully to tell an apt tale, to lend words to it.

He spoke everything that he had heard tell of Sigemund's valorous deeds, many a strange thing, the strife of Waels's son,[7] his far journeys, feuds and crimes, of which the children of men knew nothing—except for Fitela with him, to whom he would tell everything, the uncle to his nephew, for they were always friends in need in every fight. Many were the tribes of giants that they had laid low with their swords. For Sigemund there sprang up after his death-day no little glory—after he, hardy in war, had killed the dragon, keeper of the treasure-hoard: under the hoary stone the prince's son had ventured alone, a daring deed, nor was Fitela with him. Yet it turned out well for him, so that his sword went through the gleaming worm and stood fixed in the wall, splendid weapon: the dragon lay dead of the murdering stroke. Through his courage the great warrior had brought it about that he might at his own wish enjoy the ring-hoard. He loaded the sea-boat, bore into the ship's bosom the bright treasure, offspring of Waels. The hot dragon melted.

He was adventurer most famous, far and wide through the nations, for deeds of courage—he had prospered from that before, the protector of warriors—after the war-making of Heremod had come to an end, his strength and his courage.[8] Among the Jutes Heremod came into the power of his enemies, was betrayed, quickly dispatched. Surging sorrows had oppressed him too long: he had become a great care to his people, to all his princes; for many a wise man in former times had bewailed the journey of the fierce-hearted one—people who had counted on him as a relief from affliction—that that king's son should prosper, take the rank of his father, keep guard over the folk, the treasure and stronghold, the kindgom of heroes, the home of the Scyldings. The kinsman of Hygelac became dearer to his friends, to all mankind: crime took possession of Heremod.

Sometimes racing their horses they passed over the sand-covered ways. By then the morning light was far advanced, hastening on.

---

7. Waels was Sigemund's father.
8. Heremod was an unsuccessful king of the Danes, one who began brilliantly but became cruel and avaricious, ul-timately having to take refuge among the Jutes, who put him to death. His reputation was thus overshadowed by that of Sigemund.

Many a stout-hearted warrior went to the high hall to see the strange wonder. The king himself walked forth from the women's apartment, the guardian of the ring-hoards, secure in his fame, known for his excellence, with much company; and his queen with him passed over the path to the mead-hall with a troop of attendant women.

(XIV.) Hrothgar spoke—he had gone to the hall, taken his stand on the steps, looked at the high roof shining with gold, and at Grendel's hand: "For this sight may thanks be made quickly to the Almighty: I endured much from the foe, many griefs from Grendel: God may always work wonder upon wonder, the Guardian of Heaven. It was not long ago that I did not expect ever to live to see relief from any of my woes—when the best of houses stood shining with blood, stained with slaughter, a far-reaching woe for each of my counselors, for every one, since none thought he could ever defend the people's stronghold from its enemies, from demons and evil spirits. Now through the Lord's might a warrior has accomplished the deed that all of us with our skill could not perform. Yes, she may say, whatever woman brought forth this son among mankind—if she still lives —that the God of Old was kind to her in her child-bearing. Now, Beowulf, best of men, in my heart I will love you as a son: keep well this new kinship. To you will there be no lack of the good things of the world that I have in my possession. Full often I have made reward for less, done honor with gifts to a lesser warrior, weaker in fighting. With your deeds you yourself have made sure that your glory will be ever alive. May the Almighty reward you with good—as just now he has done."

Beowulf spoke, the son of Ecgtheow: "With much good will we have achieved this work of courage, that fight, have ventured boldly against the strength of the unknown one. I should have wished rather that you might have seen him, your enemy brought low among your furnishings. I thought quickly to bind him on his deathbed with hard grasp, so that because of my hand-grip he should lie struggling for life—unless his body should escape. I could not stop his going, since the Lord did not wish it, nor did I hold him firmly enough for that, my life-enemy: he was too strong, the foe in his going. Yet to save his life he has left his hand behind to show that he was here—his arm and shoulder; nor by that has the wretched creature bought any comfort; none the longer will the loathsome ravager live, hard-pressed by his crimes, for a wound has clutched him hard in its strong grip, in deadly bonds. There, like a man outlawed for guilt, he shall await the great judgment, how the bright Lord will decree for him."

Then was the warrior more silent in boasting speech of war-like deeds, the son of Ecglaf,[9] after the nobles had looked at the hand, now high on the roof through the strength of a man, the foe's fingers. The end of each one, each of the nail-places, was most like steel; the hand-spurs of the heathen warrior were monstrous spikes. Everyone said that no hard thing would hurt him, no iron good from old times would harm the bloody battle-hand of the monster.

(XV.) Then was it ordered that Heorot be within quickly adorned by hands. Many there were, both men and women, who made ready the wine-hall, the guest-building. The hangings on the walls shone with gold, many a wondrous sight for each man who looks on such things. That bright building was much damaged, though made fast within by iron bonds, and its door-hinges sprung; the roof alone came through unharmed when the monster, out-lawed for his crimes, turned in flight, in despair of his life. That is not easy to flee from—let him try it who will—but driven by need one must seek the place prepared for earth-dwellers, soul-bearers, the sons of men, the place where, after its feasting, one's body will sleep fast in its death-bed.

Then had the proper time come that Healfdene's son should go to the hall; the king himself would share in the feast. I have never heard that a people in a larger company bore themselves better about their treasure-giver. Men who were known for courage sat at the benches, rejoiced in the feast. Their kinsmen, stout-hearted Hrothgar and Hrothulf, partook fairly of many a mead-cup in the high hall. Heorot within was filled with friends: the Scylding-people had not then known treason's web.[1]

Then the son of Healfdene gave Beowulf a golden standard to reward his victory—a decorated battle-banner—a helmet and mail-shirt: many saw the glorious, costly sword borne before the war-rior. Beowulf drank of the cup in the mead-hall. He had no need to be ashamed before fighting men of those rich gifts. I have not heard of many men who gave four precious, gold-adorned things to another on the ale-bench in a more friendly way. The rim around the helmet's crown had a head-protection, wound of wire, so that no battle-hard sharp sword might badly hurt him when the shield-warrior should go against his foe. Then the people's protector commanded eight horses with golden bridles to be led into the hall, within the walls. The saddle of one of them stood shining with hand-ornaments, adorned with jewels: that had been the war-seat of the high king when the son of Healfdene would

9. I.e., Unferth, who had taunted Beowulf the night before.
1. A reference to the later history of the Danes, when, after Hrothgar's death, his nephew Hrothulf apparently drove his son and successor Hrethric from the throne.

join sword-play: never did the warfare of the wide-known one
fail when men died in battle. And then the prince of Ing's friends [2]
yielded possession of both, horses and weapons, to Beowulf: he
bade him use them well. So generously the famous prince, guardian
of the hoard, repaid the warrior's battle-deeds with horses and
treasure that no man will ever find fault with them—not he that
will speak truth according to what is right.

(XVI.) Then further the lord gave treasure to each of the
men on the mead-bench who had made the sea-voyage with
Beowulf, gave heirlooms; and he commanded that gold be paid
for the one whom in his malice Grendel had killed—as he would
have killed more if wise God and the man's courage had not
forestalled that fate. The Lord guided all the race of men then,
as he does now. Yet is discernment everywhere best, fore-
thought of mind. Many a thing dear and loath he shall live to
see who here in the days of trouble long makes use of the world.

There was song and music together before Healfdene's battle-
leader, the wooden harp touched, tale oft told, when Hrothgar's
scop should speak hall-pastime among the mead-benches . . .
[of] Finn's retainers when the sudden disaster fell upon them. . . .[3]
The hero of the Half-Danes, Hnaef of the Scyldings, was fated
to fall on Frisian battlefield. And no need had Hildeburh [4] to
praise the good faith of the Jutes: blameless she was deprived
of her dear ones at the shield-play, of son and brother; wounded
by spears they fell to their fate. That was a mournful woman.
Not without cause did Hoc's daughter lament the decree of destiny
when morning came and she might see, under the sky, the slaughter
of kinsmen—where before she had the greatest of world's joy.
The fight took away all Finn's thanes except for only a few, so
that he could in no way continue the battle on the field against
Hengest, nor protect the survivors by fighting against the prince's
thane. But they offered them peace-terms,[5] that they should clear

---

2. Ing was a legendary Danish king,
and his "friends" are the Danes.
3. The lines introducing the scop's song
seem faulty. The story itself is re-
counted in a highly allusive way, and
many of its details are obscure, though
some help is offered by an independent
version of the story given in a frag-
mentary Old English lay called *The
Fight at Finnsburg.*
4. Hildeburh, daughter of the former
Danish king Hoc and sister of the
ruling Danish king Hnaef, was married
to Finn, king of the Jutes (Frisians).
Hnaef with a party of Danes made
what was presumably a friendly visit
to Hildeburh and Finn at their home
Finnsburg, but during a feast a quarrel
broke out between the Jutes and the

Danes (since the scop's sympathies are
with the Danes, he ascribes the cause
to the bad faith of the Jutes), and in
the ensuing fight Hnaef and his nephew,
the son of Finn and Hildeburh, were
killed, along with many other Danes
and Jutes.
5. It is not clear who proposed the
peace terms, but in view of the teller's
Danish sympathies, it was probably the
Jutes that sought the uneasy truce
from Hengest, who became the Danes'
leader after Hnaef's death. The truce
imposed upon Hengest and the Danes
the intolerable condition of having to
dwell in peace with the Jutish king who
was responsible for the death of their
own king.

another building for them, hall and high seat, that they might have control of half of it with the sons of the Jutes; and at givings of treasure the son of Folcwalda [6] should honor the Danes each day, should give Hengest's company rings, such gold-plated treasure as that with which he would cheer the Frisians' kin in the high hall. Then on both sides they confirmed the fast peace-compact. Finn declared to Hengest, with oaths deep-sworn, unfeigned, that he would hold those who were left from the battle in honor in accordance with the judgment of his counselors, so that by words or by works no man should break the treaty nor because of malice should ever mention that, princeless, the Danes followed the slayer of their own ring-giver, since necessity forced them. If with rash speech any of the Frisians should insist upon calling to mind the cause of murderous hate, then the sword's edge should settle it.

The funeral pyre was made ready and gold brought up from the hoard. The best of the warriors of the War-Scyldings [7] was ready on the pyre. At the fire it was easy to see many a blood-stained battle-shirt, boar-image all golden—iron-hard swine—many a noble destroyed by wounds: more than one had died in battle. Then Hildeburh bade give her own son to the flames on Hnaef's pyre, burn his blood vessels, put him in the fire at the shoulder of his uncle. The woman mourned, sang her lament. The warrior took his place.[8] The greatest of death-fires wound to the skies, roared before the barrow. Heads melted as blood sprang out— wounds opened wide, hate-bites of the body. Fire swallowed them—greediest of spirits—all of those whom war had taken away from both peoples: their strength had departed.

(XVII.) Then warriors went to seek their dwellings, bereft of friends, to behold Friesland, their homes and high city.[9] Yet Hengest stayed on with Finn for a winter darkened with the thought of slaughter, all desolate. He thought of his land, though he might not drive his ring-prowed ship over the water—the sea boiled with storms, strove with the wind, winter locked the waves in ice-bonds—until another year came to men's dwellings, just as it does still, glorious bright weather always watching for its time. Then winter was gone, earth's lap fair, the exile was eager to go, the guest from the dwelling: [yet] more he thought of revenge for his wrongs than of the sea-journey—if he might bring about a fight where he could take account of the sons of the Jutes with his iron. So he made no refusal of the world's

---

6. I.e., Finn.
7. I.e., Hnaef.
8. The line is obscure, but it perhaps means that the body of Hildeburh's son

was placed on the pyre.
9. This seems to refer to the few survivors on the Jutish side.

custom when the son of Hunlaf [1] placed on his lap Battle-Bright, best of swords: its edges were known to the Jutes. Thus also to war-minded Finn in his turn cruel sword-evil came in his own home, after Guthlaf and Oslaf complained of the grim attack, the injury after the sea-journey, assigned blame for their lot of woes: breast might not contain the restless heart. Then was the hall reddened from foes' bodies, and thus Finn slain, the king in his company, and the queen taken. The warriors of the Scyldings bore to ship all the hall-furnishings of the land's king, whatever of necklaces, skillfully wrought treasures, they might find at Finn's home. They brought the noble woman on the sea-journey to the Danes, led her to her people.

The lay was sung to the end, the song of the scop. Joy mounted again, bench-noise brightened, cup-bearers poured wine from wonderful vessels. Then Wealhtheow came forth to walk under gold crown to where the good men sat, nephew and uncle: their friendship was then still unbroken, each true to the other. [2] There too Unferth the spokesman sat at the feet of the prince of the Scyldings: each of them trusted his spirit, that he had much courage, though he was not honorable to his kinsmen at sword-play. Then the woman of the Scyldings spoke:

"Take this cup my noble lord, giver of treasure. Be glad, gold-friend of warriors, and speak to the Geats with mild words, as a man ought to do. Be gracious to the Geats, mindful of gifts [which] [3] you now have from near and far. They have told me that you would have the warrior for your son. Heorot is purged, the bright ring-hall. Enjoy while you may many rewards, and leave to your kinsmen folk and kingdom when you must go forth to look on the Ruler's decree. I know my gracious Hrothulf, that he will hold the young warriors in honor if you, friend of the Scyldings, leave the world before him. I think he will repay our sons with good if he remembers all the favors we did to his pleasure and honor when he was a child."

Then she turned to the bench where her sons were, Hrethric and Hrothmund, and the sons of the warriors, young men together. There sat the good man Beowulf of the Geats beside the two brothers.

(XVIII.) The cup was borne to him and welcome offered

---

1. The text is open to various interpretations. The one adopted here assumes that the Dane Hunlaf, brother of Guthlaf and Oslaf, had been killed in the fight, and that ultimately Hunlaf's son demanded vengeance by the symbolical act of placing his father's sword in Hengest's lap, while at the same time Guthlaf and Oslaf reminded Hengest of the Jutes' treachery. It is not clear whether the subsequent fight in which Finn was killed was waged by the Danish survivors alone, or whether the party first went back to Denmark and then returned to Finnsburg with reinforcements.

2. See section XV, note 1, above.

3. The text seems corrupt.

in friendly words to him, and twisted gold courteously be-
stowed on him, two arm-ornaments, a mail-shirt and rings, the
largest of necklaces of those that I have heard spoken of on
earth. I have heard of no better hoard-treasure under the heavens
since Hama carried away to his bright city the necklace of the
Brosings,[4] chain and rich setting: he fled the treacherous hatred
of Eormenric, got eternal favor. This ring Hygelac of the Geats,[5]
grandson of Swerting, had on his last venture, when beneath his
battle-banner he defended his treasure, protected the spoils ot
war: fate took him when for pride he sought trouble, feud
with the Frisians. Over the cup of the waves the mighty prince
wore that treasure, precious stone. He fell beneath his shield; the
body of the king came into the grasp of the Franks, his breast-
armor and the neck-ring together. Lesser warriors plundered the
fallen after the war-harvest: people of the Geats held the place
of corpses.

The hall was filled with noise. Wealhtheow spoke, before the
company she said to him: "Wear this ring, beloved Beowulf,
young man, with good luck, and make use of this mail-shirt from
the people's treasure, and prosper well; make yourself known
with your might, and be kind of counsel to these boys: I shall
remember to reward you for that. You have brought it about
that, far and near, for a long time all men shall praise you, as
wide as the sea surrounds the shores, home of the winds. While
you live, prince, be prosperous. I wish you well of your treasure.
Much favored one, be kind of deeds to my son. Here is each
earl true to other, mild of heart, loyal to his lord; the thanes are
at one, the people obedient, the retainers cheered with drink do
as I bid."

Then she walked to her seat. There was the best of feasts, men
drank wine. They did not know the fate, the grim decree made
long before, as it came to pass to many of the earls after evening
had come and Hrothgar had gone to his chambers, the noble one
to his rest. A great number of men remained in the hall, just as
they had often done before. They cleared the benches from the
floor. It was spread over with beds and pillows. One of the beer-
drinkers, ripe and fated to die, lay down to his hall-rest. They
set at their heads their battle-shields, bright wood; there on the
bench it was easy to see above each man his helmet that towered
in battle, his ringed mail-shirt, his great spear-wood. It was their

4. The Brisings' (Brosings') necklace
had been worn by the goddess Freya.
Nothing more is known of this story of
Hama, who seems to have stolen the
necklace from the famous Gothic king
Eormenric.
5. Beowulf is later said to have pre-
sented the necklace to Hygelac's queen,
Hygd, though here Hygelac is said to
have been wearing it on his ill-fated
expedition against the Franks and
Frisians, into whose hands it fell at his
death.

custom to be always ready for war whether at home or in the field, in any case at any time that need should befall their liege lord: that was a good nation.

[GRENDEL'S MOTHER'S ATTACK]—plot event

(XIX.) Then they sank to sleep. One paid sorely for his evening rest, just as had often befallen them when Grendel guarded the gold-hall, wrought wrong until the end came, death after misdeeds. It came to be seen, wide-known to men, that after the bitter battle an avenger still lived for an evil space: Grendel's mother, woman, monster-wife, was mindful of her misery, she who had to dwell in the terrible water, the cold currents, after Cain became sword-slayer of his only brother, his own father's son. Then Cain went as an outlaw to flee the cheerful life of men, marked for his murder, held to the wasteland. From him sprang many a devil sent by fate. Grendel was one of them, hateful outcast who at Heorot found a waking man waiting his warfare. There the monster had laid hold upon him, but he was mindful of the great strength, the large gift God had given him, and relied on the Almighty for favor, comfort and help. By that he overcame the foe, subdued the hell-spirit. Then he went off wretched, bereft of joy, to seek his dying-place, enemy of mankind. And his mother, still greedy and gallows-grim, would go on a sorrowful venture, avenge her son's death.

Then she came to Heorot where the Ring-Danes slept throughout the hall. Then change came quickly to the earls there, when Grendel's mother made her way in. The attack was the less terrible by just so much as is the strength of women, the war-terror of a wife, less than an armed man's when a hard blade, forge-hammered, a sword shining with blood, good of its edges, cuts the stout boar on a helmet opposite. Then in the hall was hard-edged sword raised from the seat, many a broad shield lifted firmly in hand: none thought of helmet, of wide mail-shirt, when the terror seized him. She was in haste, would be gone out from there, protect her life after she was discovered. Swiftly she had taken fast hold on one of the nobles, then she went to the fen. He was one of the men between the seas most beloved of Hrothgar in the rank of retainer, a noble shield-warrior whom she destroyed at his rest, a man of great repute. Beowulf was not there, for earlier, after the treasure-giving, another lodging had been appointed for the renowned Geat. Outcry arose in Heorot: she had taken, in its gore, the famed hand. Care was renewed, come again on the dwelling. That was not a good bargain, that on both sides they had to pay with the lives of friends.

Then was the old king, the hoary warrior, of bitter mind when he learned that his chief thane was lifeless, his dearest man dead. Quickly Beowulf was fetched to the bed-chamber, man happy in victory. At daybreak together with his earls he went, the noble champion himself with his retainers, to where the wise one was, waiting to know whether after tidings of woe the All-Wielder would ever bring about change for him. The worthy warrior walked over the floor with his retainers—hall-wood resounded —that he might address words to the wise prince of Ing's friends, asked if the night had been pleasant according to his desires.

(XX.) Hrothgar spoke, protector of the Scyldings: "Ask not about pleasure. Sorrow is renewed to the people of the Danes: Aeschere is dead, Yrmenlaf's elder brother, my speaker of wisdom and my bearer of counsel, my shoulder-companion when we used to defend our heads in battle, when troops clashed, beat on boar-images. Whatever an earl should be, a man good from old times, such was Aeschere. Now a wandering murderous spirit has slain him with its hands in Heorot. I do not know by what way the awful creature, glorying in its prey, has made its retreat, gladdened by its feast. She has avenged the feud—that last night you killed Grendel with hard hand-grips, savagely, because too long he had diminished and destroyed my people. He fell in the fight, his life forfeited, and now the other has come, a mighty worker of wrong, would avenge her kinsman, and has carried far her revenge—as many a thane may think who weeps in his spirit for his treasure-giver, bitter sorrow in heart. Now the hand lies lifeless that was strong in support of all your desires.

"I have heard landsmen, my people, hall-counselors, say this, that they have seen two such huge walkers in the wasteland holding to the moors, alien spirits. One of them, so far as they could clearly discern, was the likeness of a woman. The other wretched shape trod the tracks of exile in the form of a man, except that he was bigger than any other man. Land-dwellers in the old days named him Grendel. They know of no father, whether in earlier times any was begotten for them among the dark spirits. They hold to the secret land, the wolf-slopes, the windy headlands, the dangerous fen-paths where the mountain stream goes down under the darkness of the hills, the flood under the earth. It is not far from here, measured in miles, that the mere stands; over it hang frost-covered woods, trees fast of root close over the water. There each night may be seen fire on the flood, a fearful wonder. Of the sons of men there lives none, old of wisdom, who knows the bottom. Though the heath-stalker, the strong-horned hart, harassed by hounds makes for the forest after long flight, rather will he give his life, his being, on the bank than save his head by entering. That is no pleasant place. From it the surging waves rise up black to the heavens when the wind stirs up awful storms, until the air becomes gloomy, the skies weep. Now once again is the cure in you alone. You do not yet know the land, the perilous place, where you might find the seldom-seen creature: seek if you dare. I will give you wealth for the feud, old treasure, as I did before, twisted gold—if you come away."

(XXI.) Beowulf spoke, the son of Ecgtheow: "Sorrow not, wise warrior. It is better for a man to avenge his friend than much mourn. Each of us must await his end of the world's life. Let him who may get glory before death: that is best for the warrior after he has gone from life. Arise, guardian of the kingdom, let us go at once to look on the track of Grendel's kin. I promise you this: she will not be lost under cover, not in the earth's bosom nor in the mountain woods nor at the bottom of the sea, go where she will. This day have patience in every woe—as I expect you to."

Then the old man leapt up, thanked God, the mighty Lord, that the man had so spoken. Then was a horse bridled for Hrothgar, a curly-maned mount. The wise king moved in state; the band of shield-bearers marched on foot. The tracks were seen wide over the wood-paths where she had gone on the ground, made her way forward over the dark moor, borne lifeless the best of retainers of those who watched over their home with Hrothgar. The son of noble forebears [6] moved over the steep rocky slopes, narrow paths where only one could go at a time, an unfamiliar trail, steep hills, many a lair of water-monsters. He went before with a few wise men to spy out the country, until suddenly he found mountain trees leaning out over hoary stone, a joyless wood: water lay beneath, bloody and troubled. It was pain of heart for all the Danes to suffer, for the friends of the Scyldings, for many a thane, grief to each earl when on the cliff over the water they came upon Aeschere's head. The flood boiled with blood—the men looked upon it—with hot gore. Again and again the horn sang its urgent war-song. The whole troop sat down to rest. Then they saw on the water many a snake-shape, strong sea-serpents exploring the mere, and water-monsters lying on the slopes of the shore such as those that in the morning often attend a perilous journey on the paths of the sea, serpents and wild beasts.

These fell away from the shore, fierce and rage-swollen: they had heard the bright sound, the war-horn sing. One of them a man of the Geats with his bow cut off from his life, his water-warring, after the hard war-arrow stuck in his heart: he was

6. I.e., Hrothgar.

weaker in swimming the lake when death took him. Straightway he was hard beset on the waves with barbed boar-spears, strongly surrounded, pulled up on the shore, strange spawn of the waves. The men looked on the terrible alien thing.

Beowulf put on his warrior's dress, had no fear for his life. His war-shirt, hand-fashioned, broad and well-worked, was to explore the mere: it knew how to cover his body-cave so that foe's grip might not harm his heart, or grasp of angry enemy his life. But the bright helmet guarded his head, one which was to stir up the lake-bottom, seek out the troubled water—made rich with gold, surrounded with splendid bands, as the weapon-smith had made it in far-off days, fashioned it wonderfully, set it about with boar-images so that thereafter no sword or battle-blade might bite into it. And of his strong supports that was not the least which Hrothgar's spokesman [7] lent to his need: Hrunting was the name of the hilted sword; it was one of the oldest of ancient treasures; its edge was iron, decorated with poison-stripes, hardened with battle-sweat. Never had it failed in war any man of those who grasped it in their hands, who dared enter on dangerous enterprises, onto the common meeting place of foes: this was not the first time that it should do work of courage. Surely the son of Ecglaf, great of strength, did not have in mind what, drunk with wine, he had spoken, when he lent that weapon to a better sword-fighter. He did not himself dare to risk his life under the warring waves, to engage his courage: there he lost his glory, his name for valor. It was not so with the other when he had armed himself for battle.

[BEOWULF ATTACKS GRENDEL'S MOTHER]

(XXII.) Beowulf spoke, the son of Ecgtheow: "Think now, renowned son of Healfdene, wise king, now that I am ready for the venture, gold-friend of warriors, of what we said before, that, if at your need I should go from life, you would always be in a father's place for me when I am gone: be guardian of my young retainers, my companions, if battle should take me. The treasure you gave me, beloved Hrothgar, send to Hygelac. The lord of the Geats may know from the gold, the son of Hrethel may see when he looks on that wealth, that I found a ring-giver good in his gifts, enjoyed him while I might. And let Unferth have the old heirloom, the wide-known man my splendid-waved sword, hard-edged: with Hrunting I shall get glory, or death will take me."

After these words the man of the Weather-Geats turned away boldly, would wait for no answer: the surging water took the warrior. Then was it a part of a day before he might see the

7. I.e., Unferth.

bottom's floor. Straightway that which had held the flood's tract a hundred half-years, ravenous for prey, grim and greedy, saw that some man from above was exploring the dwelling of monsters. Then she groped toward him, took the warrior in her awful grip. Yet not the more for that did she hurt his hale body within: his ring-armor shielded him about on the outside so that she could not pierce the war-dress, the linked body-mail, with hateful fingers. Then as she came to the bottom the sea-wolf bore the ring-prince to her house so that—no matter how brave he was —he might not wield weapons; but many monsters attacked him in the water, many a sea-beast tore at his mail-shirt with war-tusks, strange creatures afflicted him. Then the earl saw that he was in some hostile hall where no water harmed him at all, and the flood's onrush might not touch him because of the hall-roof. He saw firelight, a clear blaze shine bright.

Then the good man saw the accursed dweller in the deep, the mighty mere-woman. He gave a great thrust to his sword—his hand did not withhold the stroke—so that the etched blade sang at her head a fierce war-song. Then the stranger found that the battle-lightning would not bite, harm her life, but the edge failed the prince in his need: many a hand-battle had it endured before, often sheared helmet, war-coat of man fated to die: this was the first time for the rare treasure that its glory had failed.

But still he was resolute, not slow of his courage, mindful of fame, the kinsman of Hygelac. Then, angry warrior, he threw away the sword, wavy-patterned, bound with ornaments, so that it lay on the ground, hard and steel-edged: he trusted in his strength, his mighty hand-grip. So ought a man to do when he thinks to get long-lasting praise in battle: he cares not for his life. Then he seized by the hair Grendel's mother—the man of the War-Geats did not shrink from the fight. Battle-hardened, now swollen with rage, he pulled his deadly foe so that she fell to the floor. Quickly in her turn she repaid him his gift with her grim claws and clutched at him: then weary-hearted, the strongest of warriors, of foot-soldiers, stumbled so that he fell. Then she sat upon the hall-guest and drew her knife, broad and bright-edged. She would avenge her child, her only son. The woven breast-armor lay on his shoulder: that protected his life, with-stood entry of point or of edge. Then the son of Ecgtheow would have fared amiss under the wide ground, the champion of the Geats, if the battle-shirt had not brought help, the hard war-net—and holy God brought about victory in war; the wise Lord, Ruler of the Heavens, decided it with right, easily, when Beowulf had stood up again.

XXIII. Then he saw among the armor a victory-blessed blade,

an old sword made by the giants, strong of its edges, glory of warriors: it was the best of weapons, except that it was larger than any other man might bear to war-sport, good and adorned, the work of giants. He seized the linked hilt, he who fought for the Scyldings, savage and slaughter-bent, drew the patterned-blade; desperate of life, he struck angrily so that it bit her hard on the neck, broke the bone-rings. The blade went through all the doomed body. She fell to the floor, the sword was sweating, the man rejoiced in his work.

The blaze brightened, light shone within, just as from the sky heaven's candle shines clear. He looked about the building; then he moved along the wall, raised his weapon hard by the hilt, Hygelac's thane, angry and resolute: the edge was not useless to the warrior, for he would quickly repay Grendel for the many attacks he had made on the West-Danes—many more than the one time when he slew in their sleep fifteen hearth-companions of Hrothgar, devoured men of the Danish people while they slept, and another such number bore away, a hateful prey. He had paid him his reward for that, the fierce champion, for there he saw Grendel, weary of war, lying at rest, lifeless with the wounds he had got in the fight at Heorot. The body bounded wide when it suffered the blow after death, the hard sword-swing; and thus he cut off his head.

At once the wise men who were watching the water with Hrothgar saw that the surging waves were troubled, the lake stained with blood. Gray-haired, old, they spoke together of the good warrior, that they did not again expect of the chief that he would come victorious to seek their great king; for many agreed on it, that the sea-wolf had destroyed him.

Then came the ninth hour of the day. The brave Scyldings left the hill. The gold-friend of warriors went back to his home. The strangers sat sick at heart and stared at the mere. They wished—and did not expect—that they would see their beloved lord himself.

Then the blade began to waste away from the battle-sweat, the war-sword into battle-icicles. That was a wondrous thing, that it should all melt, most like the ice when the Father loosens the frost's fetters, undoes the water-bonds—He Who has power over seasons and times: He is the true Ruler. Beowulf did not take from the dwelling, the man of the Weather-Geats, more treasures —though he saw many there—but only the head and the hilt, bright with jewels. The sword itself had already melted, its patterned blade burned away: the blood was too hot for it, the spirit that had died there too poisonous. Quickly he was swimming, he who had lived to see the fall of his foes; he plunged up through the water. The currents were all cleansed, the great tracts of the water, when the dire spirit left her life-days and this loaned world.

Then the protector of seafarers came toward the land, swimming stout-hearted; he had joy of his sea-booty, the great burden he had with him. They went to meet him, thanked God, the strong band of thanes, rejoiced in their chief that they might see him again sound. Then the helmet and war-shirt of the mighty one were quickly loosened. The lake drowsed, the water beneath the skies, stained with blood. They went forth on the foot-tracks, glad in their hearts, measured the path back, the known ways, men bold as kings. They bore the head from the mere's cliff, toilsomely for each of the great-hearted ones: four of them had trouble in carrying Grendel's head on spear-shafts to the gold-hall —until at last they came striding to the hall, fourteen bold warriors of the Geats; their lord, high-spirited, walked in their company over the fields to the mead-hall.

Then the chief of the thanes, man daring in deeds, enriched by new glory, warrior dear to battle, came in to greet Hrothgar. Then Grendel's head was dragged by the hair over the floor to where men drank, a terrible thing to the earls and the woman with them, an awful sight: the men looked upon it.

[FURTHER CELEBRATION AT HEOROT]

(XXIV.) Beowulf spoke, the son of Ecgtheow: "Yes, we have brought you this sea-booty, son of Healfdene, man of the Scyldings, gladly, as evidence of glory—what you look on here. Not easily did I come through it with my life, the war under water, not without trouble carried out the task. The fight would have been ended straightway if God had not guarded me. With Hrunting I might not do anything in the fight, though that is a good weapon. But the Wielder of Men granted me that I should see hanging on the wall a fair, ancient great-sword—most often He has guided the man without friends—that I should wield the weapon. Then in the fight when the time became right for me I hewed the house-guardians. Then that war-sword, wavy-patterned, burnt away as their blood sprang forth, hottest of battle-sweats. I have brought the hilt away from the foes. I have avenged the evil deeds, the slaughter of Danes, as it was right to do. I promise you that you may sleep in Heorot without care with your band of retainers, and that for none of the thanes of your people, old or young, need you have fear, prince of the Scyldings—for no life-injury to your men on that account, as you did before."

Then the golden hilt was given into the hand of the old man, the hoary war-chief—the ancient work of giants. There came into the possession of the prince of the Danes, after the fall of devils, the work of wonder-smiths. And when the hostile-hearted creature, God's enemy, guilty of murder, gave up this world, and his mother too, it passed into the control of the best of worldly kings between the seas, of those who gave treasure in the Northlands.

Hrothgar spoke—he looked on the hilt, the old heirloom, on which was written the origin of ancient strife, when the flood, rushing water, slew the race of giants—they suffered terribly: that was a people alien to the Everlasting Lord. The Ruler made them a last payment through water's welling. On the sword-guard of bright gold there was also rightly marked through rune-staves, set down and told, for whom that sword, best of irons, had first been made, its hilt twisted and ornamented with snakes. Then the wise man spoke, the son of Healfdene—all were silent: "Lo, this may one say who works truth and right for the folk, recalls all things far distant, an old guardian of the land: that this earl was born the better man. Glory is raised up over the far ways—your glory over every people, Beowulf my friend. All of it, all your strength, you govern steadily in the wisdom of your heart. I shall fulfill my friendship to you, just as we spoke before. You shall become a comfort, whole and long-lasting, to your people, a help to warriors.

"So was not Heremod to the sons of Ecgwela, the Honor-Scyldings. He grew great not for their joy, but for their slaughter, for the destruction of Danish people. With swollen heart he killed his table-companions, shoulder-comrades, until he turned away from the joys of men, alone, notorious king, although mighty God had raised him in power, in the joys of strength, had set him up over all men. Yet in his breast his heart's thought grew blood-thirsty: no rings did he give to the Danes for glory. He lived joyless to suffer the pain of that strife, the long-lasting harm of the people. Teach yourself by him, be mindful of munificence. Old of winters, I tell this tale for you.

"It is a wonder to say how in His great spirit mighty God gives wisdom to mankind, land and earlship—He possesses power over all things. At times He lets the thought of a man of high lineage move in delight, gives him joy of earth in his homeland, a stronghold of men to rule over, makes regions of the world so subject to him, wide kingdoms, that in his unwisdom he may not himself have mind of his end. He lives in plenty; illness and age in no way grieve him, neither does dread care darken his heart, nor does enmity bare sword-hate, for the whole world turns to his will—he knows nothing worse—(XXV.) until his portion of pride increases and flourishes within him; then the watcher sleeps, the soul's guardian; that sleep is too sound, bound in its own cares, and the slayer most near whose bow shoots treacherously. Then is he hit in the heart, beneath his armor, with the bitter arrow—he cannot protect himself—with the crooked dark commands of the accursed spirit. What he has long held seems to him too little, angry-hearted he covets, no plated rings does he give in men's honor, and then he forgets and regards not his destiny because of what God, Wielder of Heaven, has given him before, his portion of glories. In the end it happens in turn that the loaned body weakens, falls doomed; another takes the earl's ancient treasure, one who recklessly gives precious gifts, does not fearfully guard them.

"Keep yourself against that wickedness, beloved Beowulf, best of men, and choose better—eternal gains. Have no care for pride, great warrior. Now for a time there is glory in your might: yet soon it shall be that sickness or sword will diminish your strength, or fire's fangs, or flood's surge, or sword's swing, or spear's flight, or appalling age; brightness of eyes will fail and grow dark; then it shall be that death will overcome you, warrior.

"Thus I ruled the Ring-Danes for a hundred half-years under the skies, and protected them in war with spear and sword against many nations over middle-earth, so that I counted no one as my adversary underneath the sky's expanse. Well, disproof of that came to me in my own land, grief after my joys, when Grendel, ancient adversary, came to invade my home. Great sorrow of heart I have always suffered for his persecution. Thanks be to the Ruler, the Eternal Lord, that after old strife I have come to see in my lifetime, with my own eyes, his blood-stained head. Go now to your seat, have joy of the glad feast, made famous in battle. Many of our treasures will be shared when morning comes."

The Geat was glad at heart, went at once to seek his seat as the wise one bade. Then was a feast fairly served again, for a second time, just as before, for those famed for courage, sitting about the hall.

Night's cover lowered, dark over the warriors. The retainers all arose. The gray-haired one would seek his bed, the old Scylding. It pleased the Geat, the brave shield-warrior, immensely that he should have rest. Straightway a hall-thane led the way on for the weary one, come from far country, and showed every courtesy to the thane's need, such as in those days seafarers might expect as their due.

Then the great-hearted one rested; the hall stood high, vaulted and gold-adorned; the guest slept within until the black raven, blithe-hearted, announced heaven's joy. Then the bright light came passing over the shadows. The warriors hastened, the nobles were eager to set out again for their people. Bold of spirit, the visitor would seek his ship far thence.

Then the hardy one bade that Hrunting be brought to the son of Ecglaf,[8] that he take back his sword, precious iron. He spoke thanks for that loan, said that he accounted it a good war-friend, strong in battle; in his words he found no fault at all with the sword's edge: he was a thoughtful man. And then they were eager to depart, the warriors ready in their armor. The prince who had earned honor of the Danes went to the high seat where the other was: the man dear to war greeted Hrothgar.

[Beowulf Returns Home]

(XXVI.) Beowulf spoke, the son of Ecgtheow: "Now we sea-travelers come from afar wish to say that we desire to seek Hygelac. Here we have been entertained splendidly according to our desire: you have dealt well with us. If on earth I might in any way earn more of your heart's love, prince of warriors, than I have done before with warlike deeds, I should be ready at once. If beyond the sea's expanse I hear that men dwelling near threaten you with terrors, as those who hated you did before, I shall bring you a thousand thanes, warriors to your aid. I know of Hygelac, lord of the Geats, though he is young as a guardian of the people, that he will further me with words and works so that I may do you honor and bring spears to help you, strong support where you have need of men. If Hrethric, king's son, decides to come to the court of the Geats, he can find many friends there; far countries are well sought by him who is himself strong."

Hrothgar spoke to him in answer: "The All-Knowing Lord sent those words into your mind: I have not heard a man of so young age speak more wisely. You are great of strength, mature of mind, wise of words. I think it likely if the spear, sword-grim war, takes the son of Hrethel, sickness or weapon your prince, the people's ruler, and you have your life, that the Sea-Geats will not have a better to choose as their king, as guardian of their treasure, if you wish to hold the kingdom of your kinsmen. So well your heart's temper has long pleased me, beloved Beowulf. You have brought it about that peace shall be shared by the peoples, the folk of the Geats and the Spear-Danes, and enmity shall sleep, acts of malice which they practiced before; and there shall be, as long as I rule the wide kingdom, sharing of treasures, many a man shall greet his fellow with good gifts over the sea-bird's baths; the ring-prowed ship will bring gifts and tokens of friendship over the sea. I know your people, blameless in every respect, set firm after the old way both as to foe and to friend."

Then the protector of earls, the kinsman of Healfdene, gave

8. I.e., Unferth.

him there in the hall twelve precious things; he bade him with these gifts seek his own dear people in safety, quickly come back. Then the king noble of race, the prince of the Scyldings, kissed the best of thanes and took him by his ncek: tears fell from the gray-haired one. He had two thoughts of the future, the old and wise man, one more strongly than the other—that they would not see each other again, bold men at council. The man was so dear to him that he might not restrain his breast's welling, for fixed in his heartstrings a deep-felt longing for the beloved man burned in his blood. Away from him Beowulf, warrior glorious with gold, walked over the grassy ground, proud of his treasure. The sea-goer awaited its owner, riding at anchor. Then on the journey the gift of Hrothgar was oft-praised: that was a king blameless in all things until age took from him the joys of his strength—old age that has often harmed many.

(XXVII.) There came to the flood the band of brave-hearted ones, of young men. They wore mail-coats, locked limb-shirts. The guard of the coast saw the coming of the earls, just as he had done before. He did not greet the guests with taunts from the cliff's top, but rode to meet them, said that the return of the warriors in bright armor in their ship would be welcome to the people of the Weather-Geats. There on the sand the broad sea-boat was loaded with armor, the ring-prowed ship with horses and rich things. The mast stood high over Hrothgar's hoard-gifts. He gave the boat-guard a sword wound with gold, so that thereafter on the mead-bench he was held the worthier for the treasure, the heirloom. The boat moved out to furrow the deep water, left the land of the Danes. Then on the mast a sea-cloth, a sail, was made fast by a rope. The boat's beams creaked: wind did not keep the sea-floater from its way over the waves. The sea-goer moved, foamy-necked floated forth over the swell, the ship with bound prow over the sea-currents until they might see the cliffs of the Geats, the well-known headlands. The ship pressed ahead, borne by the wind, stood still at the land. Quickly the harbor-guard was at the sea-side, he who had gazed for a long time far out over the currents, eager to see the beloved men. He [9] moored the deep ship in the sand, fast by its anchor ropes, lest the force of the waves should drive away the fair wooden vessel. Then he bade that the prince's wealth be borne ashore, armor and plated gold. It was not far for them to seek the giver of treasure, Hygelac son of Hrethel, where he dwelt at home near the sea-wall, himself with his retainers.

The building was splendid, its king most valiant, set high in the hall, Hygd [1] most youthful, wise and well-taught, though she

9. Beowulf.
1. Hygd is Hygelac's young queen. The suddenness of her introduction here is perhaps due to a faulty text.

had lived within the castle walls few winters, daughter of Hae-
reth. For she was not niggardly, nor too sparing of gifts to the
men of the Geats, of treasures. Modthryth,[2] good folk-queen, did
dreadful deeds [in her youth]: no bold one among her retainers
dared venture—except her great lord—to set his eyes on her in
daylight, but [if he did] he should reckon deadly bonds pre-
pared for him, arresting hands: that straightway after his seizure
the sword awaited him, that the patterned blade must settle it,
make known its death-evil. Such is no queenly custom for a
woman to practice, though she is peerless—that one who weaves
peace [3] should take away the life of a beloved man after pretended
injury. However the kinsman of Hemming stopped that: [4] ale-
drinkers gave another account, said that she did less harm to
the people, fewer injuries, after she was given, gold-adorned, to
the young warrior, the beloved noble, when by her father's teach-
ing she sought Offa's hall in a voyage over the pale sea. There
on the throne she was afterwards famous for generosity, while
living made use of her life, held high love toward the lord of
warriors, [who was] of all mankind the best, as I have heard,
between the seas of the races of men. Since Offa was a man
brave of wars and gifts, wide-honored, he held his native land
in wisdom. From him sprang Eomer to the help of warriors,
kinsman of Hemming, grandson of Garmund, strong in battle.[5]

(XXVIII.) Then the hardy one came walking with his troop
over the sand on the sea-plain, the wide shores. The world-candle
shone, the sun moved quickly from the south. They made their
way, strode swiftly to where they heard that the protector of
earls, the slayer of Ongentheow,[6] the good young war-king, was
dispensing rings in the stronghold. The coming of Beowulf was
straightway made known to Hygelac, that there in his home the
defender of warriors, his comrade in battle, came walking alive
to the court, sound from the battle-play. Quickly the way within
was made clear for the foot-guests, as the mighty one bade.

2. A transitional passage introducing
the contrast between Hygd's good be-
havior and Modthryth's bad behavior
as young women of royal blood seems
to have been lost. Modthryth's practice
of having those who looked into her
face put to death may reflect the folk-
motif of the princess whose unsuccessful
suitors are executed, though the text
does not say that Modthryth's victims
were suitors. Modthryth's "great lord"
was probably her father.
3. Daughters of kings were frequently
given in marriage to the king of a
hostile nation in order to bring about
peace; hence Modthryth may be called
"one who weaves peace."

4. Offa, an Angle king who according
to legend ruled Mercia in England; who
Hemming was—besides being Offa's
forebear—is not known.
5. Offa, the only person that may be
identified as English in this English
poem, receives high praise; apparently
the names of his father Garmund and
son Eomer would strike a responsive
chord in the poet's audience.
6. Ongentheow was a Scylfing (Swedish)
king, whose story is fully told below,
sections XL and XLI. In fact Hygelac
was not his slayer, but is called so
because he led the attack on the Scylf-
ings in which Ongentheow was killed.

Then he sat down with him, he who had come safe through the fight, kinsman with kinsman, after he had greeted his liege lord with formal speech, loyal, with vigorous words. Haereth's daughter moved through the hall-building with mead-cups, cared lovingly for the people, bore the cup of strong drink to the hands of the warriors. Hygelac began fairly to question his companion in the high hall, curiosity pressed him, what the adventures of the Sea-Geats had been. "How did you fare on your journey, beloved Beowulf, when you suddenly resolved to seek distant combat over the salt water, battle in Heorot? Did you at all help the wide-known woes of Hrothgar, the famous prince? Because of you I burned with seething sorrows, care of heart—had no trust in the venture of my beloved man. I entreated you long that you should in no way approach the murderous spirit, should let the South-Danes themselves settle the war with Grendel. I say thanks to God that I may see you sound."

Beowulf spoke, the son of Ecgtheow: "To many among men it is not hidden, lord Hygelac, the great encounter—what a fight we had, Grendel and I, in the place where he made many sorrows for the Victory-Scyldings, constant misery. All that I avenged, so that none of Grendel's kin over the earth need boast of that clash at night—whoever lives longest of the loathsome kind, wrapped in malice. There I went forth to the ring-hall to greet Hrothgar. At once the famous son of Healfdene, when he knew my purpose, gave me a seat with his own sons. The company was in joy: I have not seen in the time of my life under heaven's arch more mead-mirth of hall-sitters. At times the famous queen, peace-pledge of the people, went through all the hall, cheered the young men; often she would give a man a ring-band before she went to her seat. At times Hrothgar's daughter bore the ale-cup to the retainers, to the earls throughout the hall. I heard hall-sitters name her Freawaru when she offered the studded cup to warriors. Young and gold-adorned, she is promised to the fair son of Froda.[7] That has seemed good to the lord of the Scyldings, the guardian of the kingdom, and he believes of this plan that he may, with this woman, settle their portion of deadly feuds, of quarrels.[8] Yet most often after the fall of a prince in any nation the deadly spear rests but a little while, even though the bride is good.

"It may displease the lord of the Heatho-Bards and each thane of that people when he goes in the hall with the woman, [that while] the noble sons of the Danes, her retainers, [are] feasted,[9]

7. I.e., Ingeld, who succeeded his father a king of the Heatho-Bards.
8. I.e., the feud between the Danes and Heatho-Bards.
9. The text is faulty here.

the heirlooms of their ancestors will be shining on them [1]—the hard and wave-adorned treasure of the Heatho-Bards, [which was theirs] so long as they might wield those weapons, (XXIX.) until they led to the shield-play, to destruction, their dear companions and their own lives. Then at the beer he [2] who sees the treasure, an old ash-warrior who remembers it all, the spear-death of warriors—grim is his heart—begins, sad of mind, to tempt a young fighter in the thoughts of his spirit, to awaken war-evil, and speaks this word:

" 'Can you, my friend, recognize that sword, the rare iron-blade, that your father, beloved man, bore to battle his last time in armor, where the Danes slew him, the fierce Scyldings, got possession of the battle-field, when Withergeld [3] lay dead, after the fall of warriors? Now here some son of his murderers walks in the hall, proud of the weapon, boasts of the murder, and wears the treasure that you should rightly possess.' So he will provoke and remind at every chance with wounding words until that moment comes that the woman's thane, [4] forfeiting life, shall lie dead, blood-smeared from the sword-bite, 'for his father's deeds. The other escapes with his life, knows the land well. Then on both sides the oath of the earls will be broken; then deadly hate will well up in Ingeld, and his wife-love after the surging of sorrows will become cooler. Therefore I do not think the loyalty of the Heatho-Bards, their part in the alliance with the Danes, to be without deceit—do not think their friendship fast.

"I shall speak still more of Grendel, that you may readily know, giver of treasure, what the hand-fight of warriors came to in the end. After heaven's jewel had glided over the earth, the angry spirit came, awful in the evening, to visit us where, unharmed, we watched over the hall. There the fight was fatal to Hondscioh, deadly to one who was doomed. He was dead first of all, armed warrior. Grendel came to devour him, good young retainer, swallowed all the body of the beloved men. Yet not for this would the bloody-toothed slayer, bent on destruction, go from the gold-hall empty-handed; but, strong of might, he made trial of me, grasped me with eager hand. His glove [5] hung huge and wonderful, made fast with cunning clasps: it had been made all with craft, with devil's devices and dragon's skins. The fell doer of evils would

---

1. I.e., the weapons and armor which had once belonged to the Heatho-Bards and were captured by the Danes will be worn by the Danish attendants of Hrothgar's daughter Freawaru when she goes to the Heatho-Bards to marry king Ingeld.
2. I.e., some old Heatho-Bard warrior.

3. Apparently a leader of the Heatho-Bards in their unsuccessful war with the Danes.
4. I.e., the Danish attendant of Freawaru who is wearing the sword of his Heatho-Bard attacker's father.
5. Apparently a large glove that could be used as a pouch.

put me therein, guiltless, one of many. He might not do so after I had stood up in anger. It is too long to tell how I repaid the people's foe his due for every crime. My prince, there with my deeds I did honor to your people. He slipped away, for a little while had use of life's joy. Yet his right hand remained as his spoor in Heorot, and he went from there abject, mournful of heart sank to the mere's bottom.

"The lord of the Scyldings repaid me for that bloody combat with much plated gold, many treasures, after morning came and we sat down to the feast. There was song and mirth. The old Scylding, who has learned many things, spoke of times far-off. At times a brave one in battle touched the glad wood, the harp's joy; at times he told tales, true and sad; at times he related strange stories according to right custom; at times, again, the great-hearted king, bound with age, the old warrior, would begin to speak of his youth, his battle-strength. His heart welled within when, old and wise, he thought of his many winters. Thus we took pleasure there the livelong day until another night came to men.

"Then in her turn Grendel's mother swiftly made ready to take revenge for his injuries, made a sorrowful journey. Death had taken her son, war-hate of the Weather-Geats. The direful woman avenged her son, fiercely killed a warrior: there the life of Aeschere departed, a wise old counselor. And when morning came the folk of the Danes might not burn him, death-weary, in the fire, nor place him on the pyre, beloved man: she had borne his body away in fiend's embrace beneath the mountain stream. That was the bitterest of Hrothgar's sorrows, of those that had long come upon the people's prince. Then the king, sore-hearted, implored me by your life [6] that I should do a man's work in the tumult of the waters, venture my life, finish a glorious deed. He promised me reward. Then I found the guardian of the deep pool, the grim horror, as is now known wide. For a time there we were locked hand in hand. Then the flood boiled with blood, and in the war-hall I cut off the head of Grendel's mother with a mighty sword. Not without trouble I came from there with my life. I was not fated to die then, but the protector of earls again gave me many treasures, the son of Healfdene.

(XXXI.) "Thus the king of that people lived with good customs. I had lost none of the rewards, the meed of my might, but he gave me treasures, the son of Healfdene, at my own choice. I will bring these to you, great king, show my good will. On your kindnesses all still depends: I have few close kinsmen besides you, Hygelac."

Then he bade bring in the boar-banner—the head-sign—the

6. I.e., "in your name."

helmet towering in battle, the gray battle-shirt, the splendid sword
—afterwards spoke words: "Hrothgar, wise king, gave me this
armor; in his words he bade that I should first tell you about his
gift: he said that king Heorogar,[7] lord of the Scyldings, had
had it for a long time; not for that would he give it, the
breast-armor, to his son, bold Heoroweard, though he was loyal
to him. Use it all well!"

I have heard that four horses, swift and alike, followed that
treasure, fallow as apples. He gave him the gift of both horses
and treasure. So ought kinsmen do, not weave malice-nets for
each other with secret craft, prepare death for comrades. To
Hygelac his nephew was most true in hard fights, and each one
mindful of helping the other. I have heard that he gave Hygd
the neck-ring, the wonderfully wrought treasure, that Wealhtheow
had given him—gave to the king's daughter as well three horses,
supple and saddle-bright. After the gift of the necklace, her
breast was adorned with it.

Thus Beowulf showed himself brave, a man known in battles,
of good deeds, bore himself according to discretion. Drunk, he
slew no hearth-companions. His heart was not savage, but he held
the great gift that God had given him, the most strength of all
mankind, like one brave in battle. He had long been despised,[8]
so that the sons of the Geats did not reckon him brave, nor
would the lord of the Weather-Geats do him much gift-honor on
the mead-bench. They strongly suspected that he was slack, a young
man unbold. Change came to the famous man for each of his
troubles.

Then the protector of earls bade fetch in the heirloom of
Hrethel,[9] king famed in battle, adorned with gold. There was
not then among the Geats a better treasure in sword's kind. He laid
that in Beowulf's lap, and gave him seven thousand [hides of
land], a hall and a throne. To both of them alike land had been
left in the nation, home and native soil: to the other more espe-
cially wide was the realm, to him who was higher in rank.

[Beowulf and the Dragon]

Afterwards it happened, in later days, in the crashes of battle,
when Hygelac lay dead and war-swords came to slay Heardred [1]
behind the shield-cover, when the Battle-Scylfings, hard fighters,
sought him among his victorious nation, attacked bitterly the

---

7. Hrothgar's elder brother, whom
Hrothgar succeeded as king.
8. Beowulf's poor reputation as a young
man is mentioned only here.
9. Hygelac's father.
1. Hygelac's son Heardred, who suc-
ceeded Hygelac as king, was killed by
the Swedes (Heatho-Scylfings) in his
own land, as is explained more fully
below, section XXXIII. His uncle Here-
ric was perhaps Hygd's brother.

nephew of Hereric—then the broad kingdom came into Beowulf's hand. He held it well fifty winters—he was a wise king, an old guardian of the land—until in the dark nights a certain one, a dragon, began to hold sway, which on the high heath kept watch over a hoard, a steep stone-barrow. Beneath lay a path unknown to men. By this there went inside a certain man [who made his way near to the heathen hoard; his hand took a cup, large, a shining treasure. The dragon did not afterwards conceal it though in his sleep he was tricked by the craft of the thief. That the people discovered, the neighboring folk—that he was swollen with rage].[2]

(XXXII.) Not of his own accord did he who had sorely harmed him [3] break into the worm's hoard, not by his own desire, but for hard constraint; the slave of some son of men fled hostile blows, lacking a shelter, and came there, a man guilty of wrong-doing. As soon as he saw him,[4] great horror arose in the stranger; [yet the wretched fugitive escaped the terrible worm . . . When the sudden shock came upon him, he carried off a precious cup.][5] There were many such ancient treasures in the earth-house, as in the old days some one of mankind had prudently hidden there the huge legacy of a noble race, rare treasures. Death had taken them all in earlier times, and the only one of the nation of people who still survived, who walked there longest, a guardian mourning his friends, supposed the same of himself as of them—that he might little while enjoy the long-got treasure. A barrow stood all ready on the shore near the sea-waves, newly placed on the headland, made fast by having its entrances skillfully hidden. The keeper of the rings carried in the part of his riches worthy of hoarding, plated gold; he spoke few words:

"Hold now, you earth, now that men may not, the possession of earls. What, from you good men got it first! War-death has taken each man of my people, evil dreadful and deadly, each of those who has given up this life, the hall-joys of men. I have none who wears sword or cleans the plated cup, rich drinking vessel. The company of retainers has gone elsewhere. The hard helmet must be stripped of its fair-wrought gold, of its plating. The polishers are asleep who should make the war-mask shine. And even so the coat of mail, which withstood the bite of swords after the crashing of the shields, decays like its warrior. Nor may the ring-mail travel wide on the war-chief beside his warriors. There is no harp-delight, no mirth of the singing wood, no

2. This part of the manuscript is badly damaged, and the text within brackets is highly conjectural.
3. The dragon.
4. The dragon.
5. Several lines of the text have been lost.

good hawk flies through the hall, no swift horse stamps in the castle court. Baleful death has sent away many races of men."

So, sad of mind, he spoke his sorrow, alone of them all, moved joyless through day and night until death's flood reached his heart. The ancient night-ravager found the hoard-joy standing open, he who burning seeks barrows, the smooth hateful dragon who flies at night wrapped in flame. Earth-dwellers much dread him. He it is who must seek a hoard in the earth where he will guard heathen gold, wise for his winters: he is none the better for it.

So for three hundred winters the harmer of folk held in the earth one of its treasure-houses, huge and mighty, until one man angered his heart. He bore to his master a plated cup, asked his lord for a compact of peace: thus was the hoard searched, the store of treasures diminished. His requests were granted the wretched man: the lord for the first time looked on the ancient work of men. Then the worm woke; cause of strife was renewed: for then he moved over the stones, hard-hearted beheld his foe's footprints—with secret stealth he had stepped forth too near the dragon's head. (So may an undoomed man who holds favor from the Ruler easily come through his woes and misery.) The hoard-guard sought him eagerly over the ground, would find the man who had done him injury while he slept. Hot and fierce-hearted, often he moved all about the outside of the barrow. No man at all was in the emptiness. Yet he took joy in the thought of war, in the work of fighting. At times he turned back into the barrow, sought his rich cup. Straightway he found that some man had tampered with his gold, his splendid treasure. The hoard-guard waited restless until evening came; then the barrow-keeper was in rage: he would requite that precious drinking cup with vengeful fire. Then the day was gone—to the joy of the worm. He would not wait long on the sea-wall, but set out with fire, ready with flame. The beginning was terrible to the folk on the land, as the ending was soon to be sore to their giver of treasure.

(XXXIII.) Then the evil spirit began to vomit flames, burn bright dwellings; blaze of fire rose, to the horror of men; there the deadly flying thing would leave nothing alive. The worm's warfare was wide-seen, his cruel malice, near and far—how the destroyer hated and hurt the people of the Geats. He winged back to the hoard, his hidden hall, before the time of day. He had circled the land-dwellers with flame, with fire and burning. He had trust in his barrow, in his war and his wall: his expectation deceived him.

Then the terror was made known to Beowulf, quickly in its truth, that his own home, best of buildings, had melted in surging flames, the throne-seat of the Geats. That was anguish of spirit to the good man, the greatest of heart-sorrows. The wise one supposed that he had bitterly offended the Ruler, the Eternal Lord, against old law. His breast within boiled with dark thoughts— as was not for him customary. The fiery dragon with his flames had destroyed the people's stronghold, the land along the sea, the heart of the country. Because of that the war-king, the lord of the Weather-Geats, devised punishment for him. The protector of fighting men, lord of earls, commanded that a wonderful battle-shield be made all of iron. Well he knew that the wood of the forest might not help him—linden against flame. The prince good from old times was to come to the end of the days that had been lent him, life in the world, and the worm with him, though he had long held the hoarded wealth. Then the ring-prince scorned to seek the far-flier with a troop, a large army. He had no fear for himself of the combat, nor did he think the worm's war-power anything great, his strength and his courage, because he himself had come through many battles before, dared perilous straits, clashes of war, after he had purged Hrothgar's hall, victorious warrior, and in combat crushed to death Grendel's kin, loathsome race.

Nor was that the least of his hand-combats where Hygelac was slain, when the king of the Geats, the noble lord of the people, the son of Hrethel, died of sword-strokes in the war-storm among the Frisians, laid low by the blade. From there Beowulf came away by means of his own strength, performed a feat of swimming; he had on his arm the armor of thirty earls when he turned back to the sea. There was no need for the Hetware[6] to exult in the foot-battle when they bore their shields against him: few came again from that warrior to seek their homes. Then the son of Ecgtheow swam over the water's expanse, forlorn and alone, back to his people. There Hygd offered him hoard and kingdom, rings and a prince's throne. She had no trust in her son, that he could hold his native throne against foreigners now that Hygelac was dead. By no means the sooner might the lordless ones get consent from the noble that he would become lord of Heardred or that he would accept royal power.[7] Yet he held him up among the people by friendly counsel, kindly with honor, until he became older,[8] ruled the Weather-Geats.

6. I.e., a tribe, with whom the Frisians were allied.
7. I.e., Beowulf refused to take the throne from the rightful heir Heardred.
8. I.e., Beowulf supported the young Heardred.

Outcasts from over the sea sought him, sons of Ohthere.[9] They had rebelled against the protector of the Scylfings, the best of the sea-kings of those who gave treasure in Sweden, a famous lord. For Heardred that became his life's limit: because of his hospitality there the son of Hygelac got his life's wound from the strokes of a sword. And the son of Ongentheow went back to seek his home after Heardred lay dead, let Beowulf hold the royal throne, rule the Geats: that was a good king.

(XXXIV.) In later days he was mindful of repaying the prince's fall, became the friend of the destitute Eadgils;[1] with folk he supported the son of Ohthere over the wide sea, with warriors and weapons. Afterwards he got vengeance by forays that brought with them cold care: he took the king's life.

Thus he had survived every combat, every dangerous battle, every deed of courage, the son of Ecgtheow, until that one day when he should fight with the worm. Then, one of twelve, the lord of the Geats, swollen with anger, went to look on the dragon. He had learned then from what the feud arose, the fierce malice to men: the glorious cup had come to his possession from the hand of the finder: he was the thirteenth of that company, the man who had brought on the beginning of the war, the sad-hearted slave—wretched, he must direct them to the place. Against his will he went to where he knew of an earth-hall, a barrow beneath the ground close to the sea-surge, to the struggling waves: within, it was full of ornaments and gold chains. The terrible guardian, ready for combat, held the gold treasure, old under the earth. It was no easy bargain for any man to obtain. Then the king, hardy in fight, sat down on the headland; there he saluted his hearth-companions, gold-friend of the Geats. His mind was mournful, restless and ripe for death: very close was the fate which should come to the old man, seek his soul's hoard, divide life from his body; not for long then was the life of the noble one wound in his flesh.

Beowulf spoke, the son of Ecgtheow: "In youth I lived through many battle-storms, times of war. I remember all that. I was seven winters old when the lord of treasure, the beloved king of the folk, received me from my father: King Hrethel had me and kept me, gave me treasure and feast, mindful of kinship. During his life I was no more hated by him as a man in his

9. Ohthere succeeded his father Ongentheow as king of the Scylfings (Swedes), but after his death his brother Onela seized the throne, driving out Ohthere's sons Eanmund and Eadgils. They were given refuge at the Geatish court by Heardred, whom Onela attacked for this act of hospitality. In the fight Eanmund and Heardred were killed, and Onela left the kingdom in Beowulf's charge. 1. The surviving son of Ohthere was befriended by Beowulf, who supported him in his successful attempt to gain the Swedish throne and who killed the usurper Onela.

castle than any of his own sons, Herebeald and Haethcyn, or my own Hygelac. For the eldest a murder-bed was wrongfully spread through the deed of a kinsman, when Haethcyn struck him down with an arrow from his horned bow—his friend and his lord—missed the mark and shot his kinsman dead, one brother the other, with the bloody arrowhead. That was a fatal fight, without hope of recompense, a deed wrongly done, baffling to the heart; yet it had happened that a prince had to lose life unavenged.

"So it is sad for an old man to endure that his son should ride young on the gallows. Then he may speak a story, a sorrowful song, when his son hangs for the joy of the raven, and, old in years and knowing, he can find no help for him. Always with every morning he is reminded of his son's journey elsewhere. He cares not to wait for another heir in his hall, when the first through death's force has come to the end of his deeds. Sorrowful he sees in his son's dwelling the empty wine-hall, the windy resting place without joy—the riders sleep, the warriors in the grave. There is no sound of the harp, no joy in the dwelling, as there was of old. (XXXV.) Then he goes to his couch, sings a song of sorrow, one alone for one gone. To him all too wide has seemed the land and the dwelling.

— "So the protector of the Weather-Geats bore in his heart swelling sorrow for Herebeald. In no way could he settle his feud with the life-slayer; not the sooner could he wound the warrior with deeds of hatred, though he was not dear to him. Then for the sorrow that had too bitterly befallen him he gave up the joys of men, chose God's light. To his sons he left—as a happy man does—his land and his town when he went from life.

"Then there was battle and strife of Swedes and Geats, over the wide water a quarrel shared, hatred between hardy ones, after Hrethel died. And the sons of Ongentheow [2] were bold and active in war, wanted to have no peace over the seas, but about Hreosnabeorh often devised awful slaughter. That my friends and kinsmen avenged, both the feud and the crime, as is well-known, though one of them bought it with his life, a hard bargain: the war was mortal to Haethcyn, lord of the Geats. [3] Then in the morning, I have heard, one kinsman avenged the other on his slayer with the sword's edge, when Ongentheow attacked Eofor: the war-helm split, the old Scylfing fell mortally wounded: his

2. I.e., the Swedes Onela and Ohthere: the reference is, of course, to a time earlier than that referred to in section XXXIII, note 9.
3. Haethcyn had succeeded his father Hrethel as king of the Geats after his accidental killing of his brother Here-

beald. When Haethcyn was killed while attacking the Swedes, he was succeeded by Hygelac, who, as the next sentence relates, avenged Haethcyn's death on Ongentheow. The death of Ongentheow is described below, sections XL and XLI.

hand remembered feuds enough, did not withstand the life-blow.

"I repaid in war the treasures that he [4] gave me—with my bright sword, as was granted me by fate: he had given me land, a pleasant dwelling. There was not any need for him, any reason, that he should have to seek among the Gifthas or the Spear-Danes or in Sweden in order to buy with treasure a worse warrior. I would always go before him in the troop, alone in the front. And so all my life I shall wage battle while this sword endures that has served me early and late ever since I became Daeghrefn's slayer in the press—the warrior of the Hugas. [5] He could not bring armor to the king of the Frisians, breast ornament, but fell in the fight, keeper of the standard, a noble man. Nor was my sword's edge his slayer, but my warlike grip broke open his heart-streams, his bone-house. Now shall the sword's edge, the hand and hard blade, fight for the hoard."

[BEOWULF ATTACKS THE DRAGON]

Beowulf spoke, for the last time spoke words in boast: "In my youth I engaged in many wars. Old guardian of the people, I shall still seek battle, perform a deed of fame, if the evil-doer will come to me out of the earth-hall."

Then he saluted each of the warriors, the bold helmet-bearers, for the last time—his own dear companions. "I would not bear sword, weapon, to the worm, if I knew how else according to my boast I might grapple with the monster, as I did of old with Grendel. But I expect here hot battle-fire, steam and poison. Therefore I have on me shield and mail-shirt. I will not flee a foot-step from the barrow-ward, but it shall be with us at the wall as fate allots, the ruler of every man. I am confident in heart, so I forgo help against the war-flier. Wait on the barrow, safe in your mail-shirts, men in armor—which of us two may better bear wounds after our bloody meeting. This is not your venture, nor is it right for any man except me alone that he should spend his strength against the monster, do this man's deed. By my courage I shall get gold, or war will take your king, dire life-evil."

Then the brave warrior arose by his shield; hardy under helmet he went in his mail-shirt beneath the stone-cliffs, had trust in his strength—that of one man: such is not the way of the cowardly. Then he saw by the wall—he who had come through many wars, good in his great-heartedness, many clashes in battle when troops meet together—a stone arch standing, through it a stream bursting out of the barrow: there was welling of a current hot with killing fires, and he might not endure any while unburnt

4. Hygelac.   5. I.e., the Franks.

by the dragon's flame the hollow near the hoard. Then the man of the Weather-Geats, enraged as he was, let a word break from his breast. Stout-hearted he shouted; his voice went roaring, clear in battle, in under the gray stone. Hate was stirred up, the hoard's guard knew the voice of a man. No more time was there to ask for peace. First the monster's breath came out of the stone, the hot war-steam. The earth resounded. The man below the barrow, the lord of the Geats, swung his shield against the dreadful visitor. Then the heart of the coiled thing was aroused to seek combat. The good war-king had drawn his sword, the old heirloom, not blunt of edge. To each of them as they threatened destruction there was terror of the other. Firm-hearted he stood with his shield high, the lord of friends, while quickly the worm coiled itself; he waited in his armor. Then, coiling in flames, he came gliding on, hastening to his fate. The good shield protected the life and body of the famous prince, but for a shorter while than his wish was. There for the first time, the first day in his life, he might not prevail, since fate did not assign him such glory in battle. The lord of the Geats raised his hand, struck the shining horror so with his forged blade that the edge failed, bright on the bone, bit less surely than its folk-king had need, hard-pressed in perils. Then because of the battle-stroke the barrow-ward's heart was savage, he exhaled death-fire—the war-flames sprang wide. The gold-friend of the Geats boasted of no great victories: the war blade had failed, naked at need, as it ought not to have done, iron good from old times. That was no pleasant journey, not one on which the famous son of Ecgtheow would wish to leave his land; against his will he must take up a dwelling-place elsewhere—as every man must give up the days that are lent him.

It was not long until they came together again, dreadful foes. The hoard-guard took heart, once more his breast swelled with his breathing. Encircled with flames, he who before had ruled a folk felt harsh pain. Nor did his companions, sons of nobles, take up their stand in a troop about him with the courage of fighting men, but they crept to the wood, protected their lives. In only one of them the heart surged with sorrows: nothing can ever set aside kinship in him who means well.

(XXXVI.) He was called Wiglaf, son of Weohstan, a rare shield-warrior, a man of the Scylfings,[6] kinsman of Aelfhere.

6. Though in the next sentence Wiglaf is said to belong to the family of the Waegmundings, the Geatish family to which Beowulf belonged, he is here called a Scylfing (Swede), and immediately below his father Weohstan is represented as having fought for the Swede Onela in his attack on the Geats. But for a man to change his nation was not unusual, and Weohstan, who may have had both Swedish and Geatish blood, had evidently become a Geat long enough before to have brought up his son Wiglaf as one. The identity of Aelfhere is not known.

He saw his liege lord under his war-mask suffer the heat. Then he was mindful of the honors he had given him before, the rich dwelling-place of the Waegmundings, every folk-right such as his father possessed. He might not then hold back, his hand seized his shield, the yellow linden-wood; he drew his ancient sword. Among men it was the heirloom of Eanmund, the son of Ohthere: [7] Weohstan had become his slayer in battle with sword's edge—an exile without friends; and he bore off to his kin the bright-shining helmet, the ringed mail-armor, the old sword made by giants that Onela had given him,[8] his kinsman's war-armor, ready battle-gear: he did not speak of the feud, though he had killed his brother's son.[9] He [1] held the armor many half-years, the blade and the battle-dress, until his son might do manly deeds like his old father. Then he gave him among the Geats war-armor of every kind, numberless, when, old, he went forth on the way from life. For the young warrior this was the first time that he should enter the war-storm with his dear lord. His heart's courage did not slacken, nor did the heirloom of his kinsman fail in the battle. That the worm found when they had come together.

Wiglaf spoke, said many fit words to his companions—his mind was mournful: "I remember that time we drank mead, when we promised our lord in the beer-hall—him who gave us these rings—that we would repay him for the war-arms if a need like this befell him—the helmets and the hard swords. Of his own will he chose us among the host for this venture, thought us worthy of fame—and gave me these treasures—because he counted us good war-makers, brave helm-bearers, though our lord intended to do this work of courage alone, as keeper of the folk, because among men he had performed the greatest deeds of glory, daring actions. Now the day has come that our liege lord has need of the strength of good fighters. Let us go to him, help our war-chief while the grim terrible fire persists. God knows of me that I should rather that the flame enfold my body with my gold-giver. It does not seem right to me for us to bear our shields home again unless we can first fell the foe, defend the life of the prince of the Weather-Geats. I know well that it would be no recompense for past deeds that he alone of the company of

---

7. See above, section XXXIII, note 9. Not only did Weohstan support Onela's attack on the Geat king Heardred, but actually killed Eanmund whom Heardred was supporting, and it is Eanmund's sword that Wiglaf is now wielding.
8. The spoils of war belonged to the victorious king, who apportioned them among his fighters: thus Onela gave Weohstan the armor of Eanmund, whom

Weohstan had killed.
9. This ironic remark points out that Onela did not claim *wergild* or seek vengeance from Weohstan, as in other circumstances he ought to have done inasmuch as Weohstan had killed Onela's close kinsman, his nephew Eanmund: but Onela was himself trying to kill Eanmund.
1. Weohstan.

the Geats should suffer pain, fall in the fight. For us both shall there be a part in the work of sword and helmet, of battle-shirt and war-clothing."

Then he waded through the deadly smoke, bore his war-helmet to the aid of his king, spoke in few words: "Beloved Beowulf, do all well, for, long since in your youth, you said that you would not let your glory fail while you lived. Now, great-spirited noble, brave of deeds, you must protect your life with all your might. I shall help you."

After these words, the worm came on, angry, the terrible malice-filled foe, shining with surging flames, to seek for the second time his enemies, hated men. Fire advanced in waves; shield burned to the boss; mail-shirt might give no help to the young spear-warrior; but the young man went quickly under his kinsman's shield when his own was consumed with flames. Then the war-king was again mindful of fame, struck with his war-sword with great strength so that it stuck in the head-bone, driven with force: Naegling broke, the sword of Beowulf failed in the fight, old and steel-gray. It was not ordained for him that iron edges might help in the combat. Too strong was the hand that I have heard strained every sword with its stroke, when he bore wound-hardened weapon to battle: he was none the better for it.

Then for the third time the folk-harmer, the fearful fire-dragon, was mindful of feuds, set upon the brave one when the chance came, hot and battle-grim seized all his neck with his sharp fangs: he was smeared with life-blood, gore welled out in waves.

(XXXVII.) Then, I have heard, at the need of the folk-king the earl at his side made his courage known, his might and his keenness—as was natural to him. He took no heed for that head,[2] but the hand of the brave man was burned as he helped his kinsman, as the man in armor struck the hateful foe a little lower down, so that the sword sank in, shining and engraved; and then the fire began to subside. The king himself then still controlled his senses, drew the battle-knife, biting and war-sharp, that he wore on his mail-shirt: the protector of the Weather-Geats cut the worm through the middle. They felled the foe, courage drove his life out, and they had destroyed him together, the two noble kinsmen. So ought a man be, a thane at need. To the prince that was the last moment of victory for his own deeds, of work in the world.

Then the wound that the earth-dragon had caused began to burn and to swell; at once he felt dire evil boil in his breast, poison within him. Then the prince, wise of thought, went to

2. I.e., the dragon's flame-breathing head.

where he might sit on a seat near the wall. He looked on the work of giants, how the timeless earth-hall held within it stone-arches fast on pillars. Then with his hands the thane, good without limit, washed him with water, blood-besmeared, the famous prince, his beloved lord, sated with battle; and he unfastened his helmet.

Beowulf spoke—despite his wounds spoke, his mortal hurts. He knew well he had lived out his days' time, joy on earth; all passed was the number of his days, death very near. "Now I would wish to give my son my war-clothing, if any heir after me, part of my flesh, were granted. I held this people fifty winters. There was no folk-king of those dwelling about who dared approach me with swords, threaten me with fears. In my land I awaited what fate brought me, held my own well, sought no treacherous quarrels, nor did I swear many oaths unrightfully. Sick with life-wounds, I may have joy of all this, for the Ruler of Men need not blame me for the slaughter of kinsmen when life goes from my body. Now quickly go to look at the hoard under the gray stone, beloved Wiglaf, now that the worm lies sleeping from sore wounds, bereft of his treasure. Be quick now, so that I may see the ancient wealth, the golden things, may clearly look on the bright curious gems, so that for that, because of the treasure's richness, I may the more easily leave life and nation I have long held."

(XXXVIII.) Then I have heard that the son of Weohstan straightway obeyed his lord, sick with battle-wounds, according to the words he had spoken, went wearing his ring-armor, woven battle-shirt, under the barrow's roof. Then he saw, as he went by the seat, the brave young retainer, triumphant in heart, many precious jewels, glittering gold lying on the ground, wonders on the wall, and the worm's lair, the old night-flier's—cups standing there, vessels of men of old, with none to polish them, stripped of their ornaments. There was many a helmet old and rusty, many an arm-ring skillfully twisted. (Easily may treasure, gold in the ground, betray each one of the race of men, hide it who will.) Also he saw a standard all gold hang high over the hoard, the greatest of hand-wonders, linked with fingers' skill. From it came a light so that he might see the ground, look on the works of craft. There was no trace of the worm, for the blade had taken him. Then I have heard that one man in the mound pillaged the hoard, the old work of giants, loaded in his bosom cups and plates at his own desire. He took also the standard, brightest of banners. The sword of the old lord—its edge was iron—had already wounded the one who for a long time had been guardian of the treasure, waged his fire-terror, hot for the hoard, rising up fiercely at midnight, till he died in the slaughter.

The messenger was in haste, eager to return, urged on by the treasures. Curiosity tormented him, whether eagerly seeking he should find the lord of the Weather-Geats, strength gone, alive in the place where he had left him before. Then with the treasures he found the great prince, his lord, bleeding, at the end of his life. Again he began to sprinkle him with water until this word's point broke through his breast-hoard—he spoke, the king, old man in sorrow, looked on the gold: "I speak with my words thanks to the Lord of All for these treasures, to the King of Glory, Eternal Prince, for what I gaze on here, that I might get such for my people before my death-day. Now that I have bought the hoard of treasures with my old life, you attend to the people's needs hereafter: I can be here no longer. Bid the battle-renowned make a mound, bright after the funeral fire, on the sea's cape. It shall stand high on Hronesness as a reminder to my people, so that sea-travelers later will call it Beowulf's barrow, when they drive their ships far over the darkness of the seas."

He took off his neck the golden necklace, bold-hearted prince, gave it to the thane, to the young spear-warrior—gold-gleaming helmet, ring, and mail-shirt, bade him use them well. "You are the last left of our race, of the Waegmundings. Fate has swept away all my kinsmen, earls in their strength, to destined death. I have to go after." That was the last word of the old man, of the thoughts of his heart, before he should taste the funeral pyre, hot hostile flames. The soul went from his breast to seek the doom of those fast in truth.

[*Beowulf's Funeral*]

(XXXIX.) Then sorrow came to the young man that he saw him whom he most loved on the earth, at the end of his life, suffering piteously. His slayer likewise lay dead, the awful earth-dragon bereft of life, overtaken by evil. No longer should the coiled worm rule the ring-hoard, for iron edges had taken him, hard and battle-sharp work of the hammers, so that the wide-flier, stilled by wounds, had fallen on the earth near the treasure-house. He did not go flying through the air at midnight, proud of his property, showing his aspect, but he fell to earth through the work of the chief's hands. Yet I have heard of no man of might on land, though he was bold of every deed, whom it should prosper to rush against the breath of the venomous foe or disturb with hands the ring-hall, if he found the guard awake who lived in the barrow. The share of the rich treasures became

Beowulf's, paid for by death: each of the two had journeyed to the end of life's loan.

Then it was not long before the battle-slack ones left the woods, ten weak troth-breakers together, who had not dared fight with their spears in their liege lord's great need. But they bore their shields, ashamed, their war-clothes, to where the old man lay, looked on Wiglaf. He sat wearied, the foot-soldier near the shoulders of his lord, would waken him with water: it gained him nothing. He might not, though he much wished it, hold life in his chieftain on earth nor change anything of the Ruler's: the judgment of God would control the deeds of every man, just as it still does now. Then it was easy to get from the young man a grim answer to him who before had lost courage. Wiglaf spoke, the son of Weohstan, a man sad at heart, looked on the unloved ones:

"Yes, he who will speak truth may say that the liege lord who gave you treasure, the war-gear that you stand in there, when he used often to hand out to hall-sitters on the ale-benches, a prince to his thanes, helmets and war-shirts such as he could find mightiest anywhere, both far and near—that he quite threw away the war-gear, to his distress when war came upon him. The folk-king had no need to boast of his war-comrades. Yet God, Ruler of Victories, granted him that he might avenge himself, alone with his sword, when there was need for his courage. I was able to give him little life-protection in the fight, and yet beyond my power I did begin to help my kinsman. The deadly foe was ever the weaker after I struck him with my sword, fire poured less strongly from his head. Too few defenders thronged about the prince when the hard time came upon him. Now there shall cease for your race the receiving of treasure and the giving of swords, all enjoyment of pleasant homes, comfort. Each man of your kindred must go deprived of his land-right when nobles from afar learn of your flight, your inglorious deed. Death is better for any earl than a life of blame."

(XL.) Then he bade that the battle-deed be announced in the city, up over the cliff-edge, where the band of warriors sat the whole morning of the day, sad-hearted, shield-bearers in doubt whether it was the beloved man's last day or whether he would come again. Little did he fail to speak of new tidings, he who rode up the hill, but spoke to them all truthfully: "Now the joy-giver of the people of the Weathers, the lord of the Geats, is fast on his death-bed, lies on his slaughter-couch through deeds of the worm. Beside him lies his life-enemy, struck down with dagger-wounds—with his sword he might not work wounds of any kind on the monster. Wiglaf son of Weohstan sits over

Beowulf, one earl by the lifeless other, in weariness of heart holds death-watch over the loved and the hated.

"Now may the people expect a time of war, when the king's fall becomes wide-known to the Franks and the Frisians. A harsh quarrel was begun with the Hugas when Hygelac came traveling with his sea-army to the land of the Frisians, where the Hetware assailed him in battle, quickly, with stronger forces, made the mailed warrior bow; he fell in the ranks: that chief gave no treasure to his retainers. Ever since then the good will of the Merewioing king has been denied us.

"Nor do I expect any peace or trust from the Swedish people, for it is wide-known that Ongentheow took the life of Haethcyn, Hrethel's son, near Ravenswood when in their over-pride the people of the Geats first went against the War-Scylfings. Straightway the wary father of Ohthere,[3] old and terrible, gave a blow in return, cut down the sea-king,[4] rescued his wife, old woman of times past, bereft of her gold, mother of Onela and Ohthere, and then he followed his life-foes until they escaped, lordless, painfully, to Ravenswood. Then with a great army he besieged those whom the sword had left, weary with wounds, often vowed woes to the wretched band the livelong night, said that in the morning he would cut them apart with sword-blades, [hang] some on gallows-trees as sport for birds. Relief came in turn to the sorry-hearted together with dawn when they heard Hygelac's horn and trumpet, his sound as the good man came on their track with a body of retainers. (XLI.) Wide-seen was the bloody track of Swedes and Geats, the slaughter-strife of men, how the peoples stirred up the feud between them. Then the good man went with his kinsmen, old and much-mourning, to seek his stronghold: the earl Ongentheow moved further away. He had heard of the warring of Hygelac, of the war-power of the proud one. He did not trust in resistance, that he might fight off the sea-men, defend his hoard against the war-sailors, his children and wife. Instead he drew back, the old man behind his earth-wall.

"Then pursuit was offered to the people of the Swedes, the standards of Hygelac overran the stronghold as Hrethel's people pressed forward to the citadel. There Ongentheow the gray-haired was brought to bay by sword-blades, and the people's king had to submit to the judgment of Eofor alone. Wulf [5] son of Wonred had struck him angrily with his weapon so that for the blow the

---

3. I.e., Ongentheow.
4. I.e., Haethcyn, king of the Geats. Haethcyn's brother Hygelac, who succeeded him, was not present at this battle, but arrived after the death of Haethcyn with reinforcements to relieve the survivors and to pursue Ongentheow

in his retreat to his city.
5. The two sons of Wonred, Wulf and Eofor, attacked Ongentheow in turn. Wulf was struck down but not killed by the old Swedish king, who was then slain by Eofor.

blood sprang forth in streams beneath his hair. Yet not for that was he afraid, the old Scylfing, but he quickly repaid the assault with worse exchange, the folk-king, when he turned toward him. The strong son of Wonred could not give the old man a return blow, for Ongentheow had first cut through the helmet of his head so that he had to sink down, smeared with blood—fell on the earth: he was not yet doomed, for he recovered, though the wound hurt him. The hardy thane of Hygelac,[6] when his brother lay low, let his broad sword, old blade made by giants, break the great helmet across the shield-wall; then the king bowed, the keeper of the folk was hit to the quick.

"Then there were many who bound up the brother, quickly raised him up after it was granted them to control the battle-field. Then one warrior stripped the other, took from Ongentheow his iron-mail, hard-hilted sword, and his helmet, too; he bore the arms of the hoary one to Hygelac. He accepted that treasure and fairly promised him rewards among the people, and he stood by it thus: the lord of the Geats, the son of Hrethel, when he came home, repaid Wulf and Eofor for their battle-assault with much treasure, gave each of them a hundred thousand [units] of land and linked rings: there was no need for any man on middle-earth to blame him for the rewards, since they had performed great deeds. And then he gave Eofor his only daughter as a pledge of friendship—a fair thing for his home.

"That is the feud and the enmity, the death-hatred of men, for which I expect that the people of the Swedes, bold shield-warriors after the fall of princes, will set upon us after they learn that our prince has gone from life, he who before held hoard and kingdom against our enemies, did good to the people, and further still, did what a man should. Now haste is best, that we look on the people's king there and bring him who gave us rings on his way to the funeral pyre. Nor shall only a small share melt with the great-hearted one, but there is a hoard of treasure, gold uncounted, grimly purchased, and rings bought at the last now with his own life. These shall the fire devour, flames enfold—no earl to wear ornament in remembrance, nor any bright maiden add to her beauty with neck-ring; but mournful-hearted, stripped of gold, they shall walk, often, not once, in strange countries— now that the army-leader has laid aside laughter, his game and his mirth. Therefore many a spear, cold in the morning, shall be grasped with fingers, raised by hands; no sound of harp shall waken the warriers, but the dark raven, low over the doomed, shall tell many tales, say to the eagle how he fared at the feast when with the wolf he spoiled the slain bodies."

6. I.e., Eofor.

Thus the bold man was a speaker of hateful news, nor did he much lie in his words or his prophecies. The company all arose. Without joy they went below Earnaness [7] to look on the wonder with welling tears. Then they found on the sand, soulless, keeping his bed of rest, him who in former times had given them rings. Then the last day of the good man had come, when the war-king, prince of the Weather-Geats, died a wonderful death. First they saw the stranger creature, the worm lying loathsome, opposite him in the place. The fire-dragon was grimly terrible with his many colors, burned by the flames; he was fifty feet long in the place where he lay. Once he had joy of the air at night, came back down to seek his den. Then he was made fast by death, had made use of the last of his earth-caves. Beside him stood cups and pitchers, plates and rich swords lay eaten through by rust, just as they had been there in the bosom of the earth for a thousand winters. Then that huge heritage, gold of men of old, was wound in a spell, so that no one of men must touch the ring-hall unless God himself, the True King of Victories—He is men's protection—should grant to whom He wished to open the hoard—whatever man seemed fit to Him.

(XLII.) Then it was seen that the act did not profit him who wrongly kept hidden the handiworks under the wall. The keeper had first slain a man like few others, then the feud had been fiercely avenged. It is a wonder where an earl famed for courage may reach the end of his allotted life—then may dwell no longer in the mead-hall, man with his kin. So it was with Beowulf when he sought quarrels, the barrow's ward: he himself did not then know in what way his parting with the world should come. The great princes who had put it [8] there had laid on it so deep a curse until doomsday that the man who should plunder the place should be guilty of sins, imprisoned in idol-shrines, fixed with hell-bonds, punished with evils—unless the Possessor's favor were first shown the more clearly to him who desired the gold.

Wiglaf spoke, the son of Weohstan: "Often many a man must suffer distress for the will of one man, as has happened to us. We might by no counsel persuade our dear prince, keeper of the kingdom, not to approach the gold-guardian, let him lie where he long was, live in his dwelling to the world's end. He held to his high destiny. The hoard has been made visible, grimly got. What drove the folk-king thither was too powerfully fated. I have been therein and looked at it all, the rare things of the chamber, when it was granted me—not at all friendly was the journey that I was permitted beneath the earth-wall. In haste I seized with

7. The headland near where Beowulf   8. The treasure.
had fought the dragon.

my hands a huge burden of hoard-treasures, of great size, bore it out here to my king. He was then still alive, sound-minded and aware. He spoke many things, old man in sorrow, and bade greet you, commanded that for your lord's deeds you make a high barrow in the place of his pyre, large and conspicuous, since he was of men the worthiest warrior through the wide earth, while he might enjoy wealth in his castle.

"Let us now hasten to see and visit for the second time the heap of precious jewels, the wonder under the walls. I shall direct you so that you may look on enough of them from near at hand—rings and broad gold. Let the bier be made ready, speedily prepared, when we come out, and then let us carry our prince, beloved man, where he shall long dwell in the Ruler's protection."

Then the son of Weohstan, man brave in battle, bade command many warriors, men who owned houses, leaders of the people, that they carry wood from afar for the pyre for the good man. "Now shall flame eat the chief of warriors—the fire shall grow dark—who often survived the iron-shower when the storm of arrows driven from bow-strings passed over the shield-wall—the shaft did its task, made eager by feather-gear served the arrowhead."

And then the wise son of Weohstan summoned from the host thanes of the king, seven together, the best; one of eight warriors, he went beneath the evil roof. One who walked before bore a torch in his hands. Then there was no lot to decide who should plunder that hoard, since the men could see that every part of it rested in the hall without guardian, lay wasting. Little did any man mourn that hastily they should bear out the rare treasure. Also they pushed the dragon, the worm, over the cliff-wall, let the wave take him, the flood enfold the keeper of the treasure. Then twisted gold was loaded on a wagon, an uncounted number of things, and the prince, hoary warrior, borne to Hronesness.

(XLIII.) Then the people of the Geats made ready for him a funeral pyre on the earth, no small one, hung with helmets, battle-shields, bright mail-shirts, just as he had asked. Then in the midst they laid the great prince, lamenting their hero, their beloved lord. Then warriors began to awaken on the barrow the greatest of funeral-fires; the wood-smoke climbed, black over the fire; the roaring flame mixed with weeping—the wind-surge died down—until it had broken the bone-house, hot at its heart. Sad in spirit they lamented their heart-care, the death of their liege lord. And the Geatish woman, wavy-haired, sang a sorrowful song about Beowulf, said[9] again and again that she sorely feared for herself

---

9. The manuscript is badly damaged and the interpretation conjectural.

invasions of armies, many slaughters, terror of troops, humiliation, and captivity. Heaven swallowed the smoke.

Then the people of the Weather-Geats built a mound on the promontory, one that was high and broad, wide-seen by seafarers, and in ten days completed a monument for the bold in battle, surrounded the remains of the fire with a wall, the most splendid that men most skilled might devise. In the barrow they placed rings and jewels, all such ornaments as troubled men had earlier taken from the hoard. They let the earth hold the wealth of earls, gold in the ground, where now it still dwells, as useless to men as it was before. Then the brave in battle rode round the mound, children of nobles, twelve in all, would bewail their sorrow and mourn their king, recite dirges and speak of the man. They praised his great deeds and his acts of courage, judged well of his prowess. So it is fitting that man honor his liege lord with words, love him in heart when he must be led forth from the body. Thus the people of the Geats, his hearth-companions, lamented the death of their lord. They said that he was of world-kings the mildest of men and the gentlest, kindest to his people, and most eager for fame.

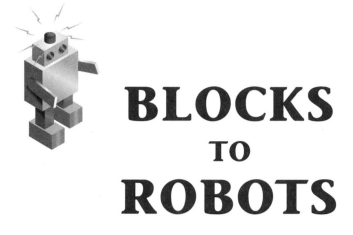

BLOCKS
TO
ROBOTS

Learning with Technology in the
Early Childhood Classroom

MARINA UMASCHI BERS

Foreword by
David Elkind

Teachers College, Columbia University
New York and London

Published by Teachers College Press, 1234 Amsterdam Avenue,
New York, NY 10027

Library of Congress Cataloging-in-Publication Data

Bers, Marina Umaschi.
    Blocks to robots : learning with technology in the early childhood
    classroom / Marina Umaschi Bers ; foreword by David Elkind.
        p.   cm.
    Includes bibliographical references and index.
    ISBN 978-0-8077-4847-3 (pbk. : alk. paper)
    ISBN 978-0-8077-4848-0 (hardcover : alk. paper)
        1. Constructivism (Education).   2. Robotics.   3. Early childhood
    education—Activity programs.   4. Technology and children.
    I. Title.
    LB1590.3.B47   2008
    372.35'8—dc22   2007028960

ISBN 978-0-8077-4847-3 (paper)
ISBN 978-0-8077-4848-0 (hardcover)

Printed on acid-free paper
Manufactured in the United States of America

15   14   13   12   11   10   09   08   8   7   6   5   4   3   2   1

This book is dedicated to the memory of my father,
    Hector Umaschi

and to my young children,
    Tali, Alan, and Nico, who are the future

Rabbi Tarfon said: It is not your obligation to complete the work, but neither are you free to desist from it.

—Pirke Avot 11:21 (*Ethics of Our Fathers*)

Contents

PART II

Using Robotic Manipulatives in
the Early Childhood Classroom • 67

Foreword

What can young children learn and when? This has become a hotly disputed subject as we move into the 21st century. On one side of the issue are those who believe that even young children can be taught the three R's and more. Many kindergartens are now teaching reading and arithmetic, not just letters and numbers. Testing and homework are also not uncommon among the preschool set. On the other side are those who argue that young children have much to learn before they should be exposed to academics, which—in any case—are inappropriate for their needs, interests, and level of mental ability.

Marina Bers now enters this controversy from an entirely different direction, namely that of electronic media and robotics. She argues that, over the last few decades, we have entered a new reality of atoms and bits, of mechanical devices that are now run by electronics. To be sure, the union of machines and electronics is not entirely new. The telegraph, the telephone, the radio, and the electric clock are all early examples of the union of mechanics and electronics.

What is new today is the miniaturization of the electronics and our vastly increased ability to become actively involved in the translation of the mechanical into the electronic. Turning on a light switch or other electrical device is the simplest form of this active translation. But this and similar on/off translations are relatively passive and automatic; they require little thought. With the introduction of the computer we have become much more active intermediaries in the translation process. And this active role has become ever more extensive with the introduction of other electronic devices such as computer games and Black-Berry® devices. Our active involvement in the conversion of the mechanical into the electronic is what is unique about our contemporary computer age. It has the potential to change the way we think about ourselves and our world (Papert, 1980).

It was Marshall McLuhan (1964) who first suggested that the "medium is the message"—that the advent of electronic media would have the same impact on culture and society as did the advent of print media in the 14th century. In moving from an oral to a print culture, McLuhan argued, we also moved from an oral culture that was based on memory to a print culture that liberated abstract thought. In the same way, McLuhan argued that electronic media would also change the way we think about and perceive our world. That was the message.

Seymour Papert (1980), Marina Bers's mentor at MIT, combined McLuhan's argument with the theory of intellectual development championed by his mentor, Jean Piaget (1950). Piaget created a constructivist epistemology in which he demonstrated that children construct and reconstruct reality out of their experiences with the environment. Piaget's view was in sharp contrast to traditional learning theory, which defined learning as "the modification of behavior as a result of experience." Instead, Piaget argued that learning could also be defined as "the modification of experience as the result of behavior." In effect, children create their own learning experiences. A child who babbles, for example, creates all of the sounds he or she needs to learn to speak his or her native language.

Papert went beyond Piaget to suggest, as McLuhan had, that electronic media can give rise to new ways of thinking. He argues that with our new technology children can now create their own objects that integrate the mechanical with the electronic. These inventive constructions give rise to a new mode of thinking that Papert calls *constructionism*. That is to say, when children build their own mechanical/electronic objects, they have created experience from which they learn new concepts of space, time, and causality. Indeed, in this self-created virtual world, space has become portable, time has become retrievable, and causality has become programmable.

It is Papert's constructionism, the idea that children create their own object realities and learn from them, combined with other contemporary ideas, that informs Bers's approach to early childhood education. She argues, as did many of the early childhood educators before her, that young children learn best through their own self-directed activity. What is different is that Bers provides an alternative to the traditional static manipulatives, such as blocks, sticks, and color skeins. Bers believes that children work just as readily with manipulatives that are dynamic.

Papert's Logo®, a program in which children learn to build and operate a turtle* electronically, is the prototype for this kind of dynamic manipulation. On the computer screen children manipulate icons that transmit signals to their self-constructed objects. These objects—robots—can then be directed to engage in a variety of simple activities. Thus, constructionism brings both design and engineering into the process of constructing and then programming objects.

Bers, however, has gone further than Papert in extending the notion of allowing children to create their own object-created environments—to the creation of social environments. The Zora program she has created allows children to construct their own spatial reality, in which they can adopt various alternative identities (Bers, 2001, 2006). In addition, she has built upon the Reggio Emilia framework (Edwards, Gandini, & Forman, 1998), as well as others, to make this approach extend to all facets of early childhood education, from curriculum to assessment to classroom management.

This groundbreaking account of Bers's work is divided into two Parts. In the first Part, Bers deals with the broad issue of childhood and technology. In Chapter 1 she presents a discussion of constructionism and its four basic subconcepts: learning by designing within a community, technological tools for learning, powerful ideas and wonderful ideas, and learning about learning with technology. In Chapter 2 she elaborates, and concretizes the theoretical discussion by showing how constructionism can be applied to social emotional learning. She further illustrates the application of these ideas with two different classroom vignettes.

The second Part of the book looks at the issue of developmentally appropriate practice with robotics. In Chapter 3 Bers describes how the construction of robotics can serve as a powerful learning tool even for young children. Chapter 4 provides guidance for teachers who are

---

*The "turtle" was originally a mobile robot shaped in the form of a large turtle. It contained a small computer that was operated by a hand-held remote control. The "turtle" moved on the floor. Eventually, the "turtle" appeared on a computer screen as a cursor in software for Atari. The child could then use the computer keyboard or mouse to move the cursor turtle to create geometric shapes of varying complexity.

interested in designing a learning environment that is centered about the use of robotics as manipulatives. These two chapters are again followed by a couple of vignettes illustrating how these ideas can be translated into classroom practice. One vignette deals with children learning about local history and the other with using design as an instructional tool.

I believe that this is a seminal work. It is suggestive as well as substantive. Because the field is so new, many of the ideas are not fully developed. Yet, in attempting to extend this atoms-and-bits approach to all facets of early childhood education, Bers has provided both teachers and researchers with many new vistas onto the domain of early childhood teaching and research. Much of the material and research she cites is probably unfamiliar to most early childhood educators. Marina Bers has thus done a most valuable service in bringing this information to their attention. In addition, she has provided abundant illustrations of how constructionism can be introduced into the early childhood classroom. In so doing, she has presented a fresh, exciting, and challenging approach to the education of young children.

—David Elkind

Playful Learning

Little Robots, Big Ideas

We are surrounded by technology—from the chairs we sit on to the computers on our desks, from the pencil to high-tech digital ink. However, in the early grades children learn very little about this world of technology. Over the past few decades and beyond, the early childhood science curriculum has focused on the natural world: bugs and insects, plants and the Arctic. While this knowledge is important, in today's society developing early knowledge about our man-made world is just as important. That area of knowledge is the realm of technology and engineering, which focuses on the development and application of tools, machines, materials, and processes that help to solve human problems.

Early childhood experience hasn't completely ignored the technological; it is common to see young children using cardboard or recycling materials to build cities and bridges. However, what is unique to our man-made world today is that atoms are not enough. Bits are just as important. Computers and electronics are as much a part of our world as gears and mechanical structures.

We go to the bathroom to wash our hands and the faucets "know" when to start dispensing water and when we are done. The elevator "knows" when someone's little hands are between the doors and they shouldn't close. Our cell phones "know" how to take pictures, send e-mails, and behave as alarm clocks. Even our cars "know" where we want to go, and they can take us there without getting lost. We live in a world in which bits and atoms are increasingly becoming integrated

(Gershenfeld, 1999). However, we continue teaching our children about atoms and bits as two separate realms of experience. In the early schooling experiences, we teach them about polar bears and cacti, which are probably further from their everyday experience than smart faucets and cell phones.

This book is about how we can start helping our young to explore the modern world of bits and atoms. The spirit of how to do this follows the early childhood teaching tradition started when Fröebel invented kindergarten in the 1800s: using manipulative materials. This book is about a new kind of material, robotic manipulatives, which integrate atoms and bits. While using these tools, children can learn about sensors, motors, and the digital domain in a playful way by building their own cars that follow a light, elevators that work with a touch sensor, or puppets that play music. Young children can become engineers by playing with gears, levers, joints, motors, sensors, and programming loops, and they can become storytellers by creating their own meaningful projects that move in response to a stimulus (either another robot or the environment). Figures 1, 2, and 3 provide exam-

FIGURE 1. A monkey robot built by a first-grader

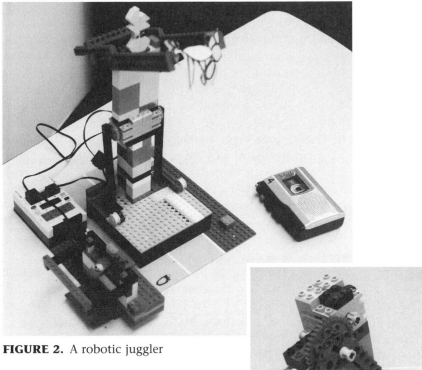

FIGURE 2. A robotic juggler

FIGURE 3. Making a swing set

ples of different LEGO®-based robotics projects done by 6- and 7-year-old children working in an after-school robotics workshop held at Tufts University's Department of Child Development.

Robotic manipulatives are a gateway for helping children learn about mathematical concepts and the scientific method of inquiry. They also help develop technological fluency early on through the introduction of engineering and programming. By extending the potential of traditional manipulatives, they engage children in using their hands and developing fine motor skills, as well as hand–eye coordination. But most importantly, robotic manipulatives invite children to participate in social interactions and negotiations while playing to learn, and learning to play.

This book presents innovative work with robotic manipulatives in early childhood that is situated within the constructionist philosophy of using computers in education, which was developed by pioneer Seymour Papert. Papert, creator of the Logo language and the LEGO MINDSTORMS® robotics concept, worked with Jean Piaget in Geneva. Readers might be familiar with Piaget's concept of *constructivism*. This book focuses instead on *constructionism,* an approach that keeps constructivism's developmental stance but is explicitly conceived for teaching and learning with technology.

Constructionism asserts that computers are powerful educational technologies when used as tools for supporting the design, the construction, and the programming of projects people truly care about (Papert, 1980). By constructing an external object to reflect upon, people also construct internal knowledge. Constructionism has its roots in Piaget's constructivism (Piaget, 1971; Papert, 1999). However, whereas Piaget's theory was developed to explain how knowledge is constructed in our heads, Papert pays particular attention to the role of constructions in the world (specifically, robotic constructions) as a support for those in the head. Thus, constructionism is both a theory of learning and a strategy for education that offers the framework for developing a technology-rich, design-based learning environment. Independent learning and discovery happen best when children can make, create, program, and design their own "objects to think with" in a playful manner. Robotic manipulatives are certainly powerful "objects to think with." However, the technology by itself is not enough. There are many ways of using a powerful technology in a disempowering way. Therefore, this book offers an educational philosophy to empower children in the use of technology.

This volume addresses questions leading to an understanding of constructionism as a philosophy and pedagogy for using technology in early childhood: What is the constructionist educational philosophy? How is it different from constructivism and instructionism? Is constructionism a philosophy that can guide developmentally appropriate practice? How can it inform the use of robotics in early childhood? How can we promote socioemotional development through the use of robotics? What cultural contexts need to be in place for this work to be successful? This set of questions is addressed in Part I: "Constructionism: Technology and Early Childhood." An interview with an expert in sociocultural theories of child development and education, Dr. Rebecca S. New, offers a different perspective on these questions by focusing on conflicting views and anxieties regarding the developmental appropriateness of children's learning opportunities with robotics. Two vignettes written by innovative educators provide examples of how robotics is currently used in early childhood classrooms.

Whereas the first Part of the book focuses on the pedagogy and the philosophy that guide the work with robotic manipulatives (or any other technology), the second Part addresses questions leading to an understanding of the potential of, and challenges of, this new generation of manipulatives—robotics, such as: Why robotics in early childhood? What can be done with this new technology to improve children's learning, in particular in the areas of math, science, and technology? How can a teacher start this work in his or her own classroom? These questions are addressed in Part II: "Using Robotic Manipulatives in the Early Childhood Classroom." Examples of curricular activities for K–2 are provided, along with vignettes about experiences of using robotics in early childhood and how to approach classroom management in this context. An interview with a master teacher, Terry Green, who has been using robotics in the public school system for over 10 years, provides further insights of the challenges, possibilities, and issues to consider when approaching this work.

Most of the projects and examples discussed in this book use LEGO Mindstorms because it is the commercial robotics kit most widely available and supported for educational uses. However, the pedagogical and developmental theories presented go beyond this particular construction kit. They apply to any robotic manipulative or technology that allows children to combine bits and atoms to design a personally meaningful project that can exhibit behaviors by responding to inputs (Resnick, 1998).

As you read this book, you might become convinced of the opportunities (and challenges) of using robotic manipulatives in early childhood. However, where do you start? Chapter 4 provides a practical guide, with resources and recommendations to orient readers interested in exploring the use of robotics in early childhood. It is not intended to be a comprehensive how-to manual but instead is a first introduction to how to approach the topic and where to find more information. Rather than offering a prescribed set of rules or a toolbox for putting a robotics program into action, this guide presents suggestions in two areas: designing the learning environment and obtaining further resources. Information is provided about other robotics kits, besides LEGO Mindstorms, that can be used in early childhood. Finally, a list of references of scholarly work focusing on robotics and early childhood is presented.

Acknowledgments

Many people have contributed, in thoughts or in deeds, to my own thinking and writing for this book. First of all, I am deeply thankful to my doctoral advisor at the Massachusetts Institute of Technology (MIT), Seymour Papert, for introducing me to these ideas. I first played with Logo when I was a child living in my homeland, Argentina, and at that time, little did I imagine that years later I would work and study with the father of Logo. When I first told Seymour about my idea to write this book, he was very excited and agreed to write a Foreword. However, a serious accident and brain injury in Hanoi prevented him from doing so. It is my hope that Seymour will soon recover, and while relearning the world around him, that he will also discover that his ideas, through this book, are now having an impact in early childhood.

I am also thankful to Mitchel Resnick, who in his course "Technological Tools for Thinking and Learning," back in the 1990s at the MIT Media Lab, taught me by example what a constructionist learning environment looks like; and to Fred Martin, who helped me understand how robotics could be integrated into any object in our lives, including soft teddy bears and cozy bunnies like the ones I developed for my master's thesis at the Media Lab under the direction of Justine Cassell. I am also thankful to Sherry Turkle, who as a member of my doctoral thesis committee showed me the impact that technology can have in our understanding of our own psychology. Other people at the MIT Media Lab played a very important role in my learning about robotics and constructionism, and I am deeply thankful to them: Claudia Urrea, David Cavallo, Jacqueline Karaslanian, Edith Ackermann, Rick Borovoy, Amy Bruckman, Mike Best, Deb Roy, and members of the Epistemology and Learning Group and the Lifelong Kindergarten group.

In Argentina I am thankful to my mentors at Buenos Aires University, Alejandro Piscitelli and Anibal Ford, now colleagues and friends, who helped me grow intellectually and inspired me with their hard academic work and sense of social responsibility when using technology. I am also deeply thankful to Rabbi Sergio Bergman and Lea Vainer, who in 1998 made it possible for me to work with families and young children to create robotic prayers in the Arlene Fern Community School. It was Rabbi Bergman who encouraged me to pursue the use of computers for teaching and learning about identity and human values.

At Tufts University, Chris Rogers, my colleague in the School of Engineering and Director of the Center for Educational Engineering Outreach (CEEO), played an important role in introducing me to the need for and challenges of bringing robotics into public schools. I am deeply thankful to Chris for supporting my work and for providing me with encouragement and resources to extend the work of the CEEO to early childhood. In addition, I thank him for carefully reading a complete draft of this book and providing me with feedback. At the CEEO I am deeply thankful to many people, in particular to Robert Rasmussen (whom I knew from his previous days at the LEGO Group) and to Kevin Staszowski and Merredith Portsmore, who have taught me so much about engineering education and young children.

In my own department of Child Development at Tufts University I am thankful to my fellow faculty colleagues, in particular the members of the Early Childhood Education Committee (past and present versions of it), who welcomed me in the department and taught me about early childhood: Betty Allen, Kate Camara, David Elkind, Mary Eisenberg, Heidi Given, Fran Jacobs, Debbie LeeKeenan, Becky New, Jayanthi Mistry, Marion Reynolds, Don Wertlieb, Janet Zeller, and George Scarlett. In particular, I am deeply thankful to Becky New, who introduced me to the world of Reggio Emilia and guided my learning about early childhood education. Debbie LeeKeenan, director of the Eliot-Pearson Children's School, welcomed the challenge and opportunity of trying something new, such as robotics. Debbie also read the manuscript for this book to provide feedback with the eyes of an early childhood educator. I am also thankful to the department chairs, Ann Easterbrooks, David Elkind, Fred Rothbaum, and Ellen Pinderhughes, who supported my work teaching robotics in the early childhood education teacher preparation program. The experience gained teaching that topic, semester after semester, helped me develop the ideas and structure for this book. Two other people play an important role as mentors in all my work at Tufts: Donald Wertlieb and Richard Lerner. I do not have enough words to thank them.

None of this work could be possible without the contributions of the hard-working and talented doctoral students in my Developmental Technologies (DevTech) Research Group: Laura Beals, Clement Chau, Natalie Rusk, and Keiko Satoh, and the large cohort of graduate and undergraduate students in my courses at Tufts, who helped me learn how to teach about robotics in the classroom in a way that makes the most sense for early childhood educators. In particular, I am grateful to Sia Haralampus, who helped me develop a first version of this manuscript, conducted interviews and a literature review, and helped with formatting and editorial work.

I am also thankful to Ioannis Miaoulis, now president and director of the Science Museum, who as Dean of Engineering at Tufts played an important role in developing the graduate program in Math, Science, Technology, and Engineering at Tufts University and had the vision to promote the hiring of interdisciplinary faculty such as myself. Thanks also go to Yvonne Spicer, Associate Director for K–12, National Center for Technological Literacy® (NCTL®) at the Museum of Science, Boston, for providing me with information on the current state of the art with respect to engineering and technology frameworks in the United States; to Christine Cunningham, now Vice President of Research at the Boston Museum of Science, for early but formative conversations about engineering education; and to Ken Berry and Natalie Rusk for providing me information about current robotics kits used in education. Many, many thanks go to my editor at Teachers College Press, Marie Ellen Larcada, for believing in this book project and helping me realize how much I have to contribute to the field of early childhood education.

Working on this book was possible thanks to the financial support provided by the Bernstein Award for Junior Faculty at Tufts University (I am deeply thankful to Jane and Leonard Bernstein); the CEEO faculty grant that allowed me to conduct a summer institute for early childhood educators where some of these ideas were piloted; and the National Science Foundation (NSF), award #0212046, "Multi-Threaded Instruction: Forming Multi-disciplinary Research Groups to Improve Undergraduate Education," and NSF Career Award #IIS-0447166NSF, "Communities of Learning and Care: Multi-user Environments that Promote Positive Youth Development."

Finally, I would like to thank my family from the bottom of my heart. My sincere thanks go to my mother, Lydia Umaschi, who had the vision to send me as a young girl in the late 1970s to participate in a workshop to pilot some of the first versions of Logo in Argentina; to my mother-in-law, Nanny Bers, who read many versions of numerous papers on the topic to correct my English; to my husband, Josh Bers, whom I first met while we were both playing with robots at MIT and my English was not very good. Josh, with his calm manner, gives me love and support so I can both work and be a mom. I love you, Joshi! And I thank my three beautiful and playful children—Tali, Alan, and Nico—who participate in every open house of my courses and serve as guinea pigs for testing some of the projects created by my students. Most importantly, they are my best teachers about early childhood and they provide me with the inspiration to do this work.

I HOPE YOU WILL ENJOY reading this book as much as I enjoyed writing it. And I hope you become convinced, as I am, that by providing children early in life with powerful tools such as robotics, which are natural digital extensions of traditional learning manipulatives such as building blocks, we can help them develop readiness to become producers, and not only consumers, of technology. We can help them invent a better world for us and for the generations to come.

PART I

Constructionism: Technology and Early Childhood

FIGURE 4. Playing to learn and learning to play in a constructionist environment

We live in an advantageous time for introducing technology in early childhood. On one hand, given the increasing federal mandate to make early childhood programs more academically challenging, technology can provide a playful bridge to integrate academic demands with personally meaningful projects. On the other hand, discussions about the appropriateness of technology in early childhood are mostly put aside, and the pressing question is not "Should we introduce computers?" but "How should we introduce them?" (Clements & Sarama, 2003). The focus has shifted from technology to pedagogy.

This first Part of the book is about pedagogy. It presents a constructionist approach to using technology, in particular robotics, in early childhood. It describes four basic principles for developing successful early childhood constructionist learning environments that are developmentally appropriate:

1. Learning by designing meaningful projects to share in the community,
2. Using concrete objects to build and explore the world,
3. Identifying powerful ideas that are both personally and epistemologically significant, and
4. Engaging in self-reflection as part of the learning process.

The first chapter, on constructionism, is followed by a second chapter on sociocultural and developmental contexts needed for constructionism to flourish. Within this chapter, a section is devoted to exploring how the early development of technological fluency can happen hand in hand with socioemotional development. An interview with Dr. Rebecca S. New, an expert in child development and sociocultural theory, situates constructionism in the light of these theoretical contributions. At the end of Part I, two vignettes written by educators are presented to illustrate the use of robotics in early childhood classrooms.

CHAPTER 1

Constructionism as Developmentally Appropriate Practice

It would be particularly oxymoronic to convey the idea of constructionism through a definition since, after all, constructionism boils down to demanding that everything be understood by being constructed.
—Seymour Papert (1991, p. 2)

C onstructionism might best be understood by educators trained in the Piagetian tradition as a constructivist approach to developing and evaluating educational programs that make use of technologies with the purpose of learning. Constructionism proposes that technologies, computers as well as tangible manipulatives such as robotics, are powerful for educational purposes when used for supporting the design, the construction, and the programming of personally and epistemologically meaningful projects (Papert, 1980; Resnick, Bruckman, & Martin, 1996a). Personally meaningful projects are those that we choose to work on because we are interested in them. Epistemologically meaningful projects are those that engage learners in exploring disciplinary realms of knowledge, as well as the nature of knowledge itself. These projects invite learners to encounter powerful ideas. This concept will be explored later in this chapter.

The notion of personally meaningful projects is not foreign to early childhood educators. Developmentally appropriate practice pays attention to the individual interests of the child as well as the community in which learning happens. In this context, learning environments should support children in their explorations, scaffold their learning, and provide interesting materials to manipulate and share with others.

In early childhood education there is general agreement about the efficacy of "learning by doing" and engaging in "project-based learning." Blocks have traditionally been used for this purpose. Constructionism suggests that computers can complement these already established

13

practices by engaging children in "learning by designing" and "learning by programming." From a constructionist perspective, there is a continuum of learning opportunities that extends from blocks to robots. When the computational power is located not only on a screen but also on a tangible object, such as a mobile autonomous robot, we are encouraging children to explore projects that integrate bits and atoms, mechanics and electronics, which are present in our everyday lives.

The origins of constructionism can be traced back to the 1960s, when Seymour Papert, a mathematician and the director of the MIT Logo Group, based first at the Artificial Intelligence Laboratory at MIT and later at the MIT Media Laboratory in Cambridge, started talking about developing programming languages for children. At the time, given that computers were sophisticated and expensive machines occupying full rooms and requiring advanced mathematical skills to manipulate them, people laughed at Papert. However, he followed his vision. In 1967, the first version of Logo, a child-friendly version of the programming language LISP, also called the language of the turtle, was developed by Papert and a team from Bolt, Beranek and Newman (a high-technology research and development company), led by Wallace Feurzeig. Widespread use of Logo began with the advancement of personal computers during the late 1970s. Logo positioned itself as one of the first programming languages for children. Now, different versions of Logo exist, it has been translated into many languages, and it is widely used all over the world (Logo Computer Systems, 1999).

Technology, however, by itself is not enough to ensure good learning. Papert's colleagues and students used to joke, "Seymour doesn't come in the box." Although Logo was software carefully conceived to put children in the role of programmers, creators, discoverers, and producers of personally meaningful projects, it was not always used as intended. A top-down curriculum and an instructionist pedagogy could turn Logo into a completely different tool in classrooms where teachers did not understand the principles of constructionism. Pedagogy for how to use Logo was needed.

Papert's constructionism became widespread in education in 1980 with the publication of his pioneering book *Mindstorms: Children, Computers and Powerful Ideas* (Papert, 1980). In *Mindstorms,* Papert advocated providing children with an opportunity to become computer programmers as a way to learn about mathematics and, more importantly, to learn about learning. Although Papert, a mathematician, focused his research and Logo implementation in math education, he was convinced that the benefits of programming would extend far beyond Logo and mathematics. Through the process of designing and debugging computer programs, children would develop a metacognitive approach toward problem-solving and learning. Douglas Clements was a pioneer in conducting experimental studies in early childhood education to evaluate these assertions (Battista & Clements, 1986; Clements, 1987; Clements & Sarama, 1997).

Designing, building, and problem-solving can happen beyond the computer screen. Constructionism recognized at an early date the importance of objects for supporting the development of concrete ways of thinking and learning about abstract phenomena. This is consistent with early childhood education and its rich tradition of learning manipulatives. Thus, the original Logo had a robotic turtle, a creature that sat on the floor and could be directed to move around by typing commands at the computer. This first robotic turtle, based on a cybernetic British tortoise, became the predecessor of many of the LEGO-based robotics programming kits. In the mid-1980s Mitchel Resnick, Steve Ocko, and Fred Martin (Resnick, Ocko, & Papert, 1988), in Papert's lab at MIT, started to develop the first LEGO–Logo program. Part II of this book presents a history of this development and descriptions of commercially available robotics construction kits to use in early childhood.

Papert's constructionism is rooted in Piaget's constructivism, in which learning is best characterized as an individual cognitive process given a social and cultural context. However, whereas Piaget's theory was developed to explain how knowledge is constructed in our heads, Papert pays particular attention to the role of constructions in the world as a support for those in the head. Thus, constructionism is both a theory of learning and a strategy for education. It offers the framework for developing a technology-rich, design-based learning environment in which learning happens best when children and adults are engaged in learning by making, creating, programming, discovering, and designing their own "objects to think with" in a playful manner.

A constructionist learning environment gives children the freedom to explore natural interests using new technologies, with the support of a community of learners that can facilitate deeper understanding (Kafai & Resnick, 1996). There is a long-standing tradition of constructionist authoring tools and programming environments that follow the Logo steps (Resnick et al., 1996a). Some are explicitly designed for children's learning about mathematics (Abelson & DiSessa, 1981; Harel & Papert, 1990), about science (Wilensky, 1999; Resnick, Berg, & Eisenberg, 2000), about storytelling (Bers & Cassell, 1999), about language

(Bruckman, 2000), and about identity (Berman & Bruckman, 2001; Bers, 2001). Others extend the notion of stand-alone computer programming. These toolkits engage learners in the creation of virtual communities to foster peer learning and collaboration (Bruckman, 1998) and support them in establishing positive and caring connections and relationships (Bers, 2006).

Constructionism is a complex philosophy and approach that has evolved over time from its initial conceptualizations. The goal of this book is not to present a theoretical foundation of constructionism but to shed light over how constructionism informs developmentally appropriate practice when using technology in general, and robotics in particular. Thus, this book presents the ideas of constructionism organized by four basic tenets: (1) learning by design, (2) objects to think with, (3) powerful ideas, and (4) thinking about thinking. The next sections address each of these tenets.

Learning by Designing Within a Community

Constructionism proposes that people learn better when provided with opportunities to design, create, and build projects that are personally and epistemologically meaningful. Projects are designed based on personal interests and community needs. As in the Reggio Emilia approach to early childhood education, which was initiated by the Municipal Infant–Toddler Centers and Preschools of Reggio Emilia in Italy after World War II, projects done by children are shared with the community (Rinaldi, 1998). In constructionist settings this can happen in the format of an open house, demonstration day, exhibition, or competition. The goal is to provide authentic opportunities for children to share the process and products of their learning with others who are invested in their learning, such as family, friends, and community members.

Given that constructionism engages children in the design of an object—either a virtual creation on the screen, a printed document, or a robotic artifact—constructionist environments provide opportunities for celebrating and sharing the tangible products of learning. They are also structured to provide opportunities for personal interests and community needs to emerge. For example, depending on curriculum requirements or children's interests, teachers might choose a general open-ended theme, such as a circus, a robotic zoo, or a town, and invite children to develop their own projects within the theme. Another approach would be to set up a discussion about the needs of the children's school or community and brainstorm different ways of using technology to solve the problem. For example, children might decide they have a problem with squirrels that eat the bulbs they have planted in their school garden, and might decide to make a robot to scare them away (Bers, Ponte, Juelich, Viera, & Schenker, 2002).

Both approaches of structuring constructionist learning environments—theme-based and needs-based—provide learning opportunities for children to create and design technological projects following their own interests and ideas. Children might have wonderful ideas. However, their understanding of the technology and their skills might be limiting to the implementation of those ideas. How do we set up structures so ideas can become products? How do we prevent the frustration of children who conceive complicated projects that cannot be put to work?

These are important challenges in constructionist learning environments. Little children have big ideas. On the one hand, we want to help them follow their ideas, but we do not want them to become frustrated to the point they quit the work. On the other hand, we do not want their success to be scripted, too easy, or without failure. One of the approaches to finding this middle path is to help them understand and follow the design process. This is similar to what engineers or software developers do in their own work. They identify a problem. They do research to understand better the problem and to address it. They brainstorm different potential solutions and evaluate the pros and cons. They choose the best possible solution and plan in advance how to implement it. They create a prototype and they implement it. They test it and redesign it based on feedback. This happens over and over. Then, finally, they share their solutions with others. The cycle is repeated multiple times. This simplified version of the engineering design process can be found in the Massachusetts Engineering/Design frameworks (see Figure 5).

Providing children with a design journal and with many opportunities to talk about their ideas, and to discuss details of their implementation early in the process, is common practice in constructionist learning environments. As children work on their projects, many iterations and revisions will be done. Design journals make transparent to the children themselves, as well as to teachers and parents, their own

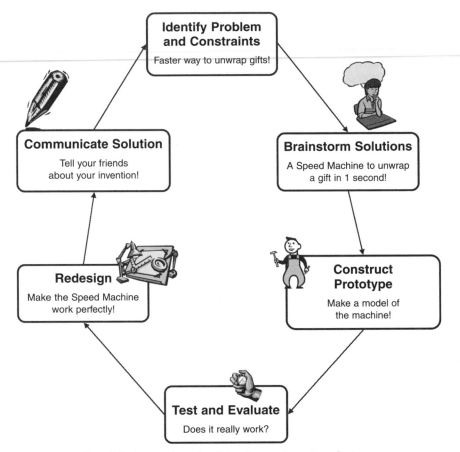

FIGURE 5. Simplified steps involved in the engineering design process, as appearing in the Massachusetts Engineering/Design Frameworks

thinking and the evolution of the project. More on this will be discussed later, in the section on thinking about thinking. Some children might choose to avoid using design journals or following a systematic design process. They do not like to plan in advance. They might belong to a group of learners that Papert and Turkle have characterized as tinkerers and bricoleurs (Turkle & Papert, 1992). They engage in dialogues and negotiations with the technology; their ideas happen as they design, build, and program. As Papert and Turkle wrote, "The bricoleur resembles the painter who stands back between brushstrokes, looks at the canvas, and only after this contemplation, decides what to do next" (Turkle & Papert, 1992, p. 169).

Constructionist learning environments allow for different epistemological styles, or ways of knowing, to flourish. Some children want and need constraints and top-down planning because they know what they want to make. Others enjoy working bottom-up and messing around with the materials to come up with ideas. Some methods of teaching robotics and programming, directly derived from engineering and computer sciences, provide structured paths for children to navigate the process from idea to product. For example, the formal steps of the engineering design process presented earlier are laid out in a design journal consisting of teacher-made worksheets. This approach might or might not work, depending on the child, the way the learning environment is set up, and the educational goals. In this book I advocate both pathways: design journals with a directive focus, in the form of questions (see Appendix C for an example), and design journals with lots of white pages, for those children who might want to invent their own strategies. Tinkerers and planners complement each other and can also learn from each other. Constructionist environments should be inviting and supportive to little engineers who thrive working with constraints and making advance plans, as well as to little tinkerers who create in dialogue with the materials.

Constructionism, like the Reggio approach, values the learning process as well as the products of learning. However, constructionism introduces a complex tension in our understanding of the learning process. A technological object—for example, a robotic car that follows the light or a Logo turtle that walks in the computer screen to make a square—either works the way it should, or it doesn't. But there are many different ways to make it work. How do we encourage a valuation in the process, if what counts is a properly working product? The secret is in structuring the constructionist learning environment to take advantage of what is not working properly. These are important "teachable moments" because they introduce the concept of debugging. Debugging, the methodical process of finding and resolving bugs, or defects and problems in a computer program, thus making it behave as expected, plays an important role in the culture of constructionism. Technology circles present a good opportunity for debugging as a community. A technology circle is a time for all, children and adults, to stop their work, put their projects on the table or floor, sit down in a circle together, and share the state of their projects. The teacher can start the technology circle by asking each child or group of children working together:

- What worked as expected and what didn't?
- What are you trying to accomplish?
- What do you think you need to know in order to make it happen?

The teacher uses children's projects and questions to highlight some of the powerful ideas illustrated by the projects. An emergent curriculum of what this particular classroom or learning community needs to know unfolds, based on authentic project needs. Before offering explanations and solutions, the teacher gives the opportunity for class members to provide responses. This is one of the most important parts of the process from a "what have they learned" point of view—but it takes substantial skill on the part of the teacher to do it right.

This approach to providing technical information on-demand, based on emerging needs, is an alternative to lecture-type introductions to the materials and skills needed. It also fosters a learning community, where peer interaction is supported and the development of different roles and forms of participation in the classroom culture is encouraged. For example, over time, there is always a child who is knowledgeable about mechanics, and thus tends to offer plausible solutions to classmates who are struggling with gears; there is a child who is very good at programming and is asked to consult on debugging; there is a child who can problem-solve when differences of opinion arise and is called on to resolve conflicts between group members. Although differentiation of roles is very important for growing a learning community, children should also be encouraged to take on new roles and to be flexible. It is sometimes easier for learners to succeed in what they are already good at, but they learn a lot more by succeeding in an area where they are weak.

Technology circles can be called as often as every 20 minutes at the beginning of a project, or only once at the end of a day of work, depending on the needs of the children and the need of the teacher to introduce new concepts. The challenging aspect of technology circles is that children might ask technical questions that the teacher is not well prepared to answer. This is an opportunity for modeling what learning with technology, and learning in general, is all about. The teacher can first disclose her or his lack of knowledge and say, "Well, I'm not sure. Let's try!" or can ask the children if someone knows the answer. If none of the above works, the teacher should then assure the children that she or he will find out by asking an expert or checking a Web site, and will bring back the answer next time.

Information-seeking, problem-solving, and learning how to find help and resources, are important activities in which workers in the information technology industry, and most professions, engage on a daily basis. Constructionist learning environments, and their emphasis on learning by designing, by creating, by programming, and by sharing with the community, provide opportunities for modeling useful lifelong learning habits.

Technological Tools for Learning: From Building Blocks to Robotics

Constructionism recognizes the importance of "objects to think with" and proposes new technologies, from software to robotics, as the new generation of learning manipulatives. The potential of using objects to think and learn with has a long-standing tradition in early childhood education. During the 1800s Montessori and Fröebel designed a number of "manipulatives" or "gifts" to help children develop a deeper understanding of mathematical concepts such as number, size, and shape (Brosterman, 1997). Today most early childhood educational settings have Cuisenaire rods, pattern blocks, DigiBlocks, and other manipulatives carefully designed to help children build and experiment. More recently, but in the same spirit, "digital manipulatives" developed by Mitchel Resnick and colleagues in the Lifelong Kindergarten Group at the MIT Media Laboratory (such as programmable building bricks and communicating beads) expand the range of concepts that children can explore (Resnick et al., 1998). For example, by embedding computational power in traditional children's toys such as blocks, beads, and balls, young children can learn about dynamic processes and "systems concepts," such as feedback and emergence, that were previously considered too advanced for them (Resnick et al., 2000).

It is within this tradition that robotics presents a wonderful opportunity to introduce children to the world of technology. Robotic manipulatives, such as the ones this book focuses on, enable children to use their hands and develop fine motor skills, as well as hand–eye coordination, and to engage in collaboration and teamwork. But they also provide a concrete and tangible way to understand abstract ideas. For example, by playing with mechanical parts to design their own robotic creatures, they explore levers, joints, and motors. The study of these simple machines becomes more concrete because children can build their own working machines. By adding gears to their machines, they explore the mathematical concept of ratio. By programming movement of these mechanical parts they start to explore the concepts of cause and effect, programming loops, and variables in a concrete and fun manner. By including sensors to detect input from the world, such as light or touch, they encounter the concept of feedback. All of these skills are fundamental stepping stones for understanding our complex world of bits and atoms.

The issue of abstract and concrete ideas is not new in education. It became prevalent with Piaget's view of children's intellectual growth as proceeding from the concrete operations stage to the more advanced stage of formal operations (Piaget, 1952). Furthermore, the emergence of the computer incited researchers, such as Sherry Turkle and Seymour Papert, to call for a "revaluation of the concrete" in education. In their breakthrough article in 1992, they identified how

> The computer stands betwixt and between the world of formal systems and physical things; it has the ability to make the abstract concrete. In the simplest case, an object moving on a computer screen might be defined by the most formal of rules and so be like a construct in pure mathematics; but at the same time it is visible, almost tangible, and allows a sense of direct manipulation that only the encultured mathematician can feel in traditional formal systems. (Turkle & Papert, 1992, p. 162)

Turkle and Papert (1992) were describing the manipulation of virtual objects in the screen, but the same process happens, and becomes even more powerful, when children are provided with objects that are physically tangible as well as digitally manipulable, such as robotic manipulatives. Furthermore, the physical characteristics of these "concrete" objects foster the development of sensorimotor skills that, in early childhood, are as important as intellectual ability.

However, using a concrete object to learn important ideas does not guarantee that the ideas will become concrete for the child (Clements, 1999). Wilensky (1991) proposes that "concreteness is not a property of an object but rather a property of a person's relationship to an object." Therefore, "concepts that were hopelessly abstract at one time can become concrete for us if we get into the 'right relationship' with them." According to Wilensky, the more relationships we can establish with an object, the more concrete it will become.

Robotic manipulatives, used in a constructionist learning environment in which children can design personally meaningful projects, allow for establishing many connections. Some children might connect with the materials as little engineers, deeply interested in the mechanisms. For example, by building with gears and motors they are likely to encounter powerful ideas such as ratio. These ideas will be studied later on, as schooling progresses, in a more abstract form, but the first personal connections will already have been established. For example, in the Foreword to his book *Mindstorms*, Seymour Papert talks about how playing with gears in his childhood fueled his later passion for mathematics. Other children might connect as little story-tellers and make robotic creatures that enact a play, more interested in the meaning of the project they are creating than in its inner work-ings. For example, a little girl in Argentina was very busy building a theater in which two robotic puppets would become friends again after a fight. Thus, she needed the puppets to shake hands, a difficult robotic movement to coordinate. She was not interested in the tech-nology itself. But she kept going until she made it work, just the way she wanted it, because it was important for her to create a project about friendship (Bers & Urrea, 2000).

Powerful Ideas and Wonderful Ideas

Papert's 1980s pioneering book was called *Mindstorms: Children, Computers and Powerful Ideas*. This last phrase, "powerful ideas," is one of the most complex concepts to understand within constructionism. Over the years, a growing community of researchers and educators have used the term *powerful ideas* to refer to a set of intellectual tools worth learning, as decided by a community of experts in each of the fields of study. However, different people have used the term in diverse ways, and among the powerful ideas community there are divergent opinions about the benefits and dangers of presenting a unified defini-tion (Papert & Resnick, 1996).

In this book, I propose a conceptualization of the term based on Papert's claim that powerful ideas afford new ways of thinking, new ways of putting knowledge to use, and new ways of making personal and epistemological connections with other domains of knowledge (Papert, 2000). Powerful ideas can be (1) content-specific, expressed as "knowing-that" or propositional knowledge with a discipline as a birthplace: for example, the concept of zero; (2) process-specific, cut-ting across different subjects and domains, and often expressed as "knowing-how" or procedural knowledge, such as how to multiply by zero; their birthplace is a skill or a set of strategies for doing something, for example, problem-solving or addition; or (3) a combination of both, "content–process" powerful ideas. For example, technological fluency is a powerful idea of the "content–process" kind. Technological fluency refers to the ability to use and apply technology in a fluent way effortlessly and smoothly, as one does with language (process), but also involves the development of knowledge within the information technology domain (content). The powerful idea of technological fluency is central to constructionism and will be explored later in this book.

Constructionism asserts that new technologies can become liberators or incubators of powerful ideas. For example, some powerful ideas existed before the computer, but the computer liberated them by making them more powerful and accessible to a wide range of people. Papert (2000) uses modeling as an example of a powerful idea that was always in the culture but, with the appearance of computers, was elevated. Scientists as well as children could start making their own models of complex phenomena and understanding them in new ways. Resnick (1994) uses decentralized systems, such as the behaviors of ant colonies and bird flocks, as an example of an idea that before computers was very hard for children to grasp. Computers did not originate decentralized systems, but they did provide good ways of thinking about them. Other ideas stemming from computers are, for example, technological fluency and debugging.

Constructionists envision the computer as a powerful carrier of new ideas and as an agent of educational change. Although school reform is a complex topic, constructionism adds to this dialogue by proposing the introduction of computers into the classroom as a way to restructure learning. Instead of facts or skills, powerful ideas can be addressed. The question would shift from "How do we develop child-centered, framework-based curriculum?" to "How do we nurture a learning environment built on powerful ideas?" The role of computers is to empower children and teachers to develop and understand powerful ideas.

The importance attributed by Papert and colleagues to the world of ideas derives from the Piagetian legacy concerned with epistemology: understanding how we know what we know, how we construct knowledge. Educational researchers such as Eleanor Duckworth (1991), from Harvard University, propose a similar concept: wonderful ideas. According to Duckworth, wonderful ideas are personal insights or revelations. Ideas can be wonderful for someone because they provide a basis for thinking about new things and questions to ask, but they may not necessarily look wonderful to the outside world. Following a Piagetian tradition, in Duckworth's vision, wonderful ideas are deeply connected with the developmental stage of the individual and with stepping onto a new stage. Wonderful ideas are results of an individual's previous knowledge combining with intellectual alertness to ask new questions and play with materials in new ways.

Although powerful and wonderful ideas have many things in common, they stress slightly different dimensions of learning. Whereas Duckworth's wonderful ideas refer to the developmental process of an individual, Papert's powerful ideas take a more cultural perspective. Certain ideas are powerful, from an epistemological perspective, and children should be given the chance to explore them. Thus, computers take on a role to help them to encounter them. Once upon a time, all the powerful ideas were wonderful ideas grounded in personal excitement and confidence to experiment. But all wonderful ideas will not become powerful ideas. Powerful ideas are wonderful ideas that stand the test of time and that are successful in the marketplace of ideas. A powerful idea needs to establish five types of connections: cultural, personal, domain, epistemological, and historical.

- *Cultural connections.* An idea must be already established in a culture before it can become powerful. It becomes powerful when the culture reaches consensus about its importance and relevance for the culture itself. At the same time, once installed in society, a powerful idea naturalizes itself and appears as if it was always there, it is taken for granted, and its power is not questioned (Barthes, 1972). For example, in a country like the United States, democracy is a powerful idea so grounded in the culture that many would not even recognize it as such. But in other countries, with recent histories of military dictatorships, democracy is not normalized. In the descriptions of the four other types of connections needed for an idea to become powerful, I will use democracy as an example to ground the theory.
- *Personal connections.* Powerful ideas evoke an emotional response in people because people can make connections between the powerful idea and their interests, passions, and experiences. People need to get to know and establish personal relationships with the ideas, in a way similar to how they get to know and establish relationships with other people. People who have experienced life in a democratic country tend to like democracy and couldn't bear to live in any other way.

- *Domain connections.* Powerful ideas serve as organizing principles for rethinking a whole domain of knowledge and connecting it with others. A domain defines specialty areas of knowledge where many diverse subjects or topics come together. For example, young children might be interested in the domain of animals, and this domain can be used to teach them about different subjects such as biology and geography. The powerful idea of democracy can serve to organize the domain of public life, and at the same time it connects to other domains such as human rights. Democracy becomes a powerful idea when people know facts such as rules that organize a democratic society and when they can connect their own situation with cases of democratic experiences. It also becomes a powerful idea when people can apply skills, such as voting, and mental processes, such as conflict resolution.
- *Epistemological connections.* Powerful ideas open up new ways of thinking, not only about a particular domain, but about thinking itself. Powerful ideas serve to make a connection with the "meta" level. To be powerful, an idea needs to reflect back on our own way of constructing knowledge about the world and ourselves. For example, democracy opens up a new way of thinking about fair organization and distribution of power. This new way of thinking applies to different domains as well as reflects back into our own way of living, thinking, and learning.
- *Historical connections.* Powerful ideas persist over time and have a very broad range of influence. They are not only a matter of fashion; their influence can be felt by many generations and can change the intellectual atmosphere of an historical period. For example, in France prior to the Revolution, democracy was not a powerful idea; it was hardly an idea at all. However, once it became powerful it had a multiplier effect, influenced the world, and persisted over the centuries.

These five dimensions of powerful ideas contribute to making the understanding of the concept difficult. Seymour Papert sometimes laments that, over the years, readers of *Mindstorms: Children, Computers and Powerful Ideas* have focused so much on the word "computers" in the title and have forgotten about "powerful ideas." The power of computers for education lies in their potential to assist children in encountering powerful ideas and to engage them in experimenting with and testing these ideas.

Early childhood education has paid particular attention to one dimension of powerful ideas: personal connections. There is agreement about the need to leverage children's own intuitions and passions. Emergent curriculum builds upon children's interests and is responsive to the ideas, excitement, and questions from the children themselves (Rinaldi, 1998). National Association for the Education of Young Children (NAEYC) guidelines for promoting integrated curricula are very close in spirit to the constructionist notion of powerful ideas. These guidelines call for powerful principles or concepts applied generatively across disciplines (i.e., principles that support the development of new ideas and concepts) and emerging from and connecting to children's personal interests (Bredekamp & Rosegrant, 1995). What is new for early childhood education is the emphasis on epistemology. Constructionism invites us to revisit the ideas we are helping our children learn through the looking glass of the five dimensions of powerful ideas.

Learning About Learning with Technology

In constructionist learning environments self-reflection and "thinking about thinking" play a very important role. Papert and colleagues (Papert, 1980; Harel & Papert, 1991) suggest that the best learning experiences occur when individuals are encouraged to explore their own thinking process and their intellectual and emotional relationship to knowledge, as well as the personal history that affects their learning experience.

For example, every semester for the last 6 years I have been asking my students, early childhood preservice teachers, to come up with examples of powerful ideas they encountered as children and continued to explore as grown-ups. To my amazement, every single time, they have difficulties recalling and talking about ideas. They remember they learned about polar bears and bats (although they are not sure what about them they learned), but they are not able to remember (probably because no one helped them make the connection) that some of the powerful ideas behind studying those animals were the concepts of habitat and adaptation. This exercise in self-reflection tends to open their eyes to the importance of not only teaching but also engaging children in reflection about the *why* behind what they are taught.

Self-reflective practice has acquired a predominant role in early childhood education with an emphasis on documentation via the Reggio approach. Documentation allows "the construction of traces (through notes, slides, videos, and so on) that not only testify to the children's learning paths and processes, but also make them possible because they are visible" (Rinaldi, 2001, p. 83).

Although computers can aid in the process of documentation by providing opportunities to develop digital portfolios, edited videos, photo books, and audio books, constructionism views the computer—in particular the ability to program the computer or a robotic creature—as a powerful means of gaining new insights into how the mind works and learns. Thus, computers are not only a tool for documentation but also a vehicle for thinking about thinking. Not surprisingly, researchers in artificial intelligence, who are fascinated with the question of how to make machines that think, write some of the most interesting philosophical essays about self and identity. Some examples are the work of Joseph Weizenbaum (1976), Marvin Minsky (1986), and Terry Winograd (Winograd & Flores, 1987).

Computers can make both learning and thinking visible. For example, the early work of Sherry Turkle explores how young children become philosophers when trying to make sense of how a computer toy works and thinks. Ultimately, children must grapple with how to distinguish what is alive from what is not alive (Turkle, 1984). Developmental psychologist Edith Ackermann (1991) studied young children's notions of control elicited by robots and other technologies.

Within the constructionist tradition, self-reflection and understanding of how knowledge is being constructed are not only goals for the teacher but also for the learner. This is an important shift from the Reggio approach, in which documentation is mostly conceived from a teacher's perspective (Malaguzzi, 1998). The Reggio approach provides teachers with a basis for modification and adjustment of teaching strategies, with a means for relationship building with different stakeholders in the educational process, with new ways of assessing children's learning, and with a tool for reflection about the teaching and learning process (Helm, Beneke, & Steinheimer, 1998).

Constructionism has paid more attention to learning than to teaching. Therefore, the tools of documentation should be put in the hands of children, who can assume responsibility for documenting their own learning process. For this purpose, the emphasis is on using design journals, pinups, and open houses in constructionist experiences. By sharing with others our own learning experiences, we start to make sense of our personal process of constructing knowledge. Public displays of the learning process and its products for members of the community, as discussed in the section "Learning by Designing Within a Community," serve a dual function: to make learning visible to others and, most importantly, to ourselves.

This chapter has explored the history and philosophy of constructionism as it relates to early childhood education. Four basic pillars have been identified as being particularly informative for our work with young children and technology: (1) the development of learning environments that encourage children to become designers of their own projects to share with a community, (2) the use of technological objects, in the tradition of early childhood learning manipulatives, for making abstract concepts more concrete, (3) the understanding of powerful ideas as the building blocks of curriculum and of computers as carriers of powerful ideas; and (4) the importance of self-reflection about our own learning process through documentation and communication.

NOW THAT WE HAVE an understanding of constructionism as a pedagogy that informs the use of technology in early childhood, the next chapter will focus on how constructionist learning environments should promote socioemotional as well as cognitive development. It will also address how different supports need to be put in place for creating developmentally appropriate, technology-based learning environments that put children in the role of designers, programmers, and builders of their own personally and epistemologically meaningful projects.

CHAPTER 2

Socioemotional and Developmental Contexts for Learning with Robotics

We have sought out the subjective computer. Computers don't just do things for us, they do things to us, including to our ways of thinking about ourselves and other people.
—Sherry Turkle (1995, p. 22)

The use of robotics has traditionally been associated with math and science education. However, in early childhood education, technology cannot be used solely with the goal of breeding little engineers, little mathematicians, and little scientists. Early childhood is not a time for specialization but a time for helping children develop holistically. Emotional and social growth is as important as cognitive development.

This chapter explores how such growth can be facilitated. It introduces the concept of positive technological development (PTD) as a learning trajectory that starts in early childhood and that leads in the direction of improving our own lives and the lives of others in the community through the use of technology (Bers, 2007a). While developing technological fluency is important for understanding the world of bits and atoms around us, it is just as important to provide children with the vision that technology can also be used to make a better world. That, in a nutshell, is the concept of PTD.

No educational experience happens in a vacuum. There are social and cultural contexts that make the work successful, and even possible. One context is institutional, and this chapter will focus on two different approaches that schools, child care centers, or family day care can use for introducing technology in the classroom: the technocentric and the systemic. The other context is the family. The chapter will conclude with a discussion of the role of families in promoting the use of technology in positive ways and in supporting the work of schools.

The Big Picture: Promoting Positive Technological Development

Over the years, practitioners and researchers in educational technologies conceived of two different ways of how children should learn with and about technology: computer literacy and technological fluency. Both approaches address the questions of what it means to be able to successfully use technology in today's world, and how to best approach teaching and learning with and about technology.

Whereas computer literacy relies heavily on developing instrumental skills, technological fluency focuses on enabling individuals to express themselves creatively with technology. In Part II, Chapter 3, in the section titled "Teaching and Learning Powerful Ideas with a Robotic Manipulative," these approaches will be explored further. For now, we need to understand that technological fluency, which is strongly linked to constructionism, emphasizes that in the process of being creative with technology, children are also likely to develop new ways of thinking. For this reason, the computer's role goes far beyond being an instrumental machine. Psychoanalyst and MIT professor Sherry Turkle's pioneering work recognizes that computers can serve psychological functions by enabling children to explore who they are (Turkle, 1984) and how they relate to others when participating in Internet-based activities (Turkle, 1995).

This recognition of the role of computers sets the stage for positive technological development. It invites educators and practitioners who are using or will use educational technologies to explore the positive role that computers and robotics can play in the socioemotional development of young children. It encourages them to pose questions such as: How can we use technology to help children think about the self in different ways? How can we design technologically rich learning environments that will allow children to explore their own psychology and their social relations? How can we develop curricula that integrate the use of technology with socioemotional development?

Technology has an impact on children's personal, social, and emotional lives from a very early age. In today's world, children need more than computer literacy and technological fluency to use technology in positive ways. Developing competence and confidence regarding computer use is a necessary step. It is also important to develop character traits that will help children use technology safely to communicate and connect with others, and to provide them with opportunities to envision a better world through the use of computers. Although in early childhood, children are not yet avid unsupervised users of the Internet, it is during this time that attitudes and ways of thinking are starting to form that will shape their adolescence. Positive technological development, as an extension of computer literacy and technological fluency, adds a psychosocial component to the possibilities of technology-rich programs to promote learning.

Like Erik Erikson (1950), developmentalists ask the question "What is the job or task of an individual at different times in his or her development?" In this spirit I encourage everyone, teachers in particular, to ask, "What is the job of a child growing up in a technologically rich period such as ours?" Computers are in children's lives, and are used differently throughout the developmental span. Children first use them at home for playing educational games, in the best cases, and for babysitting, in the worst. Later, they use technology at school for many different purposes, from writing assignments to Internet research. As they grow, children use technology to communicate with friends, to listen to and exchange music, to meet new people, to share stories with relatives, to organize civic protests, to shop for clothing, to engage in e-mail therapy, and to date (Subrahmanyam, Greenfield, Kraut, & Gross, 2001; Bers, in press).

Technology permeates children's lives. It is not limited just to school. As technologies evolve, they become a part of early childhood, a time in which a sense of self and one's role in the world is starting to develop. As educators it is our responsibility to lay a foundation for children to use technology not only to grow into better mathematicians, scientists, or engineers, but also to contribute in positive ways to themselves, their communities, and the world. That is positive technological development.

Positive technological development complements a learning trajectory initiated by computer literacy and technological fluency, which focus on cognitive development, by adding a socioemotional dimension. From a theoretical perspective, positive technological development grows out of the foundations of constructionism (with its emphasis on computational tools that provide opportunities for learning through making, designing, and programming) and applied developmental science (with its focus on understanding positive youth development).

Applied developmental scientists identify six assets or characteristics of thriving individuals, which they refer as the "six C's": competence, confidence, caring, connection, character, and contribution (Lerner et al., 2005). Taken together, these characteristics reflect a growing consensus about what is involved in healthy and positive development among people in the first two decades of their lives.

Building on this work, educational programs that make use of technologies from a framework of positive technological development should help young children develop (1) *competence* in intellectual endeavors and the acquisition of computer literacy and technological fluency; (2) *confidence* in their own learning potential through technology and their own ability to solve technical problems; (3) *caring* about others expressed by using technology to engage in collaboration and to help each other when needed; (4) *connection* with peers or adults to use technologies to form face-to-face or virtual communities and social support networks; (5) *character* to become aware of their own personal values, be respectful of other people's values, and assume a responsible use of technology; and (6) *contribution* by conceiving positive ways of using technology to make a better learning environment, community, and society.

These six C's can guide educators in creating technologically rich learning environments, from curriculum development to assessment, regardless of the particular powerful ideas in the curriculum. Part II of the book addresses some of the possibilities that robotics offers for exploring powerful ideas from different disciplinary contexts. This section focuses on how to design programs that also promote positive technological development.

How do we develop these programs? How do we know if the technologies we are using support positive technological development or are limiting in that they are only designed for teaching a particular concept or powerful idea? How do we design curricula that take into consideration positive technological development when integrating technology with disciplinary knowledge? These are legitimate questions. It is hard enough to develop an early childhood curriculum that integrates math and science with computers. It is even harder to address socioemotional aspects through the use of technology. However, as early childhood educators we are obligated to take on the challenge. A genuine concern for socioemotional growth is mandatory in developmentally appropriate practice. Thus, technology needs to be integrated with this purpose as well.

The positive technological development framework helps us to address this challenge by proposing: (1) the concept of identity construction environments; (2) questions that as educators we should ask ourselves; and (3) the "six C's by six C's" model to orient our choice of technology, curriculum development, and assessment strategies.

Identity Construction Environments

Identity construction environments are explicitly designed to promote positive technological development. There are two types: tool-centric and environment-centric. Identity construction environments can be *technological tools* purposefully designed for supporting the exploration of self and community. For example, the Zora virtual world encourages children to explore their personal and moral values while creating and inhabiting a virtual city (Bers, 2001). Or they can be *technologically rich environments* in which existing technologies, initially developed with other goals, are used with a positive development framework.

Both types of identity construction environments, tool-centric and environment-centric, are designed according to 10 principles:

1. Provide a safe space in which children can design and program personally meaningful projects that highlight and make accessible concepts and ways of thinking about identity and values.
2. Support young users to engage in self-reflection and introspection.
3. Provide opportunities to engage in interactive design-based activities to learn about self and community by becoming technologically fluent.
4. Provide tools with which users can create a complex representation of the self, highlighting its multiplicity of aspects and its change over time.
5. Provide flexibility to express and explore powerful ideas about identity in different ways (e.g., writing a story, drawing a picture, programming an interactive character, conversing with others, etc.).
6. Provide opportunities for children to engage in narrative expression, particularly in telling stories about the self.
7. Engage and motivate users for long periods in a natural and self-initiated way.
8. Make use of networked technologies to create a community to put to the test new concepts and ways of thinking and behaving.
9. Support the passage from knowledge to action. Namely, provide opportunities for learners to express their identity as well as to explore it through behaviors in the context of a community of practice.
10. Be designed following a participatory method in which potential users, both professionals and children, become partners in the different stages of the design process.

Whereas a small subset of technologies can be identified as identity construction environments (very few computational tools are specifically designed to promote positive development), most constructionist technologies can become identity construction environments if the design of the curriculum and the learning environment augment and supplement what the technology can offer. For example, children can use robotics to build, to create, and to program their own projects, thus meeting the design specifications of identity construction environments in principles 3, 4, 6, 7, and 10 of the list. The other elements, which are about the development of a community and a safe space to support learning and reflection, are not inherent to the robotics technology. However, they can be addressed by a learning environment and a curriculum developed with the goal of promoting positive youth development. This leads to the questions that, as educators, we need to ask ourselves.

Questions

The first question we need to ask is: What kind of technologies are we using to promote positive technological development? Can they be described as "identity construction environments," technologies purposefully designed to encourage children to explore issues of self and community? If the answer is "yes," we know that there is a good match between our teaching and learning goals, at least with respect to positive technological development and the technology of choice. If the answer is "no," we need to know if the technology is flexible enough that it could be incorporated into a constructionist learning environment with a curriculum based on the positive technological development approach. Robotics technology is an example of this second category. The technology by itself was not designed to promote explorations of self and community, but as a means of learning about engineering, math, and science. However, the constructionist nature of the robotics kits, which enable children to create open-ended projects, can be easily integrated into a learning environment that promotes positive technological development. For example, in Project Inter-Actions, children and their parents were invited to create robotics projects to explore an aspect of their cultural heritage (Bers, New, & Boudreau, 2004; Beals & Bers, 2006). Part II of this book will provide more examples of such activities.

If we have found a technology that is flexible and can be used in a constructionist way to engage children in the design, making, and programming of their own projects, then we need to understand how we can integrate that technology into a developmental technology framework. How do we create identity construction environments? The 10 guidelines presented earlier are a good start. But the "six C's by six C's" theoretical model (see Figure 6) provides a foundation by showing how each of the six desired positive assets or characteristics of an individual can be promoted by specific design features in the technology, the curriculum, and the learning environment that engage children on different behaviors: (1) *content creation* to promote *competence* in the use of technology; (2) *creativity* to foster *confidence* in children's own uses of technology to make meaningful projects; (3) *communication* in both synchronous and asynchronous ways to support the formation of networks of *caring*; (4) *collaboration* that enables *connection* between people; (5) *conduct* to engage in ethically and morally responsible actions guided by *character* traits; and (6) *community-building* to design and participate in environments where one can make positive *contributions*.

Following the conceptual foundation laid by the positive technological development framework, I will next focus on how robotics, a technology traditionally used for cognitive development, can be used to support socioemotional development.

Promoting Socioemotional Development Through Robotics

This chapter focuses on how robotics can be used to nurture the social and emotional aspects that are so important in early childhood, and that most work with educational technology tends to ignore. Some work on computers and early childhood education has shown that computer programs can engage children in social interactions (Wang & Ching, 2003). For example, research has shown that contrary to the view that using computers isolates young children, children at the computer spent nine times as much time talking to peers while on the computer as while doing puzzles (Muller & Perlmutter, 1985). Based on this foundation, what about robotics?

When robotics is used in the context of constructionist learning environments to promote positive technological development, two elements become important: teamwork and the management of frustration. In this section I use teamwork as an example of how to support social development, and I use the management of frustration as an example of how to support emotional development.

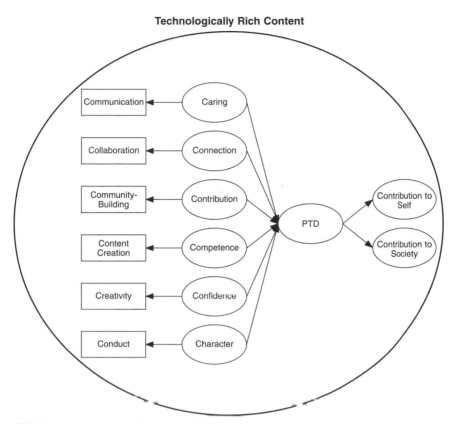

FIGURE 6. The "six C's by six C's" model of positive technological development

Teamwork is about collaboration and cooperation. It is about differentiation of roles and working together toward a common, shared goal. A child who is able to work well in a team will more likely have better learning experiences in school and better job options in adulthood. As described in Chapter 1, in constructionist learning environments children can choose to work on a technological project to address a shared interest or a shared need. Both the interest-based and the needs-based models offer opportunities for each child to express his or her individuality, while at the same time coming together in a bigger project.

Robotics provides a platform for engaging children in a joint project based on individual interests. But it can also encourage teamwork by requiring the integration of multiple skills held by different children (programming, engineering, building, etc.). Although participating in teamwork promotes the development of all six characteristics in the positive technological development framework, two of the C's play a most salient role: caring and connection. Children who work in groups to create a robotics project are not only mastering the technology, they are also learning to negotiate whose ideas will be implemented and how, while assuming a caring stance toward each other and learning how to connect with each other by asking for feedback and help.

A learning environment that supports children's development of a sense of caring and connection is designed to encourage communication and collaboration. Our choice of how to present the materials to the children can be a vehicle for promoting this. For example, if LEGO building pieces are situated in bins in the center of the room sorted by types of pieces (instead of giving an already sorted kit to each child or group), children will be learning how to take what they need without depleting the bins because someone else might need a piece. They will also learn to negotiate for the "most wanted" pieces, such as special sensors or the colorful LEGO minifigures.

When learning with robotics, managing the social relations that make possible the creation of complex projects is as important as managing our own emotions. Over the years I have often observed a sense of frustration because the technology is not doing exactly what we (teachers and children) hope it will do and because we cannot build the complex mechanic structure we had in mind. Although this frustration tends to be greater in the adults than in the children, who approach learning in a playful manner, it is important to address it instead of ignoring it. Technology works or it doesn't work. It is in our face. And it can be very frustrating to realize that, after many tries, the jaw of the crocodile doesn't open the way we want it to open, or the robotic car breaks every time it turns to the left. How do we help children manage frustration?

Some teachers want to avoid children's frustration and therefore carefully choose projects that will shield their children and provide step-by-step directions so children do not encounter pitfalls. This way of working is not consistent with the constructionist approach that I am presenting in this book. It deprives children of the authenticity of the learning experience and of the pleasures of learning by discovering.

Learning is hard. Alan Kay, pioneer in the development of the personal computer, refers to this as "hard fun," an activity that engages us because it is enjoyable but at the same time is challenging. Constructionist learning environments provide children with opportunities to have "hard fun," but should also provide ways to support the management of frustration. Some teachers set up the environment in such a way as to create a culture in which succeeding the first time is seeing as a rarity and as a sign that the child did not push him or herself that hard. "It worked on your first try, do you think you could try something a little bit more challenging? How about having a car that moves on its own with a motor, instead of a car that moves because you push it?" Other teachers always remind students that a project will break a hundred times before it works, thus anticipating the inevitable. This helps to create a safe learning environment in which it is acceptable to have things not working, breaking, and falling apart. It happens to everyone. Having fun and setting up an environment in which laughter is commonly heard is one of the best ways to help children manage their frustration when working with technology. Researchers at the Center for Educational Engineering Outreach at Tufts University have also found that if they only engage children in one or two robotics projects during the academic year, children tend to have difficulty with failure—but if they are presented with weekly opportunities to develop their projects, they learn how to learn from their failures.

Learning how to manage our frustration is associated with the development of the C of confidence when using the vocabulary of positive technological development. If we help children learn how to react when things do not work as expected, we are also helping them to become sure of themselves—confident in their ability to find a way out, either by trying multiple times, by using different strategies, or by asking for help. We are showing them that even though things might be very frustrating, we do not give up. We take an alternative path. This is an important aspect of emotional development.

Technology in the Classroom: Technocentric vs. Systemic Approaches

In Chapter 1 we learned about constructionism as a theory to guide the use of technology in a developmentally appropriate way. Then, we focused on how technology can be used to promote positive technological development. Within this context, we explored how to design technology-rich learning environments that support children's emotional and social development. However, none of the above is possible if we do not take a step back and, before introducing technology into the classroom, develop and examine our approach. Do we take a technocentric stance and understand technology as a central player in the learning environment? Or do we take a systemic approach and understand technology as one more component of a learning culture?

A technocentric approach primarily focuses on the new technology and is concerned with equipping the classroom or school with hardware and software. The budget is increased to buy new computers, and discourse centers on the new acquisitions. Seymour Papert (1987) coined the term "technocentric thinking" to capture an analogy with the egocentric stage in Piaget's developmental model of the young child. Although Piaget's egocentrism is not about the selfishness of the child, but about his or her inability to understand anything independently of the self, technocentrism refers to the tendency to give a similar centrality to technology.

Technocentric thinking is very popular among educators. Papert alerts us:

> One might imagine that "technologists" would be most likely to fall into the technocentric trap and that "humanists" would have a better understanding of the role of culture. . . . But things are not so simple. People from the humanities are often the most vulnerable to the technocentric trap. Insecurity sometimes makes a technical object loom too large in their thinking. Particularly in the case of computers, their intimidation and limited technical understanding often blind them to the fact that what they see as a property of "the computer" is often a cultural construct. (Papert, 1987, p. 25)

A technocentric approach is revealed through questions such as "What is the effect of the computer on cognitive development?" or "Does robotics work in early childhood?" The ways these questions are posed shows a tendency to see technology as the agent of change in the learning environment. However, such a context cannot change because of the sole introduction of the computer; the pedagogical approach and the people in charge of teaching and learning are more important.

A systemic approach, in contrast to a technocentric one, is concerned with the learning culture. This approach gives equal or greater importance to the training and support that teachers receive as well as to the pedagogy with which the technology is used. The budget grows or is reallocated to support professional development and the hiring of a technology coordinator for the school. Teachers are provided with opportunities to discuss how to integrate technology in their curriculum. In the process of revisiting some of the fundamental assumptions about teaching and learning, technology might play an important role as a catalyst of new dialogues. A systemic approach is revealed through questions such as "What do we need to make happen in the school so the technology can add to our teaching?" or "How can we revise our curriculum so the technology can be better integrated?"

Constructionism presents a tension between the importance of technology to support children's construction of knowledge and the dangers of "technocentric thinking." On the one hand, constructionism states that not all tools are made equal, and some are more conducive than others to helping children construct knowledge about the world. For example, tools such as Logo and the LEGO Mindstorms kit engage children in the design and programming of personally meaningful objects. Thus, there is an effort in the constructionist community to design a variety of computational construction kits (Resnick et al., 1996a). On the other hand, constructionism warns us against placing the tools at the center of educational change or viewing them as responsible for certain educational effects or learning outcomes.

This tension is a healthy one. It reminds us that both the technocentric approach and the systemic approach need to be examined and understood in order to successfully use technology in the classroom. It is my firm belief that before introducing computers or robotics to our children (or to our teachers, if we are in an administrative role), we should give some serious thought to where we stand in the continuum between technocentric and systemic approaches. This has implications for the kind of culture of learning we will be developing, the kind of discourse we will be using (among educators, as well as among the wider learning community such as parents), the efforts we will be putting toward developing assessment methods that are consistent with our approach, and the decision-making regarding budget, time, and resource allocation.

The Role of the Family: Lessons from Literacy

As shown earlier, the context of the learning environment in which technology is introduced is as important, or even more important, than the technology itself. The previous section explored the institutional context by focusing on two different approaches that schools, child care centers, or family day care homes can use for introducing technology: the technocentric and the systemic. This section explores the family context.

The educational technology community has much to learn from the family literacy movement. This growing movement in the United States and abroad emphasizes involving parents in the early years (Goodling Institute for Research on Family Literacy, 2006; National Literacy Trust, 2007). For example, research has shown that the practice of parents reading with their young children is a significant contributor to young children's learning to read (Teale, 1984; Senechal & LeFevre, 2002). As children grow, research shows that the stronger the home–school connection through parental involvement, the higher the likelihood of ensuring educational success (Fan & Chen, 2001).

In the 1960s most of the literacy intervention programs followed the "parent impact model" in which a teacher visited homes and presented pedagogy and materials to the parents. Although this model proved to be successful, critics maintained that this was a deficit model, assuming that parents lacked basic skills and methods for teaching. Later on, the success of parental involvement in Head Start led to the creation of the Parent Education Fellow programs, which promoted diverse parental participation. The goal was for parents to become genuine partners in their child's education in whatever role suited them best (i.e., teachers, volunteers, decision makers, etc.) (Wright & Church, 1986).

Some of the lessons learned from literacy education could have a strong impact in technology education. However, although most parents are comfortable helping their children with early literacy, the same is not true with technological fluency. When parents read, sing, and make rhymes with their very young children, they are immersing them in the world of language. What is the equivalent in the world of technology and engineering?

Whenever I ask groups of parents how many of them have read to their very young children or played with written words before they started formal schooling, invariably all of the hands in the audience go up. When I ask the question focusing on how many have done the equivalent in the world of technology and engineering, such as opening up a broken telephone, disassembling a bicycle, and screwing a screw, very few hands go up. And most of those belong to engineers or computer scientists.

Although at first sight reading a rhyming poem and disassembling an old television are very different, developmentally speaking they are not. Both introduce young children to the wonders and mysteries of a particular realm of knowledge. They afford opportunities to encounter powerful ideas, establish personal relationships with them, and ask questions to learn more. However, disassembling a television is more like discussing the meter and structure of a poem, than writing a poem. In the same way that we want children to be able to read and write, we want them to learn how to understand how technology works and to create their own technologies.

Following the basic premises of the Parent Education Fellow, Project Inter-Actions, a research program I created to understand how to help parents develop technological fluency along with their children offers a unique opportunity to investigate how parents can become learners simultaneously with their children, while providing support and guidance (Bers et al., 2004; Beals & Bers, 2006). Based on this work, in Part II, Chapter 4: "Designing the Environment: A Practical Guide," there is a section on how teachers can engage parents in supporting work with robotics in the classroom.

Buying multimedia applications and educational software for the home is not always the best way to engage parents in supporting children's learning. Technological fluency is measured not by how much children learn with computers and how many new skills they develop, but by children's ability and confidence to use technology to create, design, build, and program personally meaningful projects. I often find simple tools as good as some of the most sophisticated multimedia applications. For example, using the paint software and word processors that come with every computer is a good way to introduce children to the idea that they can use computers to make their own projects, such as drawing and playing with colors and lines or writing a story and changing font and type size. Although most educational software teaches new concepts and skills, it cannot teach children how to see themselves as good learners.

With the continuous advances in new technologies and applications, learning how to learn is the only viable recipe for success. Thus, parents have an important role to play—which goes beyond purchasing the latest software for their children. Parents, as in any other domain in early childhood, need to model what learning with and about technology is all about—as they do with language, by talking and engaging in conversations with their children; as they do with literacy, by reading to their children; and as they do with table manners, by using forks and knifes.

However, although most parents feel confident about their ability to sit in a proper way at the table and teach their children by example, not all parents feel the same way with respect to computers. This is not unique to technology, and parents have always struggled to support their children's learning about things they do not know themselves. In illiterate rural communities, parents face the challenge of helping their children learn their ABC's. Immigrant parents face the challenge of helping their children with homework in a second language. Parents of adolescents need to learn the popular vocabulary used by their growing children. However, there is a difference between these examples and the world of technology.

The next generation of parents of young children will be *digital natives* born after 1980 and with constant access to digital media and technology, instead of *digital immigrants* as most of us are (Prensky, 2001). These digital natives would have spent more time watching television, playing console games, and using cell phones than reading books before adulthood. Thus, they will have some familiarity with the world of bits and atoms and will not be afraid of technology. The same will be true of the early childhood teachers of tomorrow.

Today we are still in transition, and many parents (and teachers) are digital immigrants. The challenge for early childhood educators is the need to help parents who are digital immigrants to find ways to learn about technology and engage their own children in activities that will spark their curiosity and help them develop "readiness." As in any other domain of learning in early childhood, parents have an important role as the first teachers of their children. If we help parents to put themselves in the role of learners, at least three benefits can be gained. First, parents can model learning, asking questions and trying many times when things do not work as expected. Second, they can provide helpful assistance for teachers who want to use technology in the classroom but need more adult hands (this is especially true when working with robotics). Third, and most important, parents can begin to reflect about their own learning experiences and perhaps can become strong advocates for the power of learning with technology. These parents can be potential allies for teachers who are seeking systemic educational change and see the computer as an agent of that change.

In this chapter we have gained an understanding of the supports that need to be put in place for developing constructionist learning environments that promote positive technological development. We also learned that when technology is used with constructionist philosophy, socioemotional development coincides with learning powerful ideas from disciplinary realms such as math, science, computer programming, and engineering. In Part I of this book, we have been talking about technology in general, or more specifically about constructionist technologies that enable children to design, create, build, and program. Part II focuses on a particular example: robotics construction kits.

BUT BEFORE WE MOVE ON to Part II, two educators who have used robotics in early childhood discuss their experiences. First, Chris Rogers, professor of Mechanical Engineering and Director of the Center for Educational Engineering Outreach at Tufts University, shares a wealth of knowledge about classroom management while using robotics with young children. Second, Megina Baker, a preservice teacher doing her student teaching in a kindergarten class in the Eliot-Pearson Children's School, shares her experience developing and implementing a curriculum unit focused on the engineering design process. Part I concludes with an interview with an expert in sociocultural theories of child development and education, Dr. Rebecca S. New. The interview focuses on conflicting views and anxieties regarding the developmental appropriateness of children's learning opportunities with robotics.

A Well-Kept Secret

Classroom Management with Robotics

Chris Rogers

Chris Rogers is a professor in Mechanical Engineering and Director of the Center for Educational Engineering Outreach at Tufts University. He has been working closely with LEGO Education in bringing LEGO bricks and robotics into the classroom to teach math and science as well as engineering.

Why LEGO Engineering?

Ten years ago, I started working with a teacher at a local school who was simply scared of the technology involved with building and programming a robot. After 3 years of volunteers working in her classroom, she still let the volunteers direct the classroom while she watched. Even now, when she runs the classes on her own, she admits that she feels that she cannot build very effective robots and has trouble answering the children's questions. So why does she continue to do it? Robotics and engineering are hardly required in the first-grade classroom. She says she does it because she sees the excitement and enthusiasm the children have in learning through building, and because the children ask for it. She has students coming in during recess or staying after school to work on their projects. She has the whole class staying on task for over an hour. She sees them eager to learn math and science, and asking insightful and meaningful questions. Finally, she sees students that previously were disengaged (and often troublemakers) becoming engaged and better class citizens. Our Center (the Center for Engineering Education Outreach at Tufts University) works with over a thousand of these teachers around the world through LEGO Robotics and ROBOLAB™ (a product we developed that is sold by LEGO). RoboLab is currently in 15 different languages and over 30,000 classrooms. I have heard this teacher's story from teachers from almost every continent (Antarctica is the only one missing!), with children of every age, race, gender, and socioeconomic background. That is part of the reason I am convinced we have to start introducing more engineering problems into the younger grades. We can do this with a number of tool sets, but I will highlight LEGO Mindstorms because I have had the most success with it in the classroom.

Numerous teachers have shared with me their initial anxiety and concern about bringing LEGO Engineering into the classroom. A Norwegian teacher, for instance, told me how she brought out the boxes (despite her fears) and nothing worked, so she locked them away. A year later, her students convinced her to take them back out, and this time it was successful. She now talks about how impressed she is with what the children are making, how long they stay on task, and how excited they are to learn. Many teachers are motivated to bring engineering into class because of changes in student behavior. An Australian teacher told me about a child who disrupted class continuously until he found his niche in engineering. He soon became a major leader in the class. A friend of mine, who directs a school in Luxembourg, saw one student find direction and companionship through the engineering projects that helped him through a family tragedy. In all of these cases, it is the excitement, creativity, and engagement of the students that have most surprised and impressed the teachers and me. It is the fact that students of all ages are eager to improve their math and science skills that causes these teachers to bring out the LEGO bricks every year.

So is LEGO Engineering the solution to our current crisis in science and engineering education? I do not believe so. I do not think that there is any one solution that will work with all children. Further, I do not believe that any tool can be an effective teacher. The only solution to the crisis, in my mind, is to help teachers implement increasingly complex mathematical and scientific concepts in the classroom. In some cases, this implies changing how we train our teachers. We need to increase teacher self-efficacy in these fields. In other cases, this means getting the tools and curricula into the classroom. In almost all cases, it means reducing class size, changing the way we teach, increasing teacher autonomy, and allowing the teacher to create and innovate.

What Are the Obstacles and How Have Teachers Gotten Around Them?

There are a number of obstacles to bringing LEGO Engineering into the classroom, from cost to training to the current all-consuming emphasis on reading in the elementary school. Even putting these obstacles aside, teachers have a tendency to teach the way they were taught, and systemwide reform is difficult to implement. As with all other subjects, engineering builds from previous years, and so for a program to build, every classroom must be teaching the material. Whereas it is common for one or two "maverick" teachers in the grade to bring this kind of innovation into the classroom, it is much more difficult to have every teacher do it. Overcoming these obstacles requires leadership within the school and the parent community. Both groups need to understand the increasing need for engineering and technology education in our society and commit to a systemwide reform.

To properly bring hands-on learning (or engineering) into the classroom, the classroom must change from a teacher lecturing to a teacher being a mentor. Instead of the teacher driving the questions, now the students must drive the questions. Instead of everyone sitting quietly in their seats, the students are moving around, interacting, and talking. In general, where order used to reign, teachers are now teaching "through chaos." These changes are often easy to discuss but difficult to enact. It is tiring for any teacher to deal with so much activity for long periods. I have seen a number of different innovative solutions in classrooms I have visited. Some teachers reduce the chaos by giving different team members specific roles (such as programmer, builder, historian, etc.). In this way, she can pull aside a subgroup (for instance, all programmers) and discuss specific issues with the smaller group. She can send a subgroup to the library to do research, or simply have some of the programmers help each other. The students quickly identify fellow-experts and often can get all the help they need from peers. Other teachers limit options—by reducing the number of available building pieces or computers. This forces the students to collaborate more and think before building. Most of the teachers find class discussions (or circle time) at the end of the session to be invaluable in ensuring that the students are learning the material. Often it is here that the children transfer their newly learned knowledge to their environment.

How the teacher sets up her classroom can make a large difference as well. Two of the most common problems are classroom cleanup

(LEGO pieces have the ability to get everywhere) and pulling apart models. LEGO delivers sets with bins to contain all parts, and some teachers have the students continually sort the sets in an effort to keep all the pieces together. This is often difficult to do, as some of the smaller pieces get lost or end up in other people's models. Other teachers will combine all of the little parts into bins in the center of the classroom, and this way teams are only responsible for the more expensive parts (the RCX, motors, sensors, etc.). This makes cleanup faster, as there is one bin for all axles, one of all gears, and so on. The LEGO plastic bins work well as containers for the group models and can easily be stacked in the corner when not used. The second issue is how to share sets across classes. This is only an issue for schools that have a technology teacher separate from the classroom teacher. The problem is that the 10:00 class has packed away their models but the teacher needs the sets again for the 11:00 class. Because the 10:00 class will not take kindly to having their models torn apart, the teacher has a problem. Some teachers restrict the class to very simple builds, have prebuilt models, or simply do not have the 11:00 class do LEGO Engineering until the 10:00 class has completed the unit. A few schools have been able to afford enough hardware for multiple classes.

Teachers often wonder if they should have their students build from instructions or have them "free-build." Being an engineer, I always prefer the free-builds because the students appreciate the chance to be creative and produce a project different from their neighbor's. It does, however, come at a cost. Students are more likely to have problems, they will require more individual attention, the class will move forward more slowly, and the group discussions will not be as focused, because different groups will have different issues. It is these differences that can often lead to the best learning environment, as long as the teacher identifies and builds on the differences. In general, I have found that new teachers (and students) prefer to have some sort of starting instructions. Some teachers will begin the class out with an "instruction build," but then let the more advanced students modify and personalize their construction while waiting for the other students to complete their work. Once the students have more experience with designing and programming, the teacher opens up the free-building activity in the final project with a discussion of an "engineering design brief" and some of the attributes of the engineering design process (such as problem definition, brainstorming, designing, testing, and re-designing). Many teachers have the students keep engineering logs to document and assess/grade this process.

Affording the materials is challenging. Any hands-on tool set is expensive, and the LEGO bricks are no exception. The main advantage they have is that they are completely reusable, so the recurring costs are a lot less than using clay, straws, and so forth. In fact the only recurring cost is replacing lost parts, which is usually done quite cheaply. The start-up cost, however, is substantial and most teachers write grants or appeal to the community to raise the money. The most successful program I have seen in this regard was an elementary school in New Jersey that ran a "parent engineering night" that was so successful that the PTA and parent community financed materials for the fourth grade. The program at the elementary school now spans all the grades.

Finally, the last major obstacle I have seen for teachers is that there is no one right answer in the world of engineering. In reading, math, and most science in the elementary school, the answers are all known and the teacher can tell the student if he or she is on the right track or not. In engineering, there is no "right track," just some solutions that work better than others. This means that the teacher can no longer be the source of all answers, and often the teacher's response is "I do not know." Some teachers take a while to become comfortable with this approach.

But What About the Girls?

Often in the first-grade classroom, the girls have never really played with LEGO bricks but happily tell me how their brothers play with the bricks. Why is that? LEGO has spent years of market research trying to find a product that will appeal to girls. In my experience, girls approach an engineering project in substantially different ways from boys. The male is happy to just build, whereas the female often wants a reason— such as building a hospital, a city, or a ski resort. The girls often like the building time because they get to build with their friends. In fact, one first-grader we interviewed said this was the reason why she looked forward to engineering time at school yet never played with the bricks at home on her own. The boys, on the other hand, often have to be taught how to build together and would prefer being alone. My favorite difference, however, is in the approach to building. If the teacher presents a problem to a classroom and then places the LEGO bricks on the table, almost all the boys grab pieces long before they have any idea of what they are going to build. Many of the girls, however, think (and discuss with their friends) what they are going to build before choosing pieces. This causes problems with "rare" pieces disappearing early and with boy/girl groups. By the time she has figured out what she thinks they should build, he has already started to build and will not rip apart and start again. The girl gets frustrated and becomes disengaged. Teachers will often have single-sex groups or will require a drawing or a brainstorming session before bringing out the LEGO bricks to avoid these issues. The interesting thing is that I have seen this in adults as well—we do not seem to grow out of these mind-sets. I definitely grab first and think later, despite years of engineering training.

Is It All Worth It?

We are asking teachers to change the way they teach (from lecturer to mentor), we are asking them to intentionally increase the chaos in the classroom, we are asking them to teach differently from how they were taught (and how they learned), and we are asking them to learn a new subject, engineering. Finally, our tool set is not cheap, the curricular activities are relatively new, and few of their friends and colleagues have gone down this path. So the question "Is it worth it?" is very valid. The answer depends largely on the teacher, the school administrator, and the local parents. From a learning perspective, there is no doubt in my mind that the hands-on nature of engineering increases the children's enthusiasm to learn and motivates them to understand the math and science behind their constructions. There is also no doubt that the familiarity with LEGO bricks and the excitement of robotics and automation increases their enthusiasm for "LEGO time." It is teacher guidance, however, that teaches the student how to learn on her own and how to transfer this knowledge from the LEGO world to the real world. About 80% of the teachers with whom we work have decided that the added effort was worthwhile and have continued to bring LEGO Engineering into the classroom. Some teachers have completely changed how they teach, integrating engineering throughout their curriculum, whereas others have developed a number of "LEGO units" that they pull out throughout the year. Still others have replaced the LEGO world with saws, screwdrivers, and drills. In all cases, the students' excitement and pride in their accomplishments always convinces me that it is worth it.

What Next?

As more and more teachers bring engineering into the classroom, we need to build a support network and a community. I think Wikipedia is one of the best demonstrations of the power of a community that cares. Can we develop something similar for LEGO Engineering? Something where the proficient teachers can easily share their knowledge and experience? A place where new teachers can find new avenues for innovation? My dream is that someday teachers will be pushing LEGO for more innovation in their tool set, because they will have exhausted what is currently available and that school administrators will be pushing their local engineering colleges to collaborate to help increase student excitement in learning through engineering. Imagine a world where learning to build is as important as learning to read.

The Engineering Design Process in a Kindergarten Study Group

Megina Baker

Megina Baker is a graduate student in the Master of Arts in Teaching program at the Eliot-Pearson Department of Child Development at Tufts University. She works half-time as a Graduate Teaching Assistant in the kindergarten class at the Eliot-Pearson Children's School and greatly enjoyed her first experience implementing a technology curriculum.

As a new assistant teacher in the kindergarten class this year, I was excited to try out a new curriculum structure that the head teacher, Ben Mardell, uses in the classroom. Rather than selecting a theme for the entire class to focus on, Ben chooses to work in study groups. These are groups of three or four children working with a teacher to explore a topic of interest. It was October, and while planning our first round of study groups of the year, Luis gave us a wonderful idea that led to a rich learning experience for both the children and me.

Luis was the only boy new to the kindergarten class this fall. He was learning English as a second language and needed an entry point to connect with other members of the group. His mother mentioned to the teaching team that Luis "wants to become an engineer when he grows up," and this sparked the formation of the Engineering Study Group in the class. Naturally, Luis was in this group, along with three other children: Aidan, Iman, and Brian. These children had each expressed some interests in building with LEGO bricks, but we had not observed them talking about engineering before. Because I did not have previous experience working with motorized LEGO parts or the RoboLab software (used for programming our LEGO creations), I contacted the Tufts College of Engineering and was connected with two students in the Student Teacher Outreach Mentorship Program (STOMP): Mark and Dania.

These undergraduate students would be available to join our group on Friday mornings throughout the project, providing us with the LEGO materials we needed for building and programming motorized constructions and providing building and programming support. Mark worked with our group, while Dania supported a second study group.

Project Goals

My initial goals for the Engineering Study Group were that the children would have exposure to the concept of LEGO Engineering, would interact with "real" engineers who could act as positive role models, and would explore the powerful idea of the engineering design process. I hoped that the children would be able to extend their knowledge of the design process to other projects and domains, perhaps by referring to the revision process of design when troubleshooting a block structure that refuses to balance.

In addition, the project would address at least one of the National Science Education Standards for children in grades K–4 (http://www .nap.edu/readingroom/books/nses/html/6c.html):

- Abilities of technological design
- Understanding about science and technology
- Abilities to distinguish between natural objects and objects made by humans

The Initial Provocation

A firm believer in the idea of emergent curriculum, I wanted to first observe the children in my group and become aware of their interests before planning the curriculum further. Our first session, known as an "initial provocation" in the language of study groups, was an open-ended play session. During this session, a preconstructed LEGO structure was presented to the Engineering Study Group, and the children were invited to play with it using LEGO figurines, making suggestions about changes or additions that they might like to see in the structure. I was curious to see if the children would mention concepts of motion (e.g., a door that could open), which could lend itself to the next steps in our project. If the children did not explore this route, I would be

FIGURE 7. Playing while building

prepared to pose questions to them during their play that might encourage thinking about movement.

As the children played with the structure, several exciting ideas emerged. Brian and Iman began to play with the structure first, and Iman (observing the sea creatures present in the structure) announced, "It's an aquarium." As often happens in children's play, the group immediately accepted this idea, and they proceeded to use the LEGO figurines to play with the structure (see Figure 7).

This idea was followed by another: looking at two levers at the top of the rectangular wall, Brian made a suggestion that would power the rest of our engineering explorations. "Hey look!" he called to the others, "They swim when you push the levers!" As Brian used his LEGO man to move the levers, Aidan, Luis, and Iman joined him in making the sea creatures in the aquarium swim. Iman's idea of the aquarium, so readily accepted by the other children, coupled with Brian's idea to have the sea creatures move by pushing levers, had provided us with the momentum we needed to move our group toward success. With the children clearly on board, we ended the session on a high, and I set to work planning our next steps with the help of the engineering students and the kindergarten teaching team.

Curriculum Planning

Following the success of our initial provocation, I felt ready to generate a more detailed plan for the group. Because I believe it is important to maintain flexibility when designing meaningful curriculum for young children, I began with a basic plan for the flow of the project but was unsure at the outset how many sessions we would need to complete the design process (in the end, our project lasted about a month, during which we met twice weekly for 30–50 minutes at a time). Based on the children's interests in aquariums and aquatic animals, I decided to invite them to create aquatic animals of their choice from LEGO parts.

As the project progressed from planning our creatures to building and troubleshooting, I kept a documentation binder that included descriptions of our work and quotes from the children, as well as photographs and drawings of our project. This documentation was available for parents, and some portions were e-mailed out to families to keep them connected with what their children were doing at school. This documentation was also used in writing progress reports on the children at the end of the semester.

Implementing the Curriculum

Our work began by gathering background information on LEGO materials and on aquatic creatures that would later inform the design process. We spent our first session creating an aquarium habitat in the classroom, and another taking a field trip to the New England Aquarium (Session 2), where we photographed and sketched aquatic animals of interest (the children were most curious about turtles and crabs), paying attention to the ways in which they moved. Then the engineer-

FIGURE 8. Drawing before building: design journal

ing students brought in some LEGO creations (Session 3), some with motors and some without, as a provocation to pique the children's interest in motors and to open a dialogue about what motors do.

Having gained some initial information about our topic, I invited the children to start sketching their creations. I encouraged them to work together and, fortunately, this idea was received well. By the end of our fourth session together, Luis and Iman had sketched a crab and outlined its moving parts, while Aidan and Brian had engaged in a fascinating conversation about turtles' ears, ending up with a concrete sketch of a turtle, "with a little pointing mouth and four feet that swim" (see Figure 8). We were ready to begin building!

For the next five sessions, Mark, the engineering student, supported the children as they constructed a crab and a turtle using the LEGO Mindstorms technology. Mark assisted the children with the more challenging aspects of creating their creatures, such as connecting the motors to their power sources. Of course, claws fell off, and the motor cables got tangled in the turtle's feet. These were natural opportunities to reinforce the ideas of the design process, chances to encourage the children's thinking about specific problems and brainstorm new solutions (see Figure 9).

FIGURE 9. Building together

When the creatures were ready to be programmed, Mark incorporated the children's ideas about how their creatures should move ("we want the turtle to go backwards and forwards") and created simple programs to attain their goals. In a following session, we invited the children to manipulate their creatures again, this time altering the programs and the motor connections to see what they could change about the motion. We laughed together as we succeeded in making the crab's claws spin faster and faster and got the turtle to "swim" backward, and the children beamed as they shared their finished creations with the whole class.

A few weeks after our study group had come to an end, I gathered Luis, Iman, Aidan, and Brian once more to look through our study group documentation binder together. As we turned the pages, reminiscing about our challenges and successes together, the children became inspired all over again. Brian cried, "Let's do it again!" and Luis's wide grin indicated his full approval of this idea. The LEGO Mindstorms kits were brought out again, and the two boys spent the rest of that morning configuring motors and gears, competently manipulating a technology that had once eluded all of us. Best of all, when Luis asked for help connecting one of his motors, I no longer hesitated about what to do. Mark's support had made a difference to us all.

Extending Engineering

Fortunately, the kindergarten's experience with engineering and LEGO Mindstorms didn't end with the conclusion of our study group. Rather, engineering became a part of our classroom culture. Mark and Dania continued to visit our class on Friday mornings, inviting any interested children to pursue further explorations with engineering. Luis was a regular participant, spending weeks working on cars while deepening his understanding of wiring connections, circular motion with motors, and wheels. In a recent session, he created a car that spun in a circle and then reversed. The Engineering Study Group had enabled Luis to find his place in the class through a curriculum entry point that met his individual interests and skills. The whole class had come to view Luis as an "engineering expert," and we had all become engaged in the power of engineering and design.

By maintaining our relationships with the engineers, the children continued to explore the LEGO Mindstorms technology more deeply throughout their time in kindergarten. This experience left the children feeling empowered about their abilities to plan, design, and construct projects of their choosing. It certainly empowered my teaching. Given the right supports and an adventurous mind, exploring an unfamiliar technology became a uniquely rewarding challenge.

Moving from "I Know" to "I Wonder"

Revisiting Developmentally Appropriate Practices in the Light of Sociocultural Theories

Dr. Rebecca S. New is an associate professor of child development at the Eliot-Pearson Department of Child Development, Tufts University. Prior to this appointment, she was professor of education at the University of New Hampshire. Dr. New's scholarly work in the field of early childhood education has centered on the challenges of curriculum for the 21st century, culturally diverse interpretations of the constructs of quality and developmentally appropriate practices, and the necessity of expanded interpretations of teachers as researchers and parents as active participants in children's educational experiences. These foci are represented in her research on the cultural bases of children's early learning and development, including a recent collaborative study on home–school relationships in Reggio Emilia, Milan, Trento, Parma, and San Miniato, Italy.

MB (Marina Bers): *You are an expert on sociocultural theories and education. How do you think sociocultural theories can inform work with technology and young children?*

RSN (Rebecca S. New): Well, that's a wonderful question and I'll try to give a useful answer, even as I acknowledge that the question itself provokes some new thinking on my part. I believe that sociocultural theory could help us in at least three ways in our thinking and planning about children's explorations with technology. I'll begin by talking in a more general way about how sociocultural theory has helped us to understand the situated nature of children's development, the variety of interpretations of developmentally appropriate practices, and the processes of learning and development.

First of all, it is worth remembering the sources of sociocultural theory itself. Many people credit Vygotsky (1978) for helping us recognize and understand the cultural bases of human learning and development. Vygotsky's theoretical interpretations have been supported and elaborated upon by anthropologists and cultural psychologists. John and Beatrice Whiting's *Children of Six Cultures* (Whiting & Whiting, 1975) study vividly demonstrated the embeddedness of children's learning and development in *particular* places. The construct of the "developmental niche" (Super & Harkness, 1986) has since been used to illustrate this interface between children's development and the visible and invisible characteristics of their sociocultural environment. Cross-cultural research clearly demonstrates that children's developmental trajectory will vary as a function of the resources and opportunities available to them, the company that they keep (Whiting & Edwards, 1988), and the values and beliefs of those responsible for the children's early experiences. So, for example, children in middle-class American families are generally encouraged to develop and use their verbal skills at an early age, whereas children in other settings are taught to observe and respond to adult language upon request. Thus, a very talkative child in a middle-class White American family is generally regarded as competent and advantaged, whereas that same child in another cultural group might be viewed as rude, undisciplined, and poorly raised. Let me underscore this point: sociocultural theory reminds us that there are culturally distinct views of optimal child development.

A second and obviously related contribution of sociocultural theory to early childhood education is to reveal multiple interpretations of what might be considered "developmentally appropriate" educational practices. For example, our observations of classrooms in Reggio Emilia have helped us to recognize that direct instruction from teachers is not always at the expense of children's interests and capacities to engage. Indeed, those observations resulted in major changes in U.S. interpretations of developmentally appropriate practices, as evidenced by changing guidelines (Bredekamp, 1987; Bredekamp & Copple, 1997). Other differences are perhaps more provocative, such as those revealed in studies of cultural groups where it is sometimes deemed both necessary and desirable to teach children to care for one another. Japanese preschools (Tobin, Wu, & Davidson, 1989) and primary grade classrooms (Lewis, 1995) include large group sizes with explicit expectations from teachers that children will assist and evaluate each other.

In many American classrooms, in contrast, we urge and eventually expect children to mind their own business and take care of themselves. We call these competencies "self-help skills," and they are a part of most U.S. readiness assessments. I had never considered such a goal to be problematic until an Italian teacher asked why I would want to "teach children that they don't need anyone else's help." I continue to ask myself that question, even as I recognize its relationship to mainstream American values of autonomy and independence. At the least, these different views of effective and desirable teaching practices—and sociocultural theory in general—remind us that concepts of competence vary from setting to setting, as do interpretations of developmentally appropriate educational practices (Mallory & New, 1994).

A third contribution of sociocultural theory to early education—and the one that is likely the best recognized—is its illumination of pancultural and particular processes of learning. As interpreted by scholars such as Barbara Rogoff (2003) and Jerome Bruner (1990), we now have a much deeper understanding of the wide range of learning potentials that can be tapped as children apprentice to their various communities of practice. We understand now in ways previously unrecognized the inextricable relationship between cognitive development and social relationships, including the contributions of sociocultural conflict to cognitive engagement (Forman, Minick, & Stone, 1993). The theoretical construct of guided participation sheds new light on the myriad of possibilities for teachers to promote children's early learning. The notion that children utilize their experiences with one another and with adults to explore and build on ideas that are within their "zones of proximal development" has helped teachers to recognize anew *and legitimize* the potentials of children's play, of mixed-age groupings, and of long-term and open-ended projects. This work also helps us to imagine new and as yet unrealized potentials of adult–child relations and collaborative inquiry as essential components to an early childhood curriculum.

MB: *And how is this related to technology?*

RSN: Well, technology as an artifact of the 21st century is a perfect illustration of many of the premises of sociocultural theory that I have just described. Certainly in terms of adult development, there is the general expectation that if we are to be employable, it is essential that we are technologically literate. The easiest analogy is with respect to literacy. No one questions whether or not literacy is an imperative for successful adult functioning, and few find fault with literacy's primary place in educational priorities, even for very young children. Although some—myself included—are concerned that a too-early emphasis on literacy may preclude young children's exploration of other parts of the human and natural world, most agree that all young children can benefit, with pleasure, from the opportunity to explore the world of print, especially when introduced by adults and older peers with pleasure and enthusiasm. Technology is, in my view, yet another communicative tool much like the pencil, the felt-tipped pen, the paintbrush, or the telephone. It is a part of most children's lives, and to preclude their opportunity to touch, to talk about, and to explore technological tools makes no more sense than to keep children out of libraries or away from cell phones. That is *not* to say that they would benefit from an unguided exploration of such spaces or objects. Rather, the point is that children have the desire, the need, and some would say the right to observe and engage with the essential features of the world they are living in.

MB: *But many early childhood educators are also concerned because they claim that sophisticated technologies, such as the one this book discusses, might not be developmentally appropriate.*

RSN: Here is where my views of developmental appropriateness are informed by my understandings of the relationship between learning and development. Rogoff's (1990) examination of Piagetian and Vygotskian interpretations has been helpful in capturing critical differences in their theoretical interpretations of cognitive development. If we assume, as Piaget did, that development precedes and determines what can be learned, then we would be wise to keep children from exploring things that they don't yet understand. But this would suggest that the very young children should be kept out of churches or synagogues, since surely those scripted religious experiences are "over the child's head." But if we consider Vygotsky's notions of learning as a means of stretching or pushing along developmental processes, then we can recognize what we have intuited all along, which is that the child is capable of gradually appropriating what it means to be Episcopalian, or Jewish, or Muslim. This same child can, with guidance, learn to make sense of and utilize a remarkable array of contemporary tools—including cell phones as well as robotics. And to the extent that this tool use contributes to their developing capacity to engage in culturally relevant social activities and community practices, then such tool use is, by my definition, developmentally appropriate.

A second reason for allowing children to have access to and learn about technologies such as robotics comes not from child development theory but from a perspective of social justice. Technology is a lot more than a tool. It is a form of cultural knowledge that has the symbolic power of a marker of affiliation (Kantor, Elgas, & Fernie, 1993)—something that distinguishes groups of people from one another with the result that some groups are marginalized. Technological expertise is now a form of social capital that is associated with many features of economic and educational success; and schools have a responsibility, in my view, to create an equal playing ground so that no child is precluded from learning about and eventually developing such competencies (New, 1999b).

MB: *Some teachers working with robotics are afraid of losing control. The interview in the next part of this book with Terry Green, an experienced teacher, talks about chaos in the classroom.*

RSN: Teachers are trained—and I use that word with reluctance—to maintain control over their classrooms. They are also expected to have control over their curricula. And yet most would agree that control has its limits *and is limiting* when our goals include the promotion of exploration, innovation, and critical thinking. It is true that technology is not so easy to control, due in part to teachers' lack of experience in that domain but also because technology is open-ended. The child with a box of LEGO does not need to follow directions in order to construct something, any more than the child with robotics materials has to work in a particular sequence in order to learn, just as putting anatomically correct and ethnically diverse dolls in the dramatic-play corner may be of some risk. But surely some risks are worth taking, especially as they open up opportunities for both adult and child learning (New, Mardell, & Robinson, 2005).

And this leads me to my final comment about the notion of developmentally appropriate practice. When we talk about zones of proximal development, we are almost always talking about children, but adults are also in various states of readiness to learn new things. If we could imagine that, on occasion, children could be our "more competent other," then we could begin to envision schools as places where *everyone* has something new to learn. Certainly, increased technological fluency promises new interpretations of Vygotskian conjectures on the relationship between thought and language (Vygotsky, 1962). Unfortunately, such an interpretation of collaborative inquiry very rarely characterizes classrooms . . . unfortunately. We talk about collaboration among children and maybe among teachers, but not often among teachers and children, and even less do we bring parents into such collaborative learning communities. Technology has the potential to open up such pathways of discovery for multiple stakeholders.

MB: *How do you reconcile this vision of teaching and learning as collaborative inquiry with increasing demands on accountability and testing by the federal government?*

RSN: While it might be difficult to imagine, I seriously believe that technology could help teachers to accomplish more of their educational goals. While it will not make standardized testing any more responsive to the variety of ways in which children learn and demonstrate their learning, it certainly has the potential to help teachers integrate curriculum content. I can't think of anything that couldn't be taught in an enhanced way through technology. I've often thought that we effectively address most curriculum standards through two basic content areas—science and social studies. Technology, and its partner engineering, bridges those two broad bodies of knowledge. Technology in the form of Web sites can help identify the zoos that are in your state. A field trip and subsequent Web- and text-based explorations of zoos could support the study of ecosystems and animal types and feeding strategies.

MB: *And using robotics you can build your own zoo and explore the different motions and movements done by the animals and how they are related to their settings. . . .*

RSN: Yes! Yes! This example makes clear that you are teaching a lot more than robotics. How big a cage does this robotic animal need to be healthy and safe? Even very young children can be supported to examine and consider the consequences of "zoo life" on animal reproductive and mental health. How exciting such a project could be—not just for the children, but the teacher. And what a contrast this interpretation of an early childhood curriculum is to what is now standard in so many classrooms. I am convinced that if the curriculum is limited to what teachers already know how to teach, then regardless of whether or not it is of interest to children, for sure the teacher is likely to be bored and not intellectually engaged. I am confident that the very features of robotics or other forms of technology that make teachers nervous could be exactly what excites them as well, if only they allowed themselves to say, "I wonder" instead of "I know." And perhaps teachers would have the courage to be more curious if they knew that they didn't have to always be the solitary expert in the classroom. Technology has the capacity to integrate more than curriculum content; it also has the potential to integrate people, in the way that your research has illuminated (Bers et al., 2004). Current work that is taking places in countries such as Costa Rica illustrates technology's potential to inform not only child and teacher development, but also community development and social change. That's precisely what John Dewey was talking about almost 100 years ago, and he could have not imagined the tools that we have today to accomplish his vision of a transformative and integrated curriculum (New, 1999a). Yes, technology will generate conflict; but even that has been found to play a powerful and positive role in social development and cultural change (Turiel, 1999). It would be more than a missed opportunity were we not to take full advantage of what technology has to offer us. It would be a crying shame.

PART II

Using Robotic Manipulatives in the Early Childhood Classroom

FIGURE 10. A robotic scale to compare weights

Building on the basis of the constructionist theory of learning, covered in Part I, the focus of Part II is on describing robotic manipulatives, giving examples of currently available robotics construction kits, and providing lists of curricular and technical resources for taking this technology into the classroom. This Part also provides examples of powerful ideas we can help children explore by using robotics. Two vignettes are presented, in which early childhood teachers write about their experience with robotics in the classroom by sharing a project. Rebecca Merino and Kevin Staszowski tell the story of how their combined first- and second-grade class designed and built an interactive Freedom Trail after a visit to Boston. Merredith Portsmore describes different experiences of first-graders building a chair for Mr. Bear and other projects in the Engineering by Design curriculum. Part II ends with an interview with an experienced teacher in a suburban school in Massachusetts, Terry Green, who has worked with robotics in early childhood education for the last 10 years. Three appendixes, a list of references, and an index are also provided.

CHAPTER 3

Robotic Manipulatives as Learning Tools

My interest is in the process of invention of "objects-to-think-with," objects in which there is an intersection of cultural presence, embedded knowledge, and the possibility for personal identification.
—Seymour Papert (*Mindstorms*, 1980, p. 11)

I define a robotic manipulative as any construction kit for children involving two elements: construction in the physical world and programming that construction in the computer so it can become interactive and respond to stimulus in the world. After a brief history of early childhood manipulatives, I describe current robotics construction kits available for young children and how they can support learning. Then, I focus on robotics as a medium for engaging young children in developing technological fluency and learning about math and science through integrated curricula in a fun and playful environment.

What Is a Robotic Manipulative?

The word robot comes from the Slavic word *robota,* which means labor or work, and was first used by Czech writer Karel Čapek in his science fiction play *R.U.R.* (*Rossum's Universal Robots*), which premiered in 1921 in Prague. Later on, Russian-born American science fiction writer Isaac Asimov popularized the word robot in his well-known science fiction books. He first used the term *robotics* in 1941 in his short story "Runaround."

The word robot is used to refer to a wide range of machines. They take on different forms, from industrial to humanoid, and they can perform autonomous or preprogrammed tasks. Some robots perform tasks that are too dangerous or difficult for humans, such as radioactive waste clean-up and surgical procedures. Others can automate mindless but very precise repetitive tasks, such as those involved in automobile production. But all robots are capable of movement under some form of control and can be used to perform physical tasks. Thus, these two characteristics, programming and building, atoms and bits, should be present in robotics kits designed for educational purposes, regardless of the age of the children they are marketed for. Children of all ages should be able to program their robots to perform some action in the physical world.

Although in previous decades robots have captured the imagination of children through popular movies such as *Star Wars,* nowadays robots can be found in the house to help with simple tasks such as vacuum cleaning and grass cutting and to provide companionship, such as Aibo, Sony's robot pet dog. Research on social robots that can interact with each other and with humans is a booming field.

With the growing popularity of robotics, the use of robotics kits is becoming more widespread in education, particularly in high schools, middle schools, and elementary schools (Rogers & Portsmore, 2001). Using robotics requires a working knowledge of electronics, mechanics, and software programming. Thus, robotics provides a rich platform for integrating different areas of study through a compelling and engaging hands-on activity. Although early childhood education is slowly starting to develop an interest in the use of robotics for education (Bers, 2007b), most of the work has been previously limited by the complexity of the robotics kits available and the lack of a guiding philosophy for using robotics in a developmentally appropriate way. This books tackles both of these problems by presenting robotics kits that can be used with young children via constructionism.

The use of robotics in early childhood extends a long-standing tradition of learning manipulatives. Since Fröebel established the first kindergarten in 1837, and developed a set of toys (which became known as "Fröebel's gifts") with the explicit goal of teaching concepts such as number, size, shape, and color, educators like Maria Montessori have created a wide range of manipulative materials that engage children in learning through playful explorations (Brosterman, 1997).

Over time, as the gifts and manipulatives were marketed, new tools were developed that more closely resemble what is considered a construction kit today. Building bricks gave way to interlocking pieces, and the self-locking building brick was produced by LEGO in 1949. The metamorphosis of the building brick, from a strictly architectural and engineering toy to one with "technological" properties such as moving parts, starts with timber slats with linking pins, nut-and-bolt connections, wheels and pulleys and other mechanical components that were part of a variety of marketed construction kits, such as Meccano®. LEGO took on these properties as the company developed sets with mechanical parts, namely the TECHNIC I and "Early Simple Machines," which incorporated gears, shafts, and pulleys with the original plastic molded coupling brick (Parkinson, 1999). The characteristics of the pieces lend themselves to children's concrete explorations about mathematical concepts of balance, symmetry, and spatial relations. Nowadays, the use of manipulatives as a teaching tool is widespread, and most early childhood settings also have DigiBlocks, pattern blocks, Cuisenaire rods, and so forth.

In the late 1960s, Seymour Papert began experimenting with adding computation to moving machines called "floor turtles," so children could have control over the mechanical movement. In the tradition of the early manipulatives, the first robotic manipulative was born. Connected by cables to a mainframe, this ground-breaking educational robot could be programmed by children to perform various movements, such as drawing geometric designs with its mounted pen. Since then, "digital manipulatives" have continued to evolve and offer students opportunities to explore dynamic concepts such as feedback, which go beyond what traditional early childhood manipulatives could provide (Resnick, Ocko, & Papert, 1998).

Fueled by Papert's pioneering ideas, in the 1980s the MIT Media Laboratory collaborated with the LEGO Group to create a programmable construction kit. The first product of this collaboration, the LEGO tc logo (as it was named), provided an interface box for children to use Logo to program the movements of their LEGO creation. In 1987, the first prototypes of programmable bricks were used in educational research. However, they underwent many revisions before becoming "sufficiently reliable that they could truly become part of a classroom environment, honestly owned by the teachers and children who were using them" (Martin, Mikhak, Resnick, Silverman, & Berg, 2000, p. 13).

As the variations became available to schools, LEGO developed the RCX brick (Robotic Command Explorer), which became part of the LEGO Mindstorms product line, bringing robotics into the homes of children in the late 1990s (see Figure 11). Using Logo as the programming language, the software evolved into a graphical icon-based program, called "Logo Blocks" by MIT researchers and "RCX Code" for

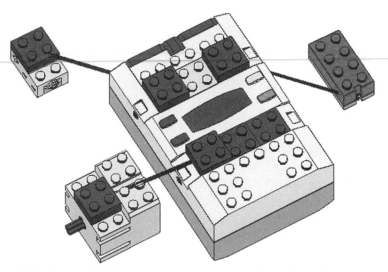

FIGURE 11. RCX brick with a motor, a touch, and a light sensor

retail LEGO kits. At the same time, Tufts University, collaborating with National Instruments and LEGO Education, developed a similar program called RoboLab, which is distributed for educational use with the Mindstorms kit and is currently used worldwide. RoboLab is built on the powerful graphical programming language LabVIEW™, developed by National Instruments. RoboLab is different from the RCX Code in that it was designed specifically for the school classroom—a place with few computers, little support, and 45-minute class periods.

In this book, most of the work described with robotics in early childhood uses the Mindstorms kit and RoboLab. The kit contains a large LEGO brick with an embedded microcomputer, called the RCX brick, an infrared USB tower that connects the RCX to the computer, and a variety of LEGO pieces in different sizes and shapes. The programs children create in the computer can be downloaded to the RCX brick. Children can use other LEGO bricks or diverse materials to build their own robots around the RCX brick, which takes the place of the "robotic brain." Once the program is downloaded into the RCX, robots can be autonomous. Some of the pieces included in the kit are familiar, such as beams, bricks, and plates. Others are unique to robotics, such as motors, light sensors, touch sensors, wires, axles, and gears. The RCX has three input connections (for the touch and light sensors) and three output connections (for motors and lights). In addition, an LCD display provides information about the motors and sensors, as well as data stored in the processor. An infrared connection allows the RCX brick to communicate both with the tower and with other RCX bricks (see Figure 12).

When introducing the RCX brick to young children and adults alike, I like to use a simplified anthropomorphic metaphor. The RCX is the brain, the motors are the legs, the touch sensors are the hands, and the light sensors are the eyes. In that way, children understand that the RCX receives information about the outside world, as the brain does, through the sensors, and can move through the motors. The kind of movement it does depends on what the brain, the RCX, tells the motors. And that is decided in the programming environment (the set of instructions the RCX brain follows). Sometimes I even have one of the children pretend to be a robot and I ask the rest of the class to program him or her to perform a simple task, such as walking toward a wall without running into anything.

Children can include the RCX brick in the building of their project. Because it does not need to be connected to the computer (the program can be downloaded through the tower), children have flexibility in the type of creations they can make, as well as in deciding the behaviors of their projects. They can create a moving car that follows the light or a merry-go-round that plays their favorite tunes. To program behaviors for their robotic creations, such as motion and reactions to stimuli (e.g., if there is light, then go forward; if the touch

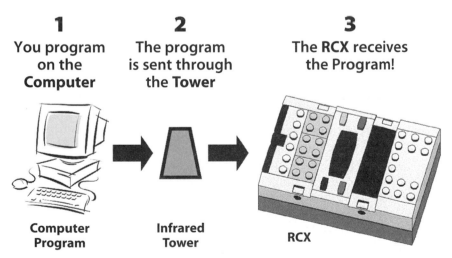

1	**2**	**3**
You program on the Computer	**The program is sent through the Tower**	**The RCX receives the Program!**
Computer Program	Infrared Tower	RCX

FIGURE 12. The three different elements involved in working with LEGO robotics kits

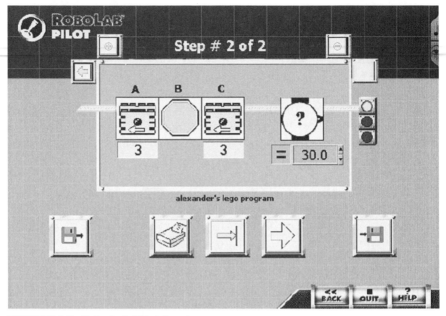

FIGURE 13. RoboLab Pilot level

sensor is pressed, then play a sound), children can use RoboLab or the Mindstorms software that comes with the LEGO Mindstorms kit from toy stores. Although both the Mindstorms software and LEGO Robo-Lab provide a drag-and-drop iconic interface that makes program-ming easy (it is possible to program without knowing how to read and write), Mindstorms is a little easier to use at first because it pro-vides the metaphor of puzzle pieces that need to come together, but it can be limiting as well.

RoboLab has several levels of difficulty and a very high ceiling, so users can tailor the functions that are available to their personal pro-gramming skills and developmental stages (Portsmore, 1999). Thus, RoboLab has been the programming language of choice for educators worldwide. When using RoboLab in early childhood classrooms I sug-gest starting with the simple levels called Pilot, which can range in complexity and make it easy to manipulate the icons (see Figure 13). These levels also work well in classrooms with very few computers, because students are able to compose and download a program in very little time.

All program levels begin with a green light and end with a red light. Icons, representing actions, are strung together by a pink wire. In the

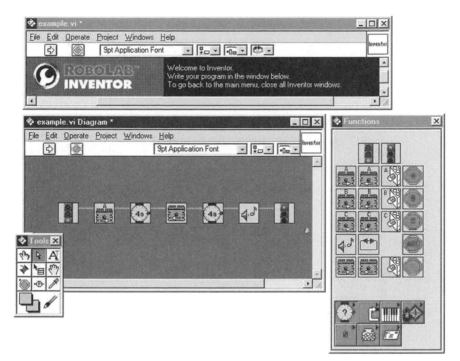

FIGURE 14. RoboLab Inventor level

Pilot levels, which range from 1 to 4, students select actions from a selection of images, and there is no need to use the pink wire. Later on, as children understand the concept of programming and they are able to better manipulate the mouse, it makes sense to switch to the Inventor levels, where students can assemble a program by selecting from a palette of multiple icons (see Figure 14). In the Pilot level, the program will always work—it might not do what children wanted but something will happen, because they are essentially picking from a limited list of behaviors. In Inventor, they are writing their own behaviors, and now they can run into standard programming problems and things might not work as expected. This then invites new possibilities for debugging and problem-solving.

This book is not intended to teach RoboLab or other programming languages for the LEGO Mindstorms robotics kit. At the end of the book, a list of resources and further references is presented. Chapter 4, "Designing the Environment: A Practical Guide," describes other commercially available robotics construction kits that can be used with very young children in the spirit of constructionism.

Teaching and Learning Powerful Ideas with a Robotic Manipulative

Robotics has traditionally been used to teach older children about engineering concepts by engaging them in teacher-directed challenges and competition. For example, robotics competitions such as the National Robotics Challenge (an open-platform robotics competition for middle school, high school, and postsecondary students) and FIRST (For Inspiration and Recognition of Science and Technology) provide a competitive forum for young people to solve an engineering design problem. As of 2005 there were over 100,000 students and 40,000 adult mentors from around the world involved in at least one of FIRST's competitions.

The concept of a competition as an event where robots must accomplish a given task (usually outperform another robot) is very appealing to some young people. However, others might be more interested in exhibitions rather than competitions. Although the use of competitive challenges is widespread in robotics education, research has shown that females do not tend to respond well to these teaching strategies (Turbak & Berg, 2002). Competitions emerge from a long-standing tradition of using challenges to help children discover concepts and develop specific skills. For example, a robotics curriculum is generally built around different design challenges that engage in step-by-step introduction to both engineering and computer programming.

Challenges and competitions might be useful in teaching specific concepts, but they may not always be appropriate in the early childhood setting. On the one hand, it is very difficult to reconcile the instructional challenges approach with notions of emergent curriculum based on children's own interest. On the other hand, the focus in early childhood on socioemotional development is more likely to engage children in collaboration rather than competition. Thus, it is important to identify an educational philosophy, such as constructionism, that is well suited for our work with young children and that understands the significance of robotic objects as carriers and incubators of powerful ideas, and not only as final products.

As stated earlier, robotics provides a platform for engaging children in exploring the man-made world, more specifically, the aspects of this world in which bits and atoms are integrated. This involves everyday objects such as automatic doors in supermarkets, motion-sensitive lights in yards, and automatic braking systems in cars. More complex objects are space shuttles, robotic surgeons, and bomb-finding robots.

Although all of these objects are interesting to study, a curriculum of powerful ideas is not built around objects. It is built around ideas.

Chapter 1 shows how powerful ideas afford new ways of thinking, new ways of putting knowledge to use, and new ways of making personal and epistemological connections with other domains of knowledge (Papert, 2000). Thus, objects such as the ones just mentioned are interesting because they can become carriers of powerful ideas about mechanics, sensing, control theory, and even artificial intelligence.

These powerful ideas afford new ways of thinking about everyday objects and also about disciplines such as physics and mathematics. For example, the gears in some of these objects invite children to think about powerful mathematical ideas such as ratios. When children are provided with opportunities to use gears in the design of their robots, personal connections with ideas such as ratio start to emerge. As schooling progresses, these ideas will be formalized through abstract equations, but the first concrete personal relationships with these powerful ideas will already have been established.

At the intersection of all these powerful ideas emerges the notion of technological fluency. This "content–process" powerful idea refers to the use and application of technology in a fluent way, effortless and smooth, as one does with language (process). It also involves the development of knowledge within the information technology domain and related areas such as physics, engineering, mathematics, and computer programming (content). Robotics construction kits provide a playful platform for developing technological fluency in an integrated way with other domains of the curriculum.

A technologically fluent person can use technology to write a story, make a drawing, model a complex simulation, or program a robotic creature (Papert & Resnick, 1996). As with learning a second language, fluency takes time to achieve and requires hard work and motivation. For example, to express ourselves through a poem, we first need to learn the alphabet. In the same spirit, to create a digital picture or program a robot, we first need to learn how to use the keyboard and to navigate the interface, how to use a Paint program and Word, or how the LEGO pieces connect together. These building blocks have come to be known as "computer literacy" or "technological literacy." However, skills with specific applications or products are necessary but not sufficient for children to grow in the information age, where new skills are constantly needed.

Although learning the alphabet is needed to write a poem, it is not enough. In the same spirit, knowing how to use software or robotics packages is not enough to become technologically fluent. As stated by the Committee on Information Technology Literacy in 1999, "the 'skills' approach lacks 'staying power'." Thus, regardless of the age or developmental stage of the child, technological literacy is a fundamental stepping stone toward technological fluency, but it should not be a goal in and of itself.

Technological fluency is knowledge about what technology is, how it works, what purposes it can serve, and how it can be used efficiently and effectively to achieve specific personal and societal goals. As of 2006, most states included engineering/technology standards in their educational frameworks (see Appendix A for a table comparing the state of the art of each state regarding these curricular frameworks).

Massachusetts is leading the nation in declaring that technology and engineering are as important to the curriculum as science, social studies, and other key subjects. For example, as early as 2001 the Massachusetts Science and Technology/Engineering Curriculum Framework mandated the teaching of technology and engineering for all students in grades pre-K–12. Although teachers have some freedom to engage their students in the discovery of powerful ideas, these days, what is taught in the classrooms is very much guided by state and federal curriculum frameworks that identify what each child should know.

Ioannis Miaoulis, president and director of the Museum of Science, played a key role in introducing engineering and technology in Massachusetts's K–12 frameworks and now, through the National Center for Technological Literacy, in taking it nationwide. He explains:

> The Federal Government has some learning requirements through the "No Child Left Behind Act" in the areas of reading, math, and soon science. Although it cannot mandate curriculum at the state level, it can mandate states to reach a certain level or standard of learning. For successfully introducing, in a wholesale way or in a national way, a new discipline like engineering, we need a strategy that works at two different levels: individual states need to include engineering when they write their standards; and any new standards that come out at the national level also should include technology and engineering. As states periodically rewrite their standards, they look at what the national standards look like. And if they see technology and engineering in the national standards then they may consider including them into their own standards. Helping at both the state and the national level is part of our efforts through the Center for Technological Literacy.
>
> However, if technology and engineering are in both the state and the national frameworks, but children do not get tested, teachers might

decide to skip this content by using the following arguments: "There are too many things to do in the day and now you are throwing us another one!?" and "I am not an engineer, how am I supposed to teach engineering?" Of course teachers are not mathematicians, but they teach mathematics; they are not writers and they teach writing, and they are not historians and they teach social studies; so it is the same thing. But engineering and technology is something new and they have to learn it. So the ideal strategy to get it taught nationally, is to put it in each state's framework and test it. Because it may be in the frameworks but if it is not tested, it is not going to be taught. Of course, then we need to talk about what kind of testing and formal assessments are best and how to implement them so children can do more creative things such as building something, designing, or put together a port-folio. (personal communication, 2006)

Both state and national frameworks are constructed around power-ful ideas. Table 1 shows how some of the powerful ideas encountered by engaging in the design of a robotics project relate to the curricular frameworks of Massachusetts. Although Massachusetts was chosen as an example because of its pioneering role, this is similar to other states in the United States and other countries that emphasize technology education.

Robotic manipulatives provide a venue through which to engage children in developing technological fluency (Miaoulis, 2001; National Academy of Engineering & National Research Council, 2002). They also offer a platform for project-based learning (Resnick et al., 2000) that promotes design processes such as iteration and testing of alternatives in problem posing and problem solving. By designing a robotics proj-ect, powerful ideas from different curricular domains can be integrated. Appendix B provides an example of how to develop a curricular web that integrates robotics with other disciplines. Last but not least, robotic manipulatives can motivate students to engage in learning complex concepts, in particular in the areas of math and science, even when they label themselves as "not good at" or "not interested in" either subject (Bers & Urrea, 2000). Table 2 presents examples of dif-ferent curricula designed and implemented around powerful ideas in several early childhood classrooms, private and public, urban and sub-urban. A more complete description of the curricula can be found at the following Web site: http://www.ase.tufts.edu/devtech/projectslibrary/projectslibrary.html.

In the spirit of Piaget, robotic manipulatives provide opportunities for both little engineers and little storytellers to develop technological

TABLE 1. Engineering and technology standards in the United States in 2006. Table provided by Yvonne Spicer, National Center for Technological Literacy (NCTL), Boston Museum of Science

Science/ Engineering Concept	Definition	Massachusetts Curriculum Technology/Engineering Frameworks, Pre-K–5
Problem solving	Inventing a solution to a given problem	General design process
Brainstorming	Using creativity during problem solving	Demonstrate methods of representing solutions to a design problem
Design process	A sequence of steps that leads one through a problem-solving challenge	Identify and explain the steps of the engineering design process
Programming sequence	The specific order in which commands are arranged to ultimately perform a task	Identify and explain how symbols are used to communicate a message
Identify constraints	Recognizing the limitations of a given problem	Explain how design features would affect construction of a prototype
Prototyping	Constructing a model of the proposed solution to a problem for testing	Describe and explain the purpose of a given prototype
Materials selection	The act of identifying the most appropriate materials for creating a solution	Identify materials used to accomplish a design task based on a specific property
Energy transfer	Changing one form of energy into another	Describe how human bodies use parts of the body as tools, and compare that with animals
Forces	A push or pull that acts on an object	Identify relevant design features for building a prototype, such as size, shape, weight
Motion	A change of position of one body with respect to another body, frame of reference, or coordinate system	Compare natural systems with mechanical systems that are designed to serve similar purposes
Wheel and axle	A simple machine consisting of a rotating rod placed in the wheel's center, thus making it easier to move objects	Identify tools and simple machines used for a specific purpose

Science/ Engineering Concept	Definition	Massachusetts Curriculum Technology/Engineering Frameworks, Pre-K–5
Lever	A simple machine consisting of an arm pivoting at a center point to easily lift objects	Identify tools and simple machines used for a specific purpose
Gear	A wheel with teeth used to transfer motion	Identify and explain the difference between simple and complex machines
Friction	The force that opposes a desired motion due to the contact of objects	Explain how design features would affect construction of a prototype
Stability	The necessary property of structures to prevent failure	Identify relevant design features of a solution
Sensors	Objects that identify a change in the immediate surrounding environment	Describe how human bodies use parts of the body as tools, and compare that with animals
Feedback	The response of sensors to a change in the surrounding environment	Identify the five elements of a universal system model
Looping	A programming method used to create an infinite program so that tasks may be repeated	Identify and explain how symbols are used to communicate a message
Input and output	Terms used for information exchanged through a computer	Identify the five elements of a universal system model
Troubleshooting/ debugging	Identifying the error(s) in a computer program	Identify and explain the steps of the engineering design process

fluency, while respecting and engaging their own epistemological styles and ways of knowing the world (Bruner, 1986). Early childhood educators have long recognized the importance of this. In good early childhood education settings we can find books as well as building blocks. When using robotics, this should be kept in mind. It is not enough to adapt the challenge-based robotics curriculum developed for upper elementary grades. As in all other domains of early childhood education, when engaging children with technology, "epistemological pluralism," diversity in ways of knowing and approaching problems and ideas, should be respected (Turkle & Papert, 1992).

TABLE 2. Powerful ideas from engineering and technology as they relate to state curriculum frameworks

Powerful Idea	Curriculum Description	Relationship to Frameworks	Level	Developer*
Metamorphosis	The teacher introduced the concept of change through several aspects of the curriculum, with an emphasis on metamorphosis. After reading *The Hungry Caterpillar*, children sequenced the story and did dramatic play, movement, and art activities to explore change. They used the Mindstorms kit to make a robotic vehicle, representing the heart of the caterpillar, that would travel the journey of the "hungry caterpillar" on an already-designed road. Children would dress up the robot/heart with puppets representing its different life cycle stages.	Life sciences: study life cycles, recognize changes in animals and plants	Preschool: 3–4 years old	Iris Ponte
Cardinal directions	The children began by directionally navigating a map of their town and developing personal connections to the town. The class next researched historical landmarks of the town and wrote illustrated fiction stories about the town. Then they created a floor map of the town to scale and built and programmed a school bus that would navigate the town floor map and stop at different locations.	Mapping, scientific method, language, literature, writing, social studies, science and technology	2nd grade	Alaina Thiel
Magnetism	The teacher designed activities in which the children explored and discussed the properties of magnets. First, a preprogrammed car was used to test the strength of magnets. Then children designed their own vehicles to follow a path on their way to a magnet.	3rd-grade topic relating to technology strand	2nd grade	Nicole Notaro
Cause and effect	Meeting the interests of the classroom boys, the teacher introduced the Mindstorms kit to a group of children as a means of collaboratively designing and creating a fire engine with light sensors. The kit was also used with the girls in the class to develop a doll cradle with touch sensors. Manipulable icons were used to promote understanding of the programming language.	Cause and effect, community helpers, programming	Preschool: 3–4 years old	Ana Zamora

82

Shadows: light/darkness, shapes, motion, relations	Within this teacher's Shadow curriculum, a child-controlled robotic car was used to carry puppets around the room as children traced the shadow's pattern of movement.	Language arts, math, science and technology, history/social science, health, arts	Preschool: 3–4 years old	Eva May
Patterns	As the children explored patterns in life, space, and time, the teacher incorporated the design and creation of a robotic space rover vehicle. The children developed patterned programs for their vehicle and were challenged to identify other groups' patterns.	Physical science: motion; math: repeating patterns	Preschool: 4–5 years old	Jo-Ellen Rowley
Measuring speed: time and distance	Robotics was used to address children's inquiries about speed and measurement. Through the exploration of the RCX and touch and light sensors, the children developed a tool for measuring the motion of objects traveling on different slopes. The information was graphed in RoboLab and the children recorded their observations with words and pictures.	Scientific inquiry, cause and effect, measurement, programming, math vocabulary, patterns, data analysis, life and physical sciences, motion, senses, technology/engineering	Preschool: 4–5 years	Maggie Beneke
Light as a source of energy	With a focus on principles of solar power, the goal of this activity was to create a robotic light-powered collhouse featuring indoor lighting, moving parts, functioning appliances, and a battery dial measuring stored energy. Children built, explored, measured, and experimented with factors involved in the process of solar power.	Identify light as a form of energy, properties of energy	1st–4th grades	Russell Sargent, Brendan Sullivan, Alex Clark, Sarah Cochrane, Aram Mead

*Developers were all students in interdisciplinary courses that I taught in technology and education at the Eliot-Pearson Department of Child Development at Tufts University between 2001 and 2005. Participants in the courses were undergraduate and graduate students from a variety of departments, including Child Development, Computer Science, and Engineering.

Although traditionally conceived as purely mechanical kits, robotic manipulatives can be inviting to both young engineers and storytellers if presented with the right educational philosophy and pedagogy. For example, whereas some children might make robotic creatures to enact a play, others might focus on building dinosaurs, lifting bridges, or racing robotic cars (Bers, 2007b). Some educational programs, such as Project Con-science in the Arlene Fern Jewish community school in Buenos Aires, Argentina, invited children to create "technological prayers," robotics projects that represent religious symbols of universal values. For example, a young boy and his father chose the value "awakening" or "call for reflection" and designed a LEGO-based Star of David. The young boy said:

> We built a "Maguen David," Star of David, as a symbol of our Jewish people and we programmed it to turn forever like the wheel of life and have flashing lights resembling candles welcoming the New Year. We also reproduced the sound of the shofar. It has three different tones that are supposed to awake us for reflection and atonement. (Bers & Urrea, 2000)

Although most uses of robotics have focused on promoting the teaching and learning of math, science, engineering, and technology, the experiences of both the Con-science and the Inter-Actions projects (Bers et al., 2004) show the potential of robotics to engage children in storytelling and exploration of identity issues (Bers, 2007b).

CHAPTER 4

Designing the Environment

A Practical Guide

Rather than stifling the children's creativity, the solution is to create an intellectual environment less dominated than the school's by the criteria of true and false.

—Seymour Papert (*Mindstorms*, 1980, p. 133)

This chapter provides initial guidelines to orient readers interested in exploring the use of robotics in early childhood. It is not intended to be a comprehensive how-to manual, but a first introduction to how to approach the work. As opposed to a prescribed set of rules for putting robotics into action, the chapter presents suggestions in four areas: designing the learning environment, obtaining further resources, curriculum starters with robotics, and engaging parents.

Designing the Learning Environment

We have learned about constructionism and have an understanding about developmentally appropriate pedagogy and philosophy for using robotics in early childhood. And we have learned about robotic manipulatives and their long-standing tradition in other learning manipulatives. How do we initiate our own work with robotics? We should start by actively designing the learning environment, not only by developing or adapting curricula. This section is organized around five different physical stations needed when designing a successful early childhood robotics learning environment: programming stations, building stations, design and art stations, floor space, and walls.

Programming Stations

In an ideal learning environment, there will be enough programming stations to accommodate every child, or at least every group of children working together on a project. However, this is not mandatory, because there are ways to develop successful learning environments even with one computer for the whole classroom. Programming stations need to provide ample space on the desk or table to accommodate the computer, the infrared tower, and the robotic construction itself. Because downloading the program to the robotic artifact is done several times during the duration of an activity, ample table space will prevent projects from falling down and breaking apart. Tables and chairs need to be accessible to children and be distributed in order to facilitate circulation. Working with robotics involves a collaborative experience, so there is a lot of moving around and gathering in front of computers. For that purpose, it is also suggested that there be multiple chairs at each computer to facilitate partner and team work. On a wall next to the programming stations it is always helpful to have a large poster displaying the icons of the programming language. It is also useful to have a white board for sketching programming flows, and to let the children experiment on the board with programming icons (see Figure 15). A projector, connected to one of the computers, is useful for sharing programming tips with the whole class. Shelves or drawers located out of reach of the children should have software boxes, manuals, and computer peripherals. A locked cabinet is useful for storing expensive documentation materials such as digital and video cameras and their corresponding supplies. Finally, it is important that all of the infrared towers point in different directions; otherwise it is easy for one group to download a program sent by another group. This is a common source of confusion in the classroom. Group A programs their RCX brick to go forward, but walks past Group B, who just hit "download." All of a sudden, Group A has a new program but does not realize it. This can be avoided if people turn off their RCXs when walking past computers and if the towers connected to neighboring computers face in different directions.

Building Stations

Robotics involves both programming in the computer and building with various materials. The building can be done with LEGO bricks or other items such as pipe cleaners, cardboard, and tape. Thus, building

FIGURE 15. Learning how to program using paper icons

stations are fundamental. These can be one or several large tables
(depending on the size of the classroom and the number of children)
located near the computer stations. Although some children like to
build while sitting down, most of them prefer to build standing up.
Thus, chairs should be positioned to accommodate both working styles.
Next to the building stations there should be shelves for storing batter-
ies, flashlights, extra pieces, and other tools that are commonly used
with robotics. These shelves can be located in the upper part of the
shelving unit, because they are primarily for teacher access. A special
shelf, protected from the clutter and perhaps also located above the
reach of the children, can be specially decorated and used as a display
station for final projects once they have been completed, and before
any public events. A different shelf, populated by empty bins and within
reach of the children, can be used to temporarily store projects in prog-
ress. It is useful for each child or team to have a labeled bin to store her
or his unfinished projects. LEGO parts can be stored in clearly labeled
bins or buckets easily accessible to all the children. Bins of different

sizes can be helpful for accommodating small or unique pieces. Near the building stations hang posters showing common building pieces and their names, as well as some basic construction tips.

Design and Art Stations

Children need to have table space where they can sit and use their design journals. For this purpose they also need to have ready access to drawing supplies. Robotics projects do not need to include LEGO parts only. Art and recyclable materials are very useful, and children tend to enjoy integrating them into their projects. Therefore, these materials, as well as glue, scissors, and tape, need to be readily available. Although in an ideal world it would be better to have different stations for the building, design, and art aspects of the work, with clearly expressed rules, such as avoiding gluing expensive LEGO parts like sensors or motors, activities can be combined using big tables with drawers or nearby cabinets to store the supplies.

Floor Space

Although much of the work with robotics happens on tables in the programming and building stations, the floor is the best place for testing. Floors without carpets are most useful because they do not cause traction problems. However, having a small carpet to unfold is always handy for technology circles. Floor color can make a big difference if using black tape so robots can follow a line by using light sensors. For example, a sensor might get "confused" on a speckled floor. However, it is not always possible to choose the type of floor in a classroom, so having a large piece of plain wood where the robots can be tested is always a good idea. Because at some point or another most robotics projects involve the creation of moving creatures, a car, a dinosaur, or a snow plow, I suggested having a minimum of 6 feet of space for forward- and backward-moving robots. Floor space is a useful element in a robotics learning environment. However, outside playgrounds or courts with concrete floors, weather permitting, or inside spaces such as corridors, can also be used for testing purposes and provide a change of scenery that children tend to enjoy.

Walls

Walls serve three very important functions in robotics learning environments: documentation, memory, and teaching. First, walls as spaces for documentation serve to illustrate the process of making robotics projects, through posters done by both children and teachers. For example, photographs of children's work as it progresses can be included. Second, walls serve as spaces for memory. Working with robotics always poses the challenge of having limited resources and therefore not being able to maintain intact robotic creations. Usually, after a project is completed it needs to be disassembled, even if this is heartbreaking for both the children who spent so much energy constructing it and the teachers who supported their work. Memory walls can be used to display pictures and short descriptions of the projects in a classroom. As the year progresses, memory walls start to fill up and serve an emotional function in allowing children to celebrate their past projects. Third, walls serve as teaching spaces for displaying posters with programming icons and diagrams describing steps involved in the building process, and for hanging chalkboards or whiteboards. In sum, wall displays vividly inform the students, teachers, parents, the school community, and visitors about the work happening with robotics technology in the early childhood classroom.

Developmentally Appropriate Robotics Construction Kits

Most of the work presented in this book uses the LEGO Mindstorms kit. This is the most widely used robotic manipulative worldwide. It provides the advantage of engaging children with a well-known material, such as the LEGO construction bricks, and engages them in exploring new possibilities by adding controlled movement to their LEGO creations. The LEGO Mindstorms kit can be purchased with two different kinds of software: RoboLab, which is sold by the educational division of LEGO to schools, and Mindstorms, which is sold in commercial toy stores. While Mindstorms offers a quick way to start programming, the power of the programming language is limited. RoboLab provides scaffolding elements and several levels to help beginners, such as the Pilot levels, to more advanced features in the Inventor levels. It also provides tools for data collection and analysis (Investigator level). Other software, such as Logo Blocks, also works with this construction kit. LEGO has made available the source code, so computer scientists and engineers have played with it and developed their own programming languages (from C to JAVA). These are not commercially available, do not provide technical support, and in the majority of cases, require advanced programming skills. Although the LEGO Mindstorms Robotics Invention

System with its RCX brick is the most popular robotics kit, other robotics kits exist in the market. However, most of them are targeted for middle school or high school students.

- The HandyCricket, which also evolved from the earlier MIT "Programmable Brick" and the Handy Board, is a tiny, programmable computer (about the size of a 9-volt battery) that can directly control motors and receive information from sensors. It can be programmed using "Cricket Logo," a simplified version of the Logo language. More information can be found at http://handyboard.com/cricket/about/
- The Vex Robotics Design System, developed by Innovation First and Radio Shack, has more than 500 parts and more than 20 accessories and can be programmed with easyC, a graphical variant on the C language used by professional programmers. Although it has substantially more power than the Mindstorms kit, construction and programming take a fair amount of time and dexterity. More information can be found at http://www.vexlabs.com/
- Machine Science, a nonprofit organization dedicated to supporting hands-on engineering programs for young people, also provides several project kits. These are very open systems, with children building their own circuits and sensors. See http://www.machinescience.com/
- Microbric is an electronic construction kit based on the construction style/concept of both LEGO and Meccano. It allows users to build complex customized electronic devices. Microbric's I-bot is targeted for elementary and middle school children. It is a small, modular, easy-to-use robot that can be put together in stages and controlled in a number of ways. For example, children can use barcodes to teach I-bot how to respond to the TV remote, and they can also write their own programs. See http://www.microbric.com/ibot/
- The Boe-Bot from Parallax can be programmed using Microsoft Robotics Studio. See http://www.parallax.com/
- OWI Robotics offers different programmable robotics kits. See http://owirobots.com/
- RoboNova is a humanoid robot that can be programmed. It is available as a kit, so students can build their own robot, or as a preassembled, "RTW" ("ready to walk") instant robot. See http://www.lynxmotion.com/Category.aspx?CategoryID=91

- IRobot Create is a programmable robot, preassembled to facilitate the development of new robots. Robot developers can program behaviors, sounds, and movements, and can even build on other electronics. Computer programming experience is required. See http://store.irobot.com/shop/index.jsp?categoryId=2597845
- GEARS Education System. The GEARS-IDS Invention and Design System provides tools for teachers to create engineering and robotics challenges in their own classrooms. See: http://www .gearseds.com/
- LEGO Mindstorms NXT. This new kit will replace the RCX in 2009. However, the latest version of RoboLab offers upgraded RCX features as well as the ability to program the NXT at all levels (Pilot, Inventor, Investigator). LEGO Engineering provides educators with resources to aid in migration of technologies including news, activities, and a database to access information. See http://mindstorms.lego.com/

Most of the robotics construction kits mentioned above offer different technological platforms for building and programming robots. However, in contrast to the Mindstorms kit, most of these focus on older children and require teachers to have a working knowledge of engineering and electronics. How about young children? What other options besides the LEGO Mindstorms kit and the RCX brick are available? In the tradition of the first "programmable bricks" at the MIT Media Lab and the Mindstorms kit, PicoCrickets is specifically geared for younger children and novice teachers. Whereas Mindstorms is created for making robots, PicoCrickets are designed especially for making artistic creations that can behave in the world. PicoCrickets are based on research of the Lifelong Kindergarten group at the MIT Media Laboratory and are sold through the Playful Invention Company (PICO). More information can be found at http://www.picocricket.com

The PicoCrickets are tiny computers, smaller than Programmable Bricks, so they are well suited for projects that need to be compact and mobile (such as electronic jewelry) and can embed in children's physical creations. PicoCrickets can control not only motors but also multicolored lights and musical devices, so children can use PicoCrickets to build more artistic and expressive projects involving light, sound, music, and motion. For example, a young person might create a cat using craft materials, and then add a light sensor and a sound-making device. She could write a program (using the PicoCricket's easy-to-use graphical programming language) that waits for the light sensor to detect someone petting the cat, and then tells the sound box to play a meowing sound. Or one can use craft materials to create an interactive garden, with flowers that dance and change colors when you clap your hands (Resnick, 2006).

A different robotics kit for young children is Roamer from Valiant Technology. Based on the first Logo turtle, Roamer is a floor robot that moves around the room following a given set of instructions. Instructions are entered by pressing the buttons on the top of the device, and the robot moves as instructed. Roamer has simple graphic buttons that can be pushed in a series of commands that allow Roamer to be controlled by the young child. Roamer can go forward, go backward, turn at specific angles, sing, and draw. See http://www.valiant-technology .com/us/pages/roamer_home.php

Engaging Parents

In Part I of the book I addressed the importance of teachers supporting parents in their work with technology with their children. In this section, I suggest four different ways in which this can be done: (1) parents working with their children at home, (2) parent volunteers at school; (3) after-school models of parent–child robotics workshops and clubs, and (4) parents as liaisons with industry and academia.

Parents Working with Their Children at Home

Teachers communicate with parents about the math and literacy curriculum by sending letters home and suggesting family activities to complement what is happening in the classroom. In the same way, they can include work with technology. For example, it might be important for the teacher at the beginning of the year to get a sense of what kind of technology children are using at home and, for example, she or he could ask families to complete a survey. The teacher can also engage families in collecting data about the simple machines and the electronic devices they have at home and share it in class; or each week the teacher can assign a different child or family to do research about how a robotic object in their house or town works.

Parents Volunteering in the Classroom

In the United States there is a long-standing tradition of inviting parents to volunteer in the classroom. Some volunteer on a weekly basis and have assigned roles, such as helping children with academics or supervising lunchtime. Others may volunteer once to share a tradition or celebration from their homeland and culture. Engaging parents in technology-related activities is a wonderful way to complement the knowledge of the teacher and to provide more support in the classroom. As mentioned earlier, many of today's parents (and sometimes grandparents as well) are computer scientists and engineers, or have jobs related to the information technology industry. Teachers need to learn how to take advantage of these tech savvy parents. These parents can come as special guests to share a specific aspect of their job. Or they can be "on call," and volunteer when technology-related activities are happening in the classroom. However, sometimes having many parents with different levels of expertise and different visions about what learning and teaching should be can be difficult. Thus, it is important to set up guidelines for how to work with young children and provide parents with basic information about how young children learn and think. For example, conducting an evening for training volunteer parents is something that has worked very well in my own experience working with parents in the classroom.

After-School Activities

In many school districts we have found that parents, after working in the classroom with robotics-based activities, see the benefits and gain confidence in their own teaching potential. They organize their own robotics clubs and parent–child robotics workshops after school. Because the materials are already in the school, organizing these types of activities is not hard. Many of the Web sites listed in this chapter provide information about how to start this work.

Regardless of the choice of how to involve parents in the work with technology with children, either at home, in the classroom, or in after-school settings, it is important to remember that different families have different interaction styles, some which are more conducive to learning than others. For example, some parents initiate and direct the work with the child, some put the child in charge, and some parent–child dyads seem to enjoy taking turns being in charge of their work. It is not easy for all the parent–child dyads to become comfortable with each other in new roles as both teachers and learners. In most of the cases, it is the parents, and not the children, who have the most difficulties adjusting. It is often anxiety-provoking for a parent to have to learn something new and, at the same time, help his or her child with his or her own learning. Based on research on Project InterActions, this is true regardless of the previous level of comfort that parents have with technology (Beals & Bers, 2006). Some parents worry about getting it right, and in some cases, this attitude can get in the way of working with their children. To address some of these concerns, I start my own work with parents by giving them the following guidelines:

- This is a learning experience. We are all exploring together.
- Families have different ways of working together. Find a way that works for you and your child.
- Learning new things is hard . . . sometimes it is harder for adults than for children.
- Learning about technology can be very frustrating and anxiety-provoking.
- Are you passing your own anxieties to your child?
- Don't worry, nobody gets it right the first time or even the tenth time. In fact, there is no "right" way.
- Adults and children can learn in very different ways.
- We are not expecting you to have perfectly working projects.
- Play with the materials and the ideas. You don't have to get it right.
- Success can mean different things for children and for adults.
- Ask questions (to your child, to us, to other families).
- Talk to each other, look at each other's projects, copy the things that you like . . . you are not cheating.
- We learn by doing and by making mistakes.
- Have fun and relax! This is a time to spend together with your child.

Parents as Liaisons with Industry and Academia

Parents can play an important role in setting up connections with both industry and academia to support technology and engineering education. Many industries that rely heavily on a workforce with math, science, and engineering knowledge are significant supporters of K–12 education. Some have generous grant programs in place such as FIRST, Engineer's Week, Explorer Scouts, and so forth, and others encourage employees to volunteer to work with students in the local community as mentors or tutors. Several companies, like Lockheed Martin, Intel, Rocketdyne, and National Instruments, have developed programs that help K–12 teachers to learn more about math, science, and engineering through courses and summer workshops. National

Instruments also provides year-round classroom support to teachers via employee volunteers. TechCorps, a national nonprofit, provides similar support by pairing technical volunteers with K–12 students and/or classrooms. The National Science Foundation also has a strong commitment to placing experts in the classroom through its GK–12 program, which provides tuition waivers and stipends to graduate student fellows pursuing advanced degrees in science, math, or engineering in exchange for the students spending 15 hours per week in K–12 classrooms. Many undergraduates in technical fields volunteer their time in school and after-school settings (Bers & Portsmore, 2005).

Placing college students or adult professionals in the classrooms provides positive outcomes for all involved: it (1) supports teachers in their work with technology with the children, while also helping them develop their own skills and confidence; (2) provides different avenues for educating children early on about technical disciplines; and (3) provides a window for college students and professionals to learn more about the education system and its challenges, allowing them to become more fully engaged civic citizens. Although teachers might lack the time and resources to investigate the myriad of existing partnership programs, parents can play an important role in information gathering, grant writing, and advocacy.

Resources

This section provides Web links that are useful for working with robotics in early childhood. Most of these sites have age-appropriate activities for young children, as well as resources for parents and educators.

Web Links

http://www.ceeo.tufts.edu/

The Web site for the Center of Educational Engineering Outreach (CEEO) at Tufts University. It describes the vision, goals, and programs of the Center and how one can get involved.

http://www.ceeo.tufts.edu/robolabatceeo/

The Web site for the RoboLab programming language at the CEEO. It provides useful tips and curriculum resources (organized around curricular frameworks) for parents and schools.

http://www.legoengineering.com
This Web site provides curricular projects, community support, and general help with LEGO Engineering.

http://www.mos.org/nctl/
The Web site of the National Center for Technological Literacy at the Boston Museum of Science provides K–12 activities, resources, and professional development opportunities for engineering and technology education.

http://llk.media.mit.edu/
The Web site of the LifeLong Kindergarten Research Group directed by Mitchel Resnick at the MIT Media Lab provides links to academic papers and innovative research projects developing technologies for children.

http://www.ase.tufts.edu/devtech/
The Web site of the Development Technologies Research Group, which the author directs at the Eliot-Pearson Department of Child Development at Tufts University, provides a link to the Early Childhood Robotics Research Program, as well as links to academic papers on early childhood and technology.

Curriculum Starters

This section presents six examples of curricula for introducing young children to the concepts of building and programming. The following activities using the LEGO Mindstorms robotics kit are reprinted with special permission from LEGOengineering.com. They are all well suited for early childhood, K–3.

The Tower

The goal of this activity is to design and construct a tower that is at least 4–6 inches high. The tower must be strong enough to withstand the weight of a stack of books.

Topics
Building, Sturdiness & Familiarity with Different LEGO Pieces

Subjects
Engineering

Building Hints

Using beams and connector pegs will help students create a sturdy structure.

Testing

Test the tower's stability by performing two tests:

1. Stack books on top of the tower
2. Stand on it

Classroom Procedure

1. Discuss sturdiness with the students and why certain structures are sturdier than others.
2. Students can work individually or in groups as long as there are enough beams, bricks, axles, and connector pegs. Each tower should be 5–6 inches high.
3. Students should build a tower that is sturdy enough to support several textbooks and/or the weight of a person.
4. Have the students test the structures and redesign as they work.
5. Spend 5 minutes at the end of the lesson discussing the walls that the students built. Have them assess which techniques worked and which did not work.
6. Be sure to exploit weaknesses so that in later exercises they will not make the same mistakes.
7. Point out the advantages of interweaving pieces, adding connector pegs and axles for support, and making supports wide for greater balance and strength.
8. Students can fill out an engineering journal.

Snail Car RCX

The goal of this activity is to design and construct a snail car capable of traveling extremely slowly. The cars compete in a snail race with the last car to cross the finish line crowned as the winner.

Topics

Gears, Gear Trains & Friction

Subjects

Math, Science, Engineering & Technology

Programming Themes

Motor Forward

Related Math & Science Concepts
Gears, Wheels and Axles, Acceleration, Velocity, Friction, Torque

Materials
RCX Car
Gears

Building Instructions
Build an RCX car that utilizes a series of gears and axles.

Programming Instructions
Using RoboLab Inventor 2, program a car to run forward for
20 seconds.

Mountain Rescue

The goal of this activity is to design and construct a car that is able
to climb a steep incline.

Topics
Gears, Friction, Torque & Speed

Subjects
Math, Science, Engineering & Technology

Programming Themes
Motor Forward

Related Math & Science Concepts
Gears, Torque, Wheel and Axle, Acceleration, Velocity, Friction, Force

Materials
RCX Brick
Gears
Ramp

Building Instructions
1. Assemble a ramp with multiple degrees of slope.
2. Build a car that is capable of climbing the ramp. The car should
   be capable of climbing a steep incline without slipping. This
   vehicle is built for power, not for speed.

Building Hints

Gearing down will slow down your car but will supply more power for climbing.

Programming Instructions

Using either RoboLab Pilot 1 or Inventor 1, program a car to run for 20 seconds.

Classroom Procedure

1. Set up the ramp that will serve as the mountain. You can use a piece of plywood as the ramp and prop it up on things of different heights to have varying steepness.
2. Students will design and build vehicles that are intended to climb steep hills. They will have to incorporate gears into their design to increase the torque.
3. If students are not familiar with gears, give them an overview on gearing up and gearing down.
4. Students should build and program their cars and then test them.
5. Have the students drive the cars up the ramps as a group. This can lead to a discussion about what works well (e.g., rubber tires) and what does not work (e.g., smooth, plastic wheels).

Scavenger Hunt RCX

The goal of this activity is to use an RCX brick and a light sensor to collect data about the light conditions of the room. Can children find light sensor readings in the range of 0–30? 60–90? 90–100? Draw conclusions and make generalizations about light intensity in the room.

Subjects

Math & Science

Topics

Light Sensors, Graphing, Data Collection & Analysis

Programming Themes

Light Sensor Data Collection

Materials

RCX
Light Sensor

Building Instructions

Attach a light sensor to the RCX and wire to an RCX input.

Programming Instructions

1. Using RoboLab Investigator Program Level 1, program the RCX to collect a light reading every second for 10 seconds.
2. Collect readings. Walk around the room in order to draw conclusions and make generalizations about light intensity in the room.
3. Upload your data. Plot your results.

Classroom Procedure

1. Students should attach a light sensor to an RCX.
2. This is a great introductory activity to introduce Investigator. Students will use a light sensor to collect data about the light conditions in the room.
3. Discuss results of data collection. Which values were difficult to find? Why do you think this was true?
4. Allow students to experiment with uploading up to four sets of data. Demonstrate how to change the color or type of graph.
5. Present the challenge of trying to find a range of light readings. For example have them look for readings in the following ranges: 0–30, 31–60, 61–80, and 81–100.
6. Next, they should open Investigator and program their RCX to take light data every second for 10 seconds.
7. Have students collect the data and upload the results.

Activity Extension: Challenge the students to keep their light readings within reading levels between 50 and 70.

Amusement Park Ride

The goal of this activity is for students to design and construct an amusement park ride.

Topics

Building & Programming

Subjects

Engineering & Technology

Related Math & Science Concepts

Forces, Structures

Materials

RCX Brick
Assortment of LEGO Pieces and Sensors

Building Instructions

Design an amusement park ride that imitates a real amusement park ride.

Programming Instructions

Select appropriate software for the RCX used in the structure and program as necessary for the design of your amusement park ride.

Line Follower

The goal of this activity is for students to design and construct an RCX car and program it to be able to closely follow a line. Don't let your car stray from the road by using light sensors only.

Topics

Light Sensors, Turning, Gearing & Friction

Subjects

Science, Engineering & Technology

Programming Themes

Motor Forward, Wait for Light/Dark, Jumps/Lands

Related Math & Science Concepts

Gears, Wheels and Axles, Acceleration, Vector Quantities, Velocity

Materials

RCX Car That Can Turn
Solid Colored Floor
Tape (Opposite of the Floor)

Building Instructions
1. Assemble two motors together.
2. Attach the motor assembly to an RCX.
3. Add wheels, skid plates (or bent arm beams), and a bracket to the car.
4. Attach a light sensor to the bracket and RCX. Wire the motors.

Building Hints

- Using a skid plate instead of two front wheels helps reduce friction.
- Friction reduction allows for ease in turning.
- Gearing down will slow down your car and make tighter turns.
- The light sensor should be facing down and as close to the floor as possible.

Programming Instructions

1. Using RoboLab Pilot 4 or RoboLab Inventor 4, program the car so that one motor runs until it sees light and then the other motor runs until it sees dark.
2. The car should be able to follow a line (either light or dark) and be able to turn both left and right.

Classroom Procedure

1. Students will use an RCX car and a light sensor to make a line follower. The car should be able to turn.
2. Discuss design criteria before they start building. Because the cars will need to turn, the design will be different from that of a car that just drives forward.
3. Completed line followers can start by using the easy course (slightly wavy line) and move on to a harder course (line with a right angle).
4. Students can fill out an engineering journal to document their project.

Building Boston Together

Local History Through Robotics

Rebecca Merino *and* Kevin Staszowski

Becky Merino completed her undergraduate degree in elementary/special education and her graduate degree in Exceptional Children at The University of Delaware. This is her ninth year of teaching elementary school. She is currently a first- and second-grade teacher at Eliot-Pearson Children's School, an inclusive laboratory school associated with the Child Development Department of Tufts University. Her classroom team consists of herself, a graduate teaching assistant, and two one-to-one instructional aides. She has always looked for ways to incorporate engineering and science into hands-on curricula for children, and has appreciated the opportunities presented by LEGO robotics.

Kevin Staszowski received his undergraduate degree in environmental engineering from Tufts University and, after working for 2 years with an environmental consulting firm, returned to Tufts University for his graduate work in Child Development. He is currently a project manager with the Center for Engineering Education Outreach, directing a National Science foundation grant that matches graduate students in engineering disciplines with teachers in the Boston area.

This is the story of collaboration between a teacher and an engineer. It is our hope that this work can inspire others to find partnerships with local universities or industries.

During the 2005–2006 academic year, we decided to use robotics technology in a first- and second-grade combination class at the Eliot-Pearson Children's School. We did not want the technology to stand alone. We wanted it to support the curriculum and to serve the purpose of integrating different curricular areas. But finding an overarching, interesting theme for our project was troublesome, as the class had such varied interests. One topic that seemed captivating to all was the local Massachusetts geography, specifically the geography of the nearby capital city of Boston. So we asked our students, "What is so great about Boston? People come here from all over the world. You live right next to it, but do you know what makes it special?"

Our long list of responses included sports teams, famous museums, famous Boston residents, and finally, the Freedom Trail. Everyone indicated that the Freedom Trail was important, but very few children knew what the Freedom Trail actually was. So, as a class, we decided to get to know Boston better by exploring sites on and around the Freedom Trail. Although we chose this as the focus of the class project, we wanted to encourage children to make their own personal connections to our city. We hoped that, with the variety of historical sites along the Freedom Trail, each child would find something of specific interest to explore further.

First, we gave the class large close-up photographs of a variety of historical buildings and sites to sketch in their "Boston Sketchpads." This drawing activity helped them to tune in to the smaller details of the Freedom Trail and to begin to form a personal connection with the places they would soon see. With their curiosity piqued, the class followed this activity by taking a subway into Boston to experience some of the historical components of the city. We rode the subway in, took a DUCK (amphibious vehicle) tour of the streets and waterways, had lunch in the cafeteria of the Prudential Center, and fed the pigeons alongside the reflections of Trinity Church at the John Hancock Tower. At school, the children also began working on sections of a 6 × 6-foot map of Boston and the Freedom Trail as a way of remembering their journey through the city. This work helped set the foundation for introducing robotics in an integrated way with the emergent curriculum.

We decided that building models would help foster ownership of the sites that the children were studying. Using LEGO bricks would add an opportunity for children to explore and further their skills in technological design and problem-solving. It would also add a more engaging way for children to recreate what was important to them. It was important to us that LEGO be a component of the curriculum without taking over the content.

Children voted for the sites they were most interested in, and small groups were formed, each studying one or two stops on the Freedom Trail. Each group met with a team of undergraduate engineering student assistants to brainstorm and sketch ideas for building their models. Within this brainstorming session, children also found ways of adding robotic LEGO components to their buildings. These initial sessions helped children tune in to details they could replicate and emphasize with LEGO bricks, especially as each building group took tours of their individual sites. Ultimately, many of those initial ideas changed as the children studied their sites in greater depth, but children understood that planning and discussion were precursors to building.

The projects took shape over the course of 2 months, during which we had weekly 60-minute building sessions. The first few meetings were used to teach the children the basics of building and programming. After this orientation period, they began building the structure of their projects out of recycled materials like cereal boxes and egg cartons. The robotic LEGO bricks were used to create the kinetic portions of their projects, and much of the free-building time was devoted to creating and programming the LEGO Mindstorms "additions."

Because there was a balance between building with recycled construction materials and with LEGO bricks, children were able to stay engaged and rarely felt frustrated. If they were waiting for teacher support for a specific component, they could work on the structure or artistic elements of their building. Everyone had the opportunity to work with LEGO bricks, and some children chose to engage deeply with the robotic LEGO bricks. Other children decided go further with different interests such as learning and writing additional facts or measuring and cutting cardboard to create buildings. Part of this process included the children also negotiating and coordinating how the robotic and nonrobotic parts of the project would fit together. When the children were not in building sessions, they continued to work on other components of the project such as sketches of their sites in Boston, reading books in class, and ongoing discussions about the challenges and successes they met with while working and building together.

Although LEGO bricks were just one part of a large project, they showcased the small details children focused during their studies, and thus became a very powerful tool for sharing what they learned. They also fostered communication and collaboration among the groups as the children needed to make shared decisions, solve building issues, and have the whole piece come together. Finally, they added a new technology to old history, so students could do more then "spit back" facts they had learned. They could present these ideas in meaningful and novel ways, showing each child's personal connection to Boston.

The Freedom Trail

We will describe the design process that one of the groups went through to recreate the Old North Church and the Copp's Hill Burying Ground. We expected the group to focus in on the two lamps hung in the Old North Church—as LEGO lights were something familiar to many of the children. The tower in the Old North Church was where, during the American Revolutionary War, Robert Newmann was to light one lantern if the British soldiers were marching on Lexington by land and two lanterns if the British were arriving by river. We also thought the group might work on creating a clock or church bell for this portion of the project. Instead, the group focused on another bit of trivia that we were unaware of—the man (Robert Newmann) who lit the lanterns in Old North Church had to jump out of the building's window to escape the British loyalists. The idea of a LEGO figurine flying out the window was very funny to the group, and we worried that the project would be too distracting. However, the group worked diligently to design a system to fling the figurine out of the Old North Church. The children actively engaged with the Mindstorms programming language instead of just using a construction-based solution, which is more typical for this age-group. Even with the programming solution, the group also went through a genuine redesign process when they found that their catapult stopped working properly when installed inside the Old North Church.

The Copp's Hill Burying Ground is the second oldest cemetery in Boston and is the resting place for many famous Boston natives. Rather than focus on the historical aspects of Copp's Hill, the group turned their attention to making the site creepy with marching LEGO skeletons. The children realized that marching LEGO skeletons would be very difficult to build, but—through brainstorming—they found a novel way to fulfill their idea for the project. Instead of making the skeletons travel across a static graveyard, the children decided to put stationary skeletons on a moving graveyard. This solution allowed the group to construct most of the Copp's Hill Burial Ground with recycled materials and use the LEGO bricks for the small portion of the project that needed to be motorized.

Our semester-long project culminated in an "art show" that was shared with the entire school and our families. Although it was called an art show, it was a chance for children to showcase their ongoing learning. Our art show opening began with a "DUCK Tour" of the

Freedom Trail. Children who finished their group project early or who wanted to work more with LEGO Mindstorms had a chance to build a LEGO car, which they covered with a paper DUCK boat. They programmed it to make stops on our 6 × 6-foot map of the Freedom Trail. When it hit a stop, the children who studied that site shared their construction, putting their robotic special effects into action. Laws popped up at the State House while the Swan Boat glided through the pond in the park. Tightrope walkers balanced at Faneuil Hall while the grasshopper on the roof spun around in frantic circles. The man who lit the lanterns came flying out the window, and the skeletons in Copp's Hill Burying Ground awoke. Paul Revere's house lit up, and he rode his horse to warn the troops. Later that month we culminated the project by visiting the last sites on the Freedom Trail: Bunker Hill Monument and the USS Constitution. We then ate lunch at the Warren Tavern (where Paul Revere used to eat) and had a lemonade toast to our exciting adventures and successful study of Boston!

Engineering by Design

Merredith Portsmore

Merredith Portsmore is a doctoral student in the Mathematics, Science, Technology, and Engineering Education program at Tufts University. She is also a program manager at Tufts Center for Engineering Educational Outreach for LEGOengineering.com, a Web site that provides resources for educators using LEGO Education products, and the STOMPnetwork.org, a network of engineering outreach programs. Her dissertation research focuses on engineering design in early elementary classrooms.

One rainy October day in a first-grade classroom during indoor recess, I saw Sam and Evan eagerly get out bins of wooden blocks and math manipulatives (pattern blocks) to build elaborate castles with towers and secret passageways. Katie, Sarah, and Sasha also got out bins of blocks to build houses for small plastic colored bears. Houses and towers were built and elaborately extended across the entire carpeted meeting area.

Blocks and the block corner are popular staples in early elementary classrooms. But thus far, we haven't put too much effort into capitalizing on young children's passion for building and designing. We can see from children's interest and proficiency with blocks that this could be a prime time to expose children to engineering design. The engineering design process introduces students to the ways of thinking involved in creating a product or process that addresses a need or problems. Ideas of posing a problem, research, planning, developing a prototype, testing, redesigning, and sharing solutions are all involved in engineering design. The design process, like the scientific method, gives students another tool for thinking and helps them engage with the world around them. In today's modern technological world an understanding of how to make and design things is as important as knowing how to obtain information and test hypotheses.

Tufts University's Center for Engineering Educational Outreach (CEEO) is dedicated to improving engineering in K–16. Although it is easy to see how engineering education can be addressed at the upper levels, engineering in early elementary school can be a challenge. I am incredibly interested in the early part of education because students are so interested in learning. Moreover, educators and school systems seem to have more flexibility in their curriculum and time in this age range. The following paragraphs describe one way of bringing engineering into early elementary school classrooms in a way that is meaningful, includes actual engineering concepts, and is age appropriate.

Engineering by Design in First Grade

A key focus of the existing engineering curriculum for young children developed at the CEEO is developing engineering readiness. We believe this is achieved through exposing students to the engineering design process and developing their facility with LEGO materials. The curriculum piece that best demonstrates the approach is "Engineering by Design," which features student activities that range from building sturdy walls to creating snow plows and their own transportation invention. The curriculum is targeted at first and second grades (6- to 8 year-olds) and was developed by first-grade teachers in cooperation with graduate and undergraduate students, including myself, at the CEEO. The teachers involved have been using this curriculum in their classrooms for several years, and the unit has received thousands of downloads via the Web. See http://130.64.87.22/robolabatceeo/k12/curriculum_units/Engineering%20by%20Design.pdf.

I have been using the unit extensively as the backbone for my dissertation research over the past 3 years, teaching 16 weeks of activities based on Engineering by Design in multiple first-grade classrooms. Activities are offered for 1 hour each week, during which I am principal instructor, assisted by the classroom teacher and volunteers or graduate students. The time I spend in the classroom is typically referred to as LEGO Engineering time. We talk about what an engineer does and read stories to better understand what engineers are involved in designing. We talk about the difference between designing something and making it, and we discuss the construction workers and manufacturers who actually make engineers' designs come to life.

Groups of two students typically work with one set of materials on engineering projects that incorporate the basic LEGO pieces as well as mechanical elements like gears, pulleys, and a motor. Sometimes little fingers have trouble with some of the smaller pieces, but in general I have found that students are able to have great success with the materials (with a little help attaching a pulley or separating small pieces).

Getting Started: From Play to Design

The initial activities in the curriculum are designed to help the pairs learn to work together and to differentiate LEGO Engineering from LEGO play. LEGO materials are heavily associated with play, so it's important to make a formal distinction. If possible, it's also best to have separate LEGO materials for planning and for engineering so both activities can easily flourish.

Students first learn the names of the pieces and their dimensions. This enables the classroom to have a common language for talking about materials. We encourage students to ask for pieces using their proper names ("Can I have a 2 × 4 brick?"). In the very first task each student is given ten 2 × 4 LEGO bricks. Each pair must build a single construction from 20 pieces. Strategies for compromising and cooperation are discussed. Students also complete a "Final Report" that consists of a drawing of what they have made and reflections on whether or not they were good partners and enjoyed the activity. This helps students practice in a low-stakes setting at being good partners and understanding how LEGO Engineering time will work.

The Engineering Design Process

A simplified version of the engineering design process found in the Massachusetts Engineering/Design frameworks guides all of the activities in the Engineering by Design activities. In the initial activities (like building a sturdy wall) the students only use two or three steps (such as test, redesign, and share). As they progress through the activities, they are introduced to more and more steps. The steps are also heavily scaffolded. In the beginning, the problem and tests are clearly defined by the teacher, but as they progress through the curriculum the students perform more of the steps independently and make their own choices.

Once students have a basic knowledge of the pieces and some strategies for working together, their next task is to create a sturdy wall. They look at real walls and study the building technique of overlapping bricks. Their wall must be able to withstand a drop test from the height of the students' knees. Typically students are familiar with the construction method of stacking LEGO bricks but are new at considering how the stacking might impact the performance of their wall. This activity also introduces students to the concept of testing and redesigning. Testing and redesigning are generally unfamiliar to young children. Young children tend to build something once and declare it done, and then move on to something else. However, testing and redesigning is an important part of engineering design and therefore needs to be introduced as part of the classroom culture of LEGO Engineering time. To do this, I clearly define the tests that a construction will have to go through and pass before the students can move on to another challenge. I always emphasize that almost everyone's construction will fail the first time, and it will probably fail many, many times. ("It could fail 5 times, it could fail 50 times, it could even fail 100 times, and that doesn't mean you aren't a great engineer.") When we share the children's final constructions we celebrate perseverance ("Did you know that Sarah and Steve's failed 10 times before they got it to work?"). While the children are testing, the educators try to have the students reflect on the outcome of their test ("Where did your wall break when you dropped it? Why did it break? How could you keep it from breaking in the same place again?")

"A Chair for Mr. Bear" is the first full engineering design problem students engage in. The students are shown Mr. Bear (a floppy stuffed animal) and told that he needs somewhere to sit. They are presented with the constraints that whatever they build needs to keep him seated upright and prevent him from falling over to the left or right. The students are asked to draw plans for their chair and to discuss them with their partner. Additional pieces and construction techniques are introduced. The constructions created by students are vastly different. Some pairs are able to build sophisticated symmetric chairs, while others struggle to construct a simple cohesive chair (see Figure 16).

As they continue through the curriculum, more of the engineering design project is presented. When the students are presented with the problem of moving snow (typically Styrofoam peanuts and wet paper towels), they start to do some research. I collect pictures of snow moving devices (snow plows, front loaders, snow blowers) into a packet that they can review. They draw plans of what their snow mover will

FIGURE 16. Two chairs for Mr. Bear, constructed by first-grade students

look like using the pictures as a source of idea. Pictures also help students get started when they have no idea what to build ("Why don't you try to build something like the blue snow plow on the second page?"). However, students often shun the research ("I have a better idea than any of the ones in the pictures that I am going to build!"). The great thing about the LEGO materials is that they allow for both types of students to build something that will be successful.

FIGURE 17. Transportation inventions

One of the culminating activities is a "Transportation Invention." In this activity, the students are allowed to choose their own problem to work on that solves some sort of transportation issue for people or animals (see Figure 17). Their work posing a problem is scaffolded through drawing and writing ("Who is your invention for? How will it help them?"). They also design their own tests for their invention ("Our tow truck must be able to drive up a hill." or "Our double-decker bus will hold 20 LEGO people."). Last year, we had cars that could transport dogs and cats, double-decker buses for 20 LEGO people, and tow trucks for toy cars.

It's amazing what 6- and 7-year-olds can create and design when they are given time to explore a tool set and build expertise in engineering design. They haven't yet begun to think, "I can't" or "This is too hard." I often see little girls who struggled at the beginning of LEGO Engineering design amazing and imaginative inventions that function perfectly well. The future challenge is to keep the students engaged in these types of activities each year so they don't forget how great they are at engineering. We hope that even this brief introduction to the engineering design process gives students tools to think about how to create their own solutions to the problems they find in their world.

Insights from Experience

From Lunar Rovers to Chaos

Sia Haralampus

Terry Green teaches science at the Lincoln Public Schools in Lincoln, Massachusetts, and has been working for over 8 years with robotics in early childhood. She has extensive experience developing curricula to integrate robotics with science education.

Sia Haralampus is an undergraduate student in Child Development at Tufts University in the teacher licensure program for Preschool to Grade 2. She is currently completing a final, year-long teaching practicum in a public first-grade classroom and looks forward to using robotics as an integrative tool in early childhood classrooms.

Sia Haralampus (SH): *You have been working for over 10 years with robotics and very young children in your suburban public school in Massachusetts. Can you tell me a little bit about the scope of what you have been doing?*

Terry Green (TG): We've been working with LEGO in this school probably for 10 years. When kids enter first grade we work on how to build sturdy: sturdy walls and sturdy structures so if you drop them they're going to not fall apart. Our goal is to show kids how you put the elements together—the LEGO pieces together—to make a sturdy structure. One of the projects I do in a unit on space is talk about Lunar Rover activity back in the early '60s, and I have the kids build a model of the rover, with one motor. In order for the kids to then get the RCX, they need to show me that if I drop the rover from my knee it's not going to break, and that it is a sturdy structure. For the accomplished builders, I introduce programming by asking, "Can you make this rover go forward for five seconds and stop?" I show them the Pilot Level 1, the simplest level in the RoboLab programming language, which has one motor icon. Sometimes I'll use bubble wrap—so they'll build their rovers and I'll have the moonscape, and they have to then drive their rovers over the bubble wrap—sometimes it involves a design element where they've got to change the wheels in order to accommodate the terrain. If I have a group of first-graders who really get it, who really understand the programming, the second step I do with them is to have them do a two-step program in reverse—that is the Pilot Level 3 program in RoboLab. And I might add the programming of a touch sensor so that if the rover runs into something, like a lunar boulder, the lunar rover will stop the motor. But that is difficult. It requires some abstract thinking for young children to be able to say, "OK I want this touch sensor to stop the car" and then be able to transfer that to a computer program that does it; that is a big leap for kids in first grade that aren't thinking abstractly—they're concrete kinds of thinkers.

In first grade I find it works best if I have helpers with me, so I use parent volunteers, adult helpers. I try to get one or two in a group of about 20 students so that I can differentiate the instruction. I can then help the children who are ready to get on to the computer programming earlier, while the other adults in the class can help the rest build a sturdy structure.

SH: *In my observations of your class, I saw you using paper cutouts for programming the robots.*

TG: The paper program is a way for the kids to think about the steps involved in programming the robot before they get to the computer. First they need to identify the activity they want the project rover to do. Then they have a response sheet I give them to cut and paste paper icons—similar to the ones they have in RoboLab. The kids have to make this program first before I let them use RoboLab in the computer. I have them use two motors, and there is a time element; they have to make the rover go forward and stop at a rock and pick up passengers. Then I give them RoboLab in the computer to test out the time element. Children sometimes like to add other elements to their program as well, such as turning things or noisemakers. I always say to my students, "You should be complimented if someone borrows your ideas," but I always ask the idea-borrowers to change them a little bit to make them their own. In any particular class, and this is certainly true for first- and second-graders, I might have five different levels of activity going on at one time, and it's messy and noisy but quite exciting. To help out with this situation I use student experts, so, for example, if I have somebody who is a little bit more advanced or has tried successfully a new element in the programming or the building aspect, then he or she is the expert on that. Their responsibility is to help other children who are coming across similar problems.

SH: *I noticed a man in the classroom . . .*

TG: He is a retired engineer, part of a volunteering organization that is interested in coming into the classrooms. He's been here about 5 years now. He is really important because he helps a lot. For example, when you came to observe, he was working with a child who had missed the last class and therefore she didn't know what she needed to about gears. He worked with her to get her up to speed. What's really great about him is that my physics is rusty—it's been a while since I've taken any force and motion courses—and he's really good at keeping me on track.

SH: *What were some of your early expectations for children's learning with robotics?*

TG: When I first started I would not have expected kids to be using the program until probably fourth grade. So, I have to admit, I was a little reluctant to bring that in, because at that point in my understanding—I didn't understand it enough to be able to see the potential with young kids. But I am finding that kids intuitively understand computers and how they work, having grown up with that. And so getting on the computer is pretty natural for them. And it's a matter of putting the pieces in place so that when they are on the computer they are really doing the work needed to be productive. To be honest, at the beginning it was quite chaotic, and as teachers, you don't really want chaos in the classroom because it appears that learning isn't going on if the classroom is so chaotic. And for me, I learned that it's okay to have a chaotic classroom because it doesn't mean that learning isn't going on, it just means learning is going on differently.

Management is also an issue—material management and classroom management. I like groups of two, and I typically do boy groups and girl groups. I just like the way they work together. The thing is you'll have 10 projects that are in different stages of completion that need to be saved. You have to have insight about management issues and how to deal with all that "stuff"; so when the kids come in next week they can pick up from where they are. You have to have checks in place, so that when the kids come in they can remember where they were to make that time valuable for them. It took me a couple of years to figure all that out. I had projects all over the room at one point, and I'll have younger kids come in and of course they want to touch them. It's about management, really, managing your materials and figuring out the best way to store those.

SH: *Based on your early expectations, how have your approaches changed over the years? How have you changed the way you bring these elements into the classroom?*

TG: I think kids need time to explore the materials because young children are naturally curious. It is important to have materials available for them to explore, and then slowly introduce things they are ready for, and slowly introduce pieces that can expand what they already have. And they need a lot of time. In the beginning it worried me—"Oh it looks like they're just playing"—whereas play is, well you can call it play, but I call it investigating. They're exploring. Exploring and investigating have an element in it that is more than just play, it's learning about something and being able to communicate what they have learned. I ask children to draw pictures of what they're thinking or what they've found out. And I have them write a little bit about it, especially in second grade. For example, today's class was really about exploring gears and noticing that some are fast and some are slow, depending on how you mesh them. I let them play with the gears because that is when they are going to remember, not if I tell them that gearing up is when the follower does this or that. We've been doing hands-on learning since the '70s . . . but this is experiential learning where you're giving materials to kids, in a controlled place, where you have clear expectations—you know when we're done. I know that I want children to know *this* about the topic. So I've got clear expectations and before the kids leave for the day I can go back to that to make sure that the expectations have been met.

SH: *What sort of suggestions can you make for teachers thinking about implementing a robotics curriculum with young children?*

TG: The hardest thing about using this kind of robotics in the classroom is being comfortable with not knowing the answer. We might have our expectations, but the answer we are expecting might not be the one the kids come to! The first few years were very hard for me because I didn't know what to expect. I had never built these kinds of structures; in fact I had never used LEGOs when I was a young child at all. But I learned that within a classroom community you're always going to have a handful of kids that intuitively have their own answers. I think it's important that teachers are learning along with the kids, and that we don't really have all the answers. And that's what engineering really is. We need citizens of the future that are going to use technology to improve our lives. I think these kids are going to do it. I am hoping that when I am in the nursing home, they are coming up with things to make my life better!

Conclusion

FIGURE 18. Building and playing

This book presents an innovative approach for using technology in early childhood. The approach is guided by the constructionist philosophy developed by Seymour Papert, which suggests that the best way to help children learn with computers is by providing them with tools flexible enough that they can create their own computational projects. As shown in this book, robotics is one such project. Not only can children design, build, and program their own interactive artifacts while having fun, but they can also learn how to work in groups and develop socioemotional skills. In the process, they encounter powerful ideas from the realms of math, science, technology, and engineering. As opposed to limiting children's interactions to a computer screen, robotics invites children to play and to engage in sensory-motor activities, which are fundamental for the healthy development of young children.

Robotics continues a long-standing tradition of learning manipulatives in early childhood. It also opens up a world of possibilities by exposing children early on to traditionally abstract and mechanical concepts such as gears, levers, joints, motors, sensors, programming loops, and variables in a concrete and fun manner, while engaging them in most of the steps involved in the engineering design process. In a world in which technology plays such an important role in our lives, it is wise to expand the range of content and contexts that young children learn about by welcoming explorations of objects made out of both bits and atoms—for example, everyday objects such as automatic doors, motion-sensitive lights, and automatic braking systems in cars, and more complex objects such as space shuttles, robotic surgeons, and bomb-finding robots. However, although all of these objects are interesting to study, a curriculum should not be built around objects, but around ideas themselves.

Given the increasing federal mandate to revisit early childhood programs and make them more academically demanding to meet stepped-up achievement requirements in later schooling, it is a perfect time to rethink what we are teaching our children and how we are teaching it. As this book shows, robotics projects provide an opportunity to focus on a pedagogy that embraces playful learning through the creation of personally meaningful projects while simultaneously enhancing curricula to strengthen the teaching of math, science, technology, and engineering.

One of the obstacles to incorporating robotics into the early childhood classroom is that early childhood educators have had little or no experience with technology or engineering concepts and processes. There is a lack of resources and theoretically accepted guidelines for working with younger children in this area. Thus, many early childhood educators are unaware of the potential of robotics construction kits as appropriate learning manipulatives. This book provides a window into these issues by presenting a theoretical approach, practical guidelines for doing the work, and information on further resources. Most of the projects and examples in this book use LEGO Mindstorms because this is the commercial robotics kit most widely available and supported for educational uses. The pedagogical and developmental theories discussed here go beyond this particular construction kit, however, and apply to any robotic manipulative or technology that allows children to combine bits and atoms to design a personally meaningful project that can exhibit behaviors by responding to inputs.

The core message of this book is that by providing children very early on with powerful tools such as robotics, which are natural digital extensions of traditional learning manipulatives, we can help them develop readiness to become producers, and not only consumers, of technology. Thus, children will develop the skills and ways of thinking needed to solve problems using technology, not only in the classroom but in society at large.

Engineering and Technology Standards in the United States

The table on the following pages is a state-by-state summary of standards for education in engineering and technology in the United States as of 2006. At the time of compilation of the data, most states included separate engineering/technology standards within their curricular frameworks. Missouri was the only state with no standards for education in engineering and technology.

Information presented in the table was provided by Yvonne Spicer, National Center for Technological Literacy (NCTL), Boston Museum of Science.

For complete, up-to-date information regarding technology and engineering frameworks, check the NCTL website: http://www.mos.org/nctl/

State	Standards by Subject					Notes on Standards	Standards by Grade Level		
	None	Separate Academic	Sci-Eng Academic	Technol Ed	Vocational		Elementary	Middle School	High School
TOTALS:	1	4	23	11	31				
Alaska			✓		✓	Industrial and Engineering Technology. Science, technology, engineering, and math industry-driven set of standards for course and program content. Involves technological design		✓	✓
Alabama					✓	Technology Education framework covers use of technology. Career Technology (Technology Education) covers applications of technology and engineering related concepts		✓	✓
Arkansas					✓	Exploring Industrial Technology. Courses and standards at middle and high school levels. Pre-engineering course sequence		✓	✓
Arizona			✓			Technology Education Standards cover computer literacy K–12. Science Standards Strand 3, Science in Personal and Social Perspectives, has design expectations	✓	✓	✓
California					✓	Engineering and Design Strand in Career and Technical Education. Contains 5 engineering pathways		✓	✓

State				Description					
Colorado	✓	✓	✓	Science frameworks integrate science, technology, and human impact. Some design elements are covered. Most of the standards involve "describe"; however, elementary does have an "invent" standard and high school a "demonstrate" standard	✓	✓	✓		
Connecticut	✓	✓	✓	Connecticut Framework K–12 Curricular Goals and Standards—Technology Education. Standards in science include design concepts and problem-solving using engineering processes		✓	✓		
Washington, DC	✓			Science Technology and Society in Science Strand		✓	✓		
Delaware	✓	✓	✓	Technology Education Standards: 2000. Public K–12 technology education standards. Science Curriculum Framework Standard One: Nature and Application of Science and Technology	✓	✓	✓		
Florida	✓	✓		Standardized courses for engineering technology. Science standards are K–12; technology education standards are middle and high school	✓	✓	✓		
Georgia	✓	✓		Technology education standards related to courses middle through high school. Assessment requirements for course completion		✓	✓		

State	Standards by Subject					Notes on Standards	Standards by Grade Level		
	None	Separate Academic	Sci-Eng Academic	Technol Ed	Vocational		Elementary	Middle School	High School
Hawaii			✓	✓		Technological design is integrated into a number of subject matter areas. Science has two technology standards related to society and impact of science/technology. Technology design is part of Career and Technology in K–12. Elementary uses KITS materials	✓	✓	
Iowa					✓	Industrial technology			✓
Idaho			✓	✓	✓	Standards for technology and engineering are in different divisions. Science standards include technology (technology design) and personal/social perspectives. Technology education is under the Division of Professional and Technical Education. Statewide standards are from 2001, grades K–12	✓	✓	✓
Illinois			✓		✓	Illinois Learning Standards are for mathematics, English language arts, and science (with science, technology and society, and technological design sections). Industrial technology state curriculum slated for 2006			

State				Notes			
Indiana	✓	✓		Most middle school students in Indiana take a technology and engineering course. The curriculum is designed for 36 weeks. Not all schools offer it, but the majority do. Science K–8 has "understanding science and technology" as Strand 1; has some limited "engineering" applications		✓	✓
Kansas	✓	✓	✓	Technology Education, Science and Technology (which includes design), and Science in Personal and Environmental Perspectives (social impacts of technology), K–12	✓	✓	✓
Kentucky	✓	✓		Curriculum Framework for Technology Education. Science standard mentions use of science in technological design and relations of science and technology to society	✓	✓	✓
Louisiana	✓	✓		Technology Content Standards	✓	✓	✓
Massachusetts	✓	✓	✓	Part of the Science and Engineering/Technology Curriculum Frameworks. Massachusetts also has a Vocational Technical Education Curriculum Framework for Engineering Technology	✓	✓	✓
Maryland	✓	✓		Technology education standards: "Technology education is a state graduation requirement"		✓	✓

State	Standards by Subject					Notes on Standards	Standards by Grade Level		
	None	Separate Academic	Sci-Eng Academic	Technol Ed	Vocational		Elementary	Middle School	High School
Maine			✓			1997 standards for science and technology	✓	✓	✓
Michigan					✓	Education technology standards centered around using technology to problem-solve, etc. Science: students must be aware of how technology affects society	✓	✓	✓
Minnesota			✓		✓	Technology Education Teachers Association is supporting implementation of the national standards			
Missouri	✓					Standards for core curriculum only. Missouri is the only state with no standards for education in engineering and technology			
Mississippi				✓	✓	Frameworks for two courses at the secondary level: Technology Discovery and Technology Applications			✓
Montana			✓			Science Content Standard 5 includes technology. State has "Technology" standards that relate to the use of computers	✓	✓	✓
North Carolina				✓		Technology education courses and standards		✓	✓

State				Notes			
North Dakota	✓	✓	✓	Science standard makes distinction between science and technology. Includes "Technological Design"	✓	✓	
Nebraska	✓	✓	✓	Covers some engineering and technical literacy concepts. A separate section on technology and society covers design and application areas		✓	
New Hampshire	✓	✓	✓	Frameworks for Science Literacy, K–12, integrate design technology, tools, and social issues into each science discipline	✓	✓	
New Jersey	✓	✓	✓	Curriculum frameworks for technological literacy, K–12, include both computer/career and engineering/technology activities			✓
New Mexico	✓	✓	✓		✓		
Nevada	✓	✓	✓	Under Science standards, students get only an "understanding"; they do not actually build, design, or test technology. Computer and Technology standards integrate activities for students to design and test technology	✓	✓	
New York	✓	✓	✓	Technology education covered under the Mathematics, Science, and Technology Learning Standards	✓	✓	

| | Standards by Subject | | | | | | Standards by Grade Level | | |
State	None	Separate Academic	Sci-Eng Academic	Technol Ed	Voca-tional	Notes on Standards	Elemen-tary	Middle School	High School
Ohio		✓		✓	✓	Technology Academic Standards. Included is a section on technical literacy described as skills needed to live in a technical society and understanding of the engineering process	✓	✓	✓
Oklahoma				✓		Technology education focused on interdisciplinary application to design and technical projects. Curriculum standards for grades 6–10 and 11–12		✓	✓
Oregon					✓		✓		✓
Pennsylvania			✓			Academic Standards for Science and Technology (2002), K–12	✓	✓	✓
Rhode Island			✓			Grade Span Expectations for Engineering Technology are segmented into grade spans of K–4, 5–8, and 9–12	✓	✓	✓
South Carolina				✓	✓			✓	✓
South Dakota					✓	Technology Education Content Standards. Science standard also includes technological design at the high school level	✓	✓	✓

State					Notes			
Tennessee				✓	Engineering Technology Education. Five courses	✓	✓	✓
Texas		✓	✓	✓	Technology Education, Industrial Education	✓	✓	✓
Utah			✓		Engineering standard is under Technology Education	✓	✓	✓
Virginia				✓	Standardized courses with specific task lists for each course. Courses in technology education include many engineering options	✓	✓	✓
Vermont				✓	Engineering technology is a content area under Career and Technical Education. It focuses on the high school level and has specific competencies for each engineering course in the sequence			✓
Washington		✓		✓	Science standards with some embedded technology/design concepts cover all grades	✓	✓	✓
Wisconsin	✓				Standards for Technology Education are integrated for all elementary grades	✓	✓	✓
West Virginia			✓		Content standards under Career and Technical Education. Technology education courses	✓	✓	✓
Wyoming				✓			✓	✓

APPENDIX B

Sample Curriculum Starter

The next page shows an example of how to develop a curricular web that integrates robotics with other disciplines. It was developed by Marina Bers and Debbie LeeKennan as part of an Early Childhood Teachers Summer Institute conducted in August 2006 at Tufts University.

During the institute educators learned how new robotics technologies could be used with young children and integrated with the math, science, technology, and engineering (MSTE) curriculum. They received (1) one free LEGO Mindstorms robotics kit after completion of the institute, (2) access to our free lending library of robotics kits to use in the classroom, (3) the opportunity to conduct guided observations of young children learning and using these materials in our Early Robotics Summer Camp, (4) a package with already-developed activities that make use of this technology with this age group, and (5) 18 PDP points. By using a curricular web, educators developed and implemented their own robotics curriculum.

Curriculum Starter

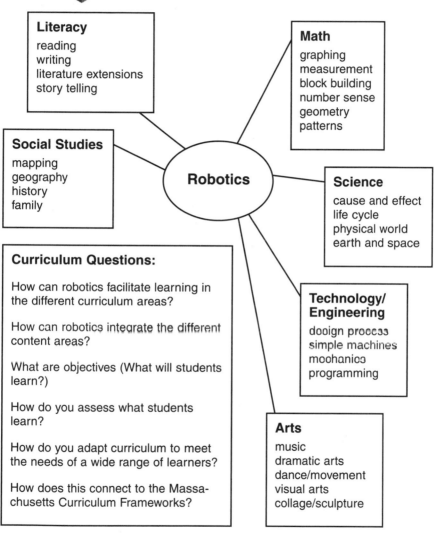

Literacy
reading
writing
literature extensions
story telling

Math
graphing
measurement
block building
number sense
geometry
patterns

Social Studies
mapping
geography
history
family

Robotics

Science
cause and effect
life cycle
physical world
earth and space

**Technology/
Engineering**
dooign prooooo
simple machines
moohanioo
programming

Arts
music
dramatic arts
dance/movement
visual arts
collage/sculpture

Curriculum Questions:

How can robotics facilitate learning in the different curriculum areas?

How can robotics integrate the different content areas?

What are objectives (What will students learn?)

How do you assess what students learn?

How do you adapt curriculum to meet the needs of a wide range of learners?

How does this connect to the Massachusetts Curriculum Frameworks?

APPENDIX C

Sample Design Journal

The design journal shown on the following pages was developed by Kevin Staszowski for an early childhood robotics summer camp conducted at Tufts University in August 2006. The theme of the camp was the circus as a starting point for children to build robotic projects.

Children were exposed to a curriculum that taught them the basics of building and programming with robotics by inviting them to create a flying trapeze, a music box, and men traveling across a tightrope, who, when hit by a spotlight (a flashlight), jumped down into a net. As a grand finale, during the last two days of the workshop, children created their own open-ended projects, such as a machine that delivers candy or a monkey that can jump up and down. Families and friends were invited to the open house to see the projects. Children used this design journal to write down their ideas for projects and to reflect on their learning experience. At the end of the workshop the journal was taken home, where it served as a way for the children to share their experience with their parents.

For a free, printable version of this Appendix, visit www.teachers collegepress.com

Circus Program

My name is _____

My partner's name is _____

 Draw what you think you and your partner are going to build:

What did you draw?_____

_____

_____

What is its name?_____

_____

What are three things you want your project to do?

1._____

_____

2._____

_____

3._____

_____

I will build_____

_____

_____

My partner will build_____

_____

_____

BUILDING NOTES

This is a picture of what my partner
and I worked on today

We finished working on _____

_____

_____

We still need to work on _____

_____

_____

BUILDING NOTES

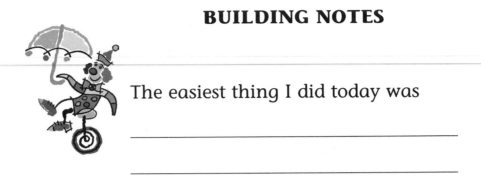

The easiest thing I did today was

_____

_____

_____

_____

_____

The hardest thing I did today was_____

_____

_____

_____

_____

What is an idea you got from another team or an adult?_____

_____

_____

_____

* This is a picture of my partner
and me with our final project

When I run my project, it _____

_____

_____

_____

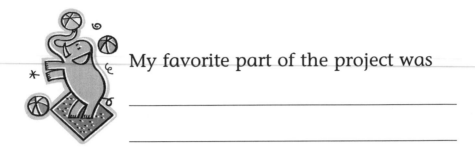 My favorite part of the project was

_____

_____

_____

_____

_____

When I worked on my project, I learned how to

_____

_____

_____

_____

My favorite part of working with my partner was

_____

_____

_____

_____

References

Abelson, H., & DiSessa, A. (1981). *Turtle geometry: The computer as a medium for exploring mathematics.* Cambridge, MA: MIT Press.

Ackermann, E. (1991). The "agency" model of transactions: Toward an understanding of children's theory of control. In J. Montangero & A. Tryphon (Eds.), *Psychologie génétique et sciences cognitives* (pp. 63–73). Geneva: Fondation Archives Jean Piaget.

Barthes, R. (1972). *Mythologies* (A. Lavers, Trans.). New York: Hill and Wang.

Battista, M. T., & Clements, D. H. (1986). The effects of Logo and CAI problem-solving environments on problem-solving abilities and mathematics achievement. *Computers in Human Behavior, 2,* 183–193.

Beals, L., & Bers, M. (2006). Robotic technologies: When parents put their learning ahead of their child's. *Journal of Interactive Learning Research, 17*(4), 341–366.

Berman, J., & Bruckman, A. (2001). The Turing game: Exploring identity in an online environment. *Convergence, 7*(3), 83–102.

Bers, M. (2001). Identity construction environments: Developing personal and moral values through the design of a virtual city. *The Journal of the Learning Sciences, 10*(4), 365–415.

Bers, M. (2006). The role of new technologies to foster positive youth development. *Applied Developmental Science, 10*(4), 200–219.

Bers, M. (2007a). Positive technological development: Working with computers, children, and the Internet. *MassPsych, 51*(1), 5–7, 18–19.

Bers, M. (2007b). Engineers and storytellers: Using robotic manipulatives to develop technological fluency in early childhood. In O. N. Saracho & B. Spodek (Eds.), *Contemporary perspectives on science and technology in early childhood education* (pp. 103–123). Charlotte, NC: Information Age Publishers.

Bers, M. (in press). Civic identities, on-line technologies: From designing civics curriculum to supporting civic experiences. In Lance Bennett (Ed.), *Digital media and civic engagement* (MacArthur series on digital media). Cambridge, MA: MIT Press.

Bers, M., & Cassell, J. (1999). Interactive storytelling systems for children: Using technology to explore language and identity. *Journal of Interactive Learning Research, 9*(2), 603–609.

Bers, M., New, B., & Boudreau, L. (2004). Teaching and learning when no one is expert: Children and parents explore technology. *Early Childhood Research &*

Practice, 6(2). Retrieved August 29, 2007, from http://ecrp.uiuc.edu/v6n2/bers.html

Bers, M., Ponte, I., Juelich, K., Viera, A., & Schenker, J. (2002). Integrating robotics into early childhood education. *Information Technology in Childhood Education Annual, 2002*(1), 123–145.

Bers, M., & Portsmore, M. (2005). Teaching partnerships: Early childhood and engineering students teaching math and science through robotics. *Journal of Science Education and Technology, 14*(1), 59–73.

Bers, M., & Urrea, C. (2000). Technological prayers: Parents and children working with robotics and values. In A. Druin & J. Hendler (Eds.), *Robots for kids: Exploring new technologies for learning experiences* (pp. 194–217). New York: Morgan Kaufman.

Bredekamp, S. (Ed.). (1987). *Developmentally appropriate practice in early childhood programs serving children from birth through age 8*. Washington, DC: National Association for the Education of Young Children.

Bredekamp, S., & Copple, C. (1997). *Developmentally appropriate practice in early childhood programs* (Rev. ed.). Washington, DC: National Association for the Education of Young Children.

Bredekamp, S., & Rosegrant, T. (Eds.). (1995). *Reaching potentials: Transforming early childhood curriculum and assessment* (Vol. 2). Washington, DC: National Association for the Education of Young Children.

Brosterman, N. (1997). *Inventing kindergarten*. New York: Harry N. Adams, Inc.

Bruckman, A. (1998). Community support for constructionist learning. *CSCW (Computer Supported Collaborative Work): The Journal of Collaborative Computing, 7*, 47–86.

Bruner, J. S. (1986). *Actual minds, possible words*. New York: Plenum Press.

Bruner, J. (1990). *Acts of meaning*. Cambridge, MA: Harvard University Press.

Clements, D. (1999). Young children and technology. In *Dialogue on early childhood science, mathematics, and technology education*. Washington, DC: American Association for the Advancement of Science. Available at http://www.project2061.org/publications/earlychild/online/experience/clements.htm

Clements, D. H. (1987). Longitudinal study of the effects of Logo programming on cognitive abilities and achievement. *Journal of Educational Computing Research, 3*, 73–94.

Clements, D. H., & Sarama, J. (1997). Research on Logo: A decade of progress. *Computers in the Schools, 14*(1–2), 9–46.

Clements, D. H., & Sarama, J. (2003). Strip mining for gold: Research and policy in educational technology—A response to "*Fool's Gold.*" *Educational Technology Review, 11*(1), 7–69.

Committee on Information Technology Literacy. (1999). *Being fluent with information technology*. Washington, DC: National Research Council, National Academy Press.

Duckworth, E. (1991). *The having of wonderful ideas and other essays*. New York: Teachers College Press.

Edwards, C., Gandini, L., & Forman, G. (Eds.). (1998). *The hundred languages of children*. Greenwich, CT: Ablex.

Erikson, E. (1950). *Childhood and society*. New York: Norton.

Fan, X., & Chen, M. (2001). Parental involvement and students' academic achievement: A meta-analysis. *Educational Psychology Review, 13*(1), 1–22.

Forman, E. A., Minick, M., & Stone, C. A. (Eds.). (1993). *Context for learning: Sociocultural dynamics in children's development.* New York: Oxford University Press.

Gershenfeld, N. A. (1999). *The nature of mathematical modeling.* Cambridge, UK: Cambridge University Press.

Goodling Institute for Research on Family Literacy. (2006). Annotated bibliography. University Park: Pennsylvania State University. Available at http://www.ed.psu.edu/goodlinginstitute/pdf/Annotated_Bibliography.pdf

Harel, I., & Papert, S. (1990). Software design as a learning environment. *Interactive Learning Environments, 1*(1), 1–32.

Harel, I., & Papert, S. (1991). *Constructionism.* Norwood, NJ: Ablex

Helm, J. H., Beneke, S., & Steinheimer, K. (1998). *Windows on learning: Documenting young children's work.* New York: Teachers College Press.

Kafai, Y., & Resnick, M. (Eds.). (1996). *Constructionism in practice: Designing, thinking, and learning in a digital world.* Mahwah, NJ: Lawrence Erlbaum.

Kantor, R., Elgas, P., & Fernie, D. (1993). Cultural knowledge and social competence within a preschool peer culture group. *Early Childhood Research Quarterly, 8*(2), 125–147.

Lerner, R., Lerner, J. V., Almerigi, J. B., Theokas, C., Phelps, E., Gestsdottir, S., Naudeau, S., Jelicic, H., Alberts, A., Ma, L., Smith, L. M., Bobek, D. L., Richman-Raphael, D., Simpson, I., DiDenti Christiansen, E., & von Eye, A. (2005). Positive youth development, participation in community youth development programs, and community contributions of fifth-grade adolescents. *The Journal of Early Adolescence, 25*(1), 17–71.

Lewis, C. (1995). *Educating hearts and minds: Reflections on Japanese preschools.* Cambridge, UK: Cambridge University Press.

Logo Computer Systems. (1999). *Logo philosophy and implementation.* Westmount, Quebec, Canada: Logo Computer Systems, Inc.

Malaguzzi, L. (1998). History, ideas, and basic philosophy: An interview with Lella Gandini. In C. Edwards, L. Gandini, & G. Forman (Eds.), *The hundred languages of children: The Reggio Emilia approach—advanced reflections* (2nd ed., pp. 49–98). Greenwich, CT: Ablex.

Mallory, B., & New, R. (Eds.). (1994). *Diversity and developmentally appropriate practices: Challenges for early childhood education.* New York: Teachers College Press.

Martin, F., Mikhak, B., Resnick, M., Silverman, B., & Berg, R. (2000). To Mindstorms and beyond: Evolution of a construction kit for magical machines. In A. Druin & J. Hendler (Eds.), *Robots for kids: Exploring new technologies for learning* (pp. 9–33). San Francisco, CA: Morgan Kaufmann.

McLuhan, M. (1964). *Understanding media: The extensions of man.* New York: McGraw-Hill. [Reissued in 1994 by MIT Press, Cambridge, MA.]

Miaoulis, I. (2001). Introducing engineering into the K–12 learning environments. *Environmental Engineering, 37*(4), 7–10.

Minsky, M. (1986). *The society of mind.* New York: Simon & Schuster.

Muller, A. A., & Perlmutter, M. (1985). Preschool children's problem-solving interactions at computers and jigsaw puzzles. *Journal of Applied Developmental Psychology, 6*(2–3), 173–186.

146   References

National Academy of Engineering and National Research Council. (2002). *Technically speaking: Why all Americans need to know more about technology.* Washington, DC: National Academy Press.

National Literacy Trust. (2007). *Research on parental involvement and family literacy.* Retrieved August 29, 2007, from http://www.literacytrust.org.uk/research/parents index.html

New, R. (1999a). A new take on an integrated curriculum. In C. Seefeldt (Ed.), *The early childhood curriculum: A review of current research* (3rd ed.). New York: Teachers College Press.

New, R. (1999b). Playing fair and square: Issues in equity in early childhood mathematics, science, and technology. In *Dialogue on early childhood science, mathematics, and technology education.* Washington, DC: American Association for the Advancement of Science. Available at http://www.project2061.org/publications/earlychild/online/fostering/new.htm

New, R., Mardell, B., & Robinson, D. (2005). Early childhood education as risky business: Going beyond what's "safe" to discovering what's possible. *Early Childhood Research & Practice, 7*(2). Retrieved August 29, 2007, from http://ecrp.uiuc.edu/v7n2/new.html

Papert, S. (1980). *Mindstorms: Children, computers, and powerful ideas* (1st ed.). New York: Harper Collins.

Papert, S. (1987). Information technology and education: Computer criticism vs. technocentric thinking. *Educational Researcher, 16*(1), 22–30.

Papert, S. (1991). Situating constructionism. In I. Harel & S. Papert (Eds.), *Constructionism.* Norwood, NJ: Ablex Publishing Corporation.

Papert, S. (1999, March 29). Papert on Piaget. *Time, 153,* 105. [Special issue on "The Century's Greatest Minds."]

Papert, S. (2000). What's the big idea? Towards a pedagogy of idea power. *IBM Systems Journal, 39*(3–4), 720–729.

Papert, S., & Resnick, M. (1996, November). Paper presented at *Rescuing the powerful ideas,* an NSF-sponsored symposium at MIT, Cambridge, MA.

Parkinson, E. (1999). Re-constructing the construction kit—Re-constructing childhood: A synthesis of the influences which have helped to give shape and form to kit-based construction activities in the primary school classroom. *International Journal of Technology and Design Education, 9,* 173–194.

Piaget, J. (1950). *The psychology of intelligence.* London: Routledge & Kegan Paul.

Piaget, J. (1952). *The origin of intelligence in children.* New York: Basic Books.

Piaget, J. (1971). The theory of stages in cognitive development. In D. R. Green (Ed.), *Measurement and Piaget* (pp. 1–11). New York: McGraw.

Portsmore, M. (1999, Spring/Summer). ROBOLAB: Intuitive robotic programming software to support life long learning. *Apple Learning Technology Review,* pp. 26–39.

Prensky, M. (2001). Digital natives, digital immigrants. *On the Horizon* (Nebraska: NCB University Press) *9*(5).

Resnick, M. (1994). *Turtles, termites, and traffic jams: Explorations in massively parallel microworlds.* Cambridge, MA: MIT Press.

Resnick, M. (1998). Technologies for lifelong kindergarten. *Educational Technology Research & Development, 46*(4), 43–55.

Resnick, M. (2006). Computer as paintbrush: Technology, play, and the creative society. In D. Singer, R. M. Golinkoff, & K. Hirsh-Pasek (Eds.), *Play = learning: How play motivates and enhances children's cognitive and social-emotional growth* (pp. 192–208). Oxford University Press.

Resnick, M., Berg, R., & Eisenberg, M. (2000). Beyond black boxes: Bringing transparency and aesthetics back to scientific investigation. *Journal of the Learning Sciences, 9*(1), 7–30.

Resnick, M., Bruckman, A., & Martin, F. (1996a). Pianos not stereos: Creating computational construction kits. *Interactions, 3*(5), 40–50.

Resnick, M., Martin, F., Berg, R., Borovoy, R., Colella, V., Kramer, K., & Silverman, B. (1998, April). Digital manipulatives. In *Proceedings of the CHI '98 conference,* Los Angeles.

Resnick, M., Martin, F., Sargent, R., & Silverman, B. (1996b). Programmable bricks: Toys to think with. *IBM Systems Journal, 35*(3–4), 443–452.

Resnick, M., Ocko, S., & Papert, S. (1988). LEGO, Logo, and design. *Children's Environments Quarterly, 5*(4), 14–18.

Rinaldi, C. (1998). Projected curriculum constructed through documentation—Progettazione: An interview with Lella Gandini. In C. Edwards, L. Gandini, & G. Forman (Eds.), *The hundred languages of children: The Reggio Emilia approach—Advanced reflections* (2nd ed., pp. 113–126). Greenwich, CT: Ablex.

Rinaldi, C. (2001). Documentation and assessment: What is the relationship? In C. Giudici, C. Rinaldi, & M. Krechevsky (Eds.), *Making learning visible: Children as individual and group learners* (pp. 78–89). Reggio Emilia, Italy: Reggio Children.

Rogers, C., & Portsmore, M. (2001). Data acquisition in the dorm room: Teaching experimentation techniques using LEGO Materials. In *Proceedings of the 2001 American Society of Engineering Education Annual Conference and Exhibition, Albuquerque, NM.* Washington, DC: American Society of Engineering Education.

Rogoff, B. (1990). *Apprenticeship in thinking: Cognitive development in social context.* New York: Oxford University Press.

Rogoff, B. (2003). *The cultural nature of human development.* New York: Oxford University Press.

Senechal, M., & LeFevre, J. (2002). Parental involvement in the development of children's reading skill: A five-year longitudinal study. *Child Development, 73*(2), 445–460.

Subrahmanyam, K., Greenfield, P., Kraut, R., & Gross, E. (2001). The impact of computer use on children's and adolescents' development. *Applied Developmental Psychology, 22,* 7–30.

Super, C., & Harkness, S. (1986). The developmental niche: A conceptualization at the interface of child and culture. *International Journal of Behavioral Development, 9,* 545–569.

Teale, W. H. (1984). Reading to young children: Its significance for literacy development. In H. Goelman, A. Oberg, & F. Smith (Eds.), *Awakening to literacy* (pp. 110–121). Portsmouth, NH: Heinemann Educational Books.

Tobin, J., Wu, D. Y., & Davidson, D. H. (1989). *Preschool in three cultures.* New Haven, CT: Yale University Press.

Turbak, F., & Berg, R. (2002). Robotic design studio: Exploring the big ideas of engineering in a liberal arts environment. *Journal of Science Education and Technology, 11*(3), 237–253.

Turiel, E. (1999). Conflict, social development, and cultural change. In E. Turiel (Ed.), *Development and cultural change: Reciprocal processes. New directions for child and adolescent development, No. 83* (pp. 77–92). San Francisco: Jossey-Bass.

Turkle, S. (1984). *The second self: Computers and the human spirit.* New York: Simon & Schuster.

Turkle, S. (1995). *Life on the screen: Identity in the age of the Internet.* New York: Simon & Schuster.

Turkle, S., & Papert, S. (1992). Epistemological pluralism and the revaluation of the concrete. *Journal of Mathematical Behavior, 11*(1), 3–33.

Vygotsky, L. S. (1962). *Thought and language.* Cambridge, MA: MIT Press.

Vygotsky, L. S. (1978). *Mind in society: The development of higher psychological processes.* Cambridge, MA: Harvard University Press.

Wang, X. C., & Ching, C. C. (2003). Social construction of computer experience in a first-grade classroom: Social processes and mediating artifacts. *Early Education and Development, 14*(3), 335–361.

Weizenbaum, J. (1976). *Computer power and human reason: From judgment to calculation.* San Francisco: W. H. Freeman.

Whiting, B., & Edwards, C. (1988). *Children of different worlds: The formation of social behavior.* Cambridge, MA: Harvard University Press.

Whiting, B. B., & Whiting, J. W. M. (1975). *Children of six cultures: A psycho-cultural analysis.* Cambridge, MA: Harvard University Press.

Wilensky, U. (1991). Abstract meditations on the concrete and concrete implications for mathematics education. In I. Harel & S. Papert (Eds.), *Constructionism.* Norwood, NJ: Ablex.

Wilensky, U. (1999). GasLab—An extensible modeling toolkit for exploring micro- and macro-views of gases. In N. Roberts, W. Feurzeig, & B. Hunter (Eds.), *Computer modeling and simulation in science education.* Berlin: Springer Verlag.

Winograd, T., & Flores, F. (1987). *Understanding computers and cognition: A new foundation for design.* Norwood, NJ: Ablex.

Wright, J. L., & Church, M. (1986). The evolution of an effective home–school microcomputer connection. *Education & Computing, 2,* 67–74.

Index

Page numbers followed by an *f* or *t* indicate figures or tables, respectively.

About the Author

MARINA UMASCHI BERS is an assistant professor at the Eliot-Pearson Department of Child Development and an adjunct professor in the Computer Science Department at Tufts University. She is also a scientific research associate at Boston Children's Hospital. Her research involves the design and study of innovative learning technologies to promote children's positive development.

Dr. Bers is from Argentina, where she did her undergraduate studies in Social Communication at Buenos Aires University. In 1994 she came to the United States. She received a Master's degree in Educational Media and Technology from Boston University and a Master of Science and Ph.D. from the MIT Media Laboratory.

Professor Bers received the 2005 Presidential Early Career Award for Scientists and Engineers (PECASE), the highest honor given by the U.S. government to outstanding investigators in the early stages of their careers. She also received a National Science Foundation (NSF) Young Investigator's Career Award, a five-year grant to support her work on virtual communities, and the American Educational Research Association's (AERA) Jan Hawkins Award for Early Career Contributions to Humanistic Research and Scholarship in Learning Technologies.

Over the past twelve years, Professor Bers has conceived and designed diverse technological tools ranging from robotics to virtual worlds. She has conducted studies in after-school programs, museums, and hospitals, as well as in schools in the United States, Argentina, Colombia, Spain, Costa Rica, and Thailand. She has also taught seminars on learning technologies for educators in many of these countries.

BLOCKS to ROBOTS